Not All Wives

Not All Wives

WOMEN OF COLONIAL PHILADELPHIA

Karin Wulf

PENN

University of Pennsylvania Press
Philadelphia

First published 2000 by Cornell University Press
Copyright © 2000 Cornell University Press
All rights reserved
Printed in the United States of America on acid-free paper

10 9 8 7 6 5 4 3 2 1

Paperback edition first published 2005 by
University of Pennsylvania Press
Philadelphia, Pennsylvania 19104-4122

ISBN 0-8122-1917-1

A CIP catalog record for this book is available from the Library of Congress.

For My Family
Lofgrens,
Swensons,
and Wulfs

Contents

[vii]

Contents

Contents

Illustrations

Tables

Preface

Although much of the research for this book derives from my 1993 Johns Hopkins dissertation, the idea for the book has earlier origins and owes much to the inspiration of a handful of excellent teachers. I first started thinking about the historical and analytical problem of unmarried women when I was a student at American University in visiting professor Joan Hoff's seminar on women and the Constitution. Women's "status" was still very much occupying historians' attention in the mid-1980s, and it struck me that it was specifically married women's status that was the subject of this scrutiny. Rather than focusing on coverture's effects on married women, I thought that examining those women who by law were not "covered," but who were very likely still restricted by the gendered ideals of submission and dependence associated with wives, would make a good study. I went to Johns Hopkins with a very different dissertation in mind, but I returned to the subject of unmarried women after an invigorating seminar on family and gender history with Toby Ditz. I especially want to thank my advisor, Jack P. Greene, for his willingness to be won over to the topic. I continue to value his model of scholarly energy, rigor, and productivity. I also want to thank my undergraduate mentor, now my colleague and friend, Roger Brown, who first taught me to love the eighteenth century and the historian's craft.

It is a very great pleasure to acknowledge the help and support of the many people and institutions who contributed to this project, including the exceptionally talented staff at Philadelphia area archives and special-collections libraries. These include Louise Jones and Linda Stanley, both formerly of the Historical Society of Pennsylvania; James Green, Philip Lapsansky, and John Van Horne of the Library Company of Philadelphia; Elisabeth Potts Brown, Diana Franzusoff Peterson, and Ann Upton of the Quaker Collection at Haverford College; and Jane Bryan of the University of Pennsylvania's Van Pelt Library. I am also grateful to the amazing, irrepressible Emma Lapsansky, curator of the Quaker Collection, who adopted me and my work at a critical stage. Much of this work was undertaken while I held a dissertation fellowship from the Philadelphia Center for Early American Studies (now the McNeil Center for Early American Studies). Richard Dunn, founder and director of the center, has created an unparalleled scholarly community of which I am very grateful to be part. Other institutions supported my research and writing through grants and fellowships, including the American Historical Association, Haverford College, The Library Company of Philadelphia, the National Endowment for the Humanities, Johns Hopkins University, Old Dominion University, and American University.

I have much appreciated the generosity of my professional colleagues. Those who shared their work-in-progress and commented on individual chapters of this book include Dickson Bruce, Deborah Cohen, Pattie Cowell, Cornelia Hughes Dayton, Mary Maples Dunn, Bernie Herman, Ruth Herndon, Craig Horle, John Kolp, Erik Seeman, Beverly Smaby, Terri Snyder, Jean Soderlund, Fredrika Teute, Lorett Treese, and the Early American Seminar at the University of Maryland. At a very early stage in the research, Billy Smith kindly opened his own research notes on taxation in Philadelphia. Going above and beyond, Richard Breitman, Roger Brown, Julie Hardwick, Susan Klepp, Robert Olwell, and David Shields read the entire manuscript. As readers for Cornell University Press, Nina Dayton and Billy Smith gave cogent analysis and sound advice. Both went far beyond their readers' reports in this regard, for which I am especially grateful. Thanks to Carl Keyes for the index.

My terrific colleagues and friends at Old Dominion University and American University have been incredibly supportive, particularly my current department chair, Allan Lichtman, who has been extraordinarily solicitous down the final stretch. I also want to thank Peter Agree, my editor at Cornell, for his encouragement, his professionalism, and his help in bringing the book to print. Grey Osterud was midwife to this project in its final stages. I am grateful for her incisive commentary, her sterling editorial skills, and her informed enthusiasm for the subject.

I owe more than I can say to Jane, Jim, Sophie, and Thomas Bryan, who are in a category by themselves. They fed and sheltered me during the years I spent researching in Philadelphia. Far beyond those contributions, however, they offered me friendships, fun, and a share in their family life.

I am lucky to have very good friends who are also very good historians. Over the years Alison Games, Ruth Wallis Herndon, Carolyn Lawes, and Brendan McConville have done their best to improve both this book and its author. For the better part of a decade, Julie Hardwick, Bob Olwell, and now Rose Hardwick Olwell, have been stalwart friends. I thank them particularly for a zillion e-mails and phone calls, many long visits, and untold effort expended on behalf of this book, and I promise that work on the next one will not begin until after New Year's.

My mother, Dixie Swenson, and my father, William Wulf, have together and singly made plain their commitment to my education and career. I thank them, my step-mother, Anita Jones, and my step-father, Keith Swenson, for their love and their confidence in me. My sister, Ellen Wulf Epstein, long ago allowed herself to be dragooned into tabulating and re-tabulating some of Philadelphia's tax records. I often say that in Joyce and John Lofgren I have the very best in-laws in the world; in ways large and small the evidence mounts. John also provided essential computer supplies and support at various stages.

Stephen and John William Lofgren deserve my last, best thanks. Steve has read everything I have ever written and has wielded his editorial pen with alternating glee and grim determination. I thank him for his sustaining faith in me and this project. Jack's principal contribution to this book was arriving the day after the first draft had been packaged up to send to Cornell. But his contributions to the author are immeasurable. He has inherited his father's gifts for making me laugh, for making me crazy, and for making life without him utterly unimaginable.

KARIN WULF

Bethesda, Maryland

Abbreviations

APS   American Philosophical Society
CPP   College of Physicians of Philadelphia
FHL   Friends Historical Library, Swarthmore College
GSP   Genealogical Society of Pennsylvania
HSP   Historical Society of Pennsylvania
LCHS   Lancaster County Historical Society
LCP   Library Company of Philadelphia
MCC   *Minutes of the Common Council of the City of Philadelphia, 1704–1776* (Philadelphia, 1847)
PCA   Philadelphia City Archives
PG   *The Pennsylvania Gazette* Accessible Archives, Folios I–III
PDW   Philadelphia Department of Wills
PMHB   *Pennsylvania Magazine of History and Biography*
QC   Quaker Collection, Haverford College
SMC   Society Miscellaneous Collection, Historical Society of Pennsylvania
WMQ   *William and Mary Quarterly*
VPL   Special Collections Department, Van Pelt Library, University of Pennsylvania

Not All Wives

INTRODUCTION

"Not All Wives": The Problem
of Marriage in Early America

Amid the turmoil of England's seventeenth-century civil wars, women petitioners to Parliament openly questioned the gender distinctions in English legal practice, which treated men as individuals but women collectively as dependents. Should "any of our lives, limbs, liberties or goods to be taken from us more than from men," they asked, except "by due process of law?"[1] Such petitions ran up against the bulwark of early modern English patriarchy: the idea that women, like children and servants, were inherently dependent creatures. Thus Parliament, in those cases when it responded to the women at all, suggested that they go back to their homes, to the fold of their husbands' protection and rule, and that they rely on their husbands to represent the interests of their households in public. The women's varied responses identified a problem that remained central to the battle that Anglo-American seventeenth- and eighteenth-century feminists waged over the relationship of gender to power, state and otherwise. The English petitioners put it most succinctly when they claimed their right to be heard, because "we are *not all wives*."[2]

To conflate women and wives was to assume subordinance and dependence; to distinguish between the two, as these petitioners demanded, was to understand the legal and cultural constructions that bound all wives but not all women. This book sets out to meet the challenge of incorporating into our historical knowledge these seventeenth-century petitioners' insight. In particular this study explores how ideas about gender, rooted in assumptions about women's positions as wives,

1. Quoted in Ellen A. McArthur, "Women Petitioners and the Long Parliament," *English Historical Review* 24 (1909): 708.
2. Quoted in Merry E. Wiesner, *Women and Gender in Early Modern Europe* (Cambridge, 1993), 245 (emphasis added).

came to apply to all women regardless of their marital status, as well as the ways in which unmarried women were free from some inequities that historians have assumed applied to all women. This book is about how unmarried women in a specific historical and geographical context perceived and experienced their status and how their culture in turn perceived and experienced the presence of women who were "not all wives."

Eighteenth-century Philadelphia provides a compelling setting for studying both the interplay of gender and marital status in female identity and the lives and experiences of unmarried women. As heads of their own households and as occupants of others' households, unmarried women—women who had yet to marry, women who never married, and women who were widowed or separated—comprised a statistically and culturally significant population in colonial Philadelphia. The city's early culture, affected in large measure by the presence of religious groups such as Quakers and Moravians who held alternative views of gender and marriage, provided a more expansive space for the development of positive models of femininity outside marriage. By the mid-eighteenth century, however, aspects of transatlantic Anglo-American culture, including an increasingly masculine (and martial) public culture, made Philadelphia look in many respects more like other cities in the British empire. A greater emphasis on masculine independence made female independence increasingly culturally anomalous despite the preponderance of unmarried women still populating the city. Thus, *Not All Wives* explores essential aspects of the early modern world, while locating processes of change in a particular spatial and temporal context.

Understanding and delineating the distinctions between wives and women who were not wives are essential to the history of women and gender in the early modern period. As the civil war petitioners perceived so clearly, marital status was a defining feature of female identity throughout the early modern European world and was reflected in law, culture, and economy. Yet in various social contexts, the connection of women to marriage was worked out somewhat differently. Law was a critical component of these differences. In France, where customary law gave women greater access to the property that they brought to a marriage than did the common law of England, the maintenance of a patriarchal state was nonetheless seen as dependent on the legal and cultural confluence of woman and wife.[3] The structural inequities of Anglo-

3. On the implications of Burgundian law, see Julie Hardwick, "Women Working the Law in Seventeenth-Century France," *Journal of Women's History* (October 1997), and on the creation of the patriarchal state through the application of laws constraining female

American marriage, encoded in law and scripted in culture, provide essential background for understanding differentiated notions of woman and woman in marriage. In England and its colonies, the common law of coverture placed married women under the legal wing of their husbands. Once married, women had no right, by law or custom, to act or speak as individuals. They were literally in law and essentially by custom *covered* by their husbands. This system was the foundation of the Anglo-American form of household patriarchy. Using what English legal commentator William Blackstone articulated as the "principle of legal unity," a *feme covert*'s personal property became her husband's outright upon marriage, and any real estate she brought to the marriage became his to manage. In any event, few women inherited realty; inheritance practices that favored granting real estate to sons and personalty to daughters ensured that property would pass unencumbered from male to male. Married women could not own personal property in their own names, could not make contracts, including for the management of any realty, wills, or even for their own labor, and could not, with few exceptions, appear in court. Coverture, therefore, not only deprived women of property, the most significant source of political power and status in early modern society, but it also denied them access to the legal system. A feme covert had no legal authority and no legal identity separate from her husband. The interests of married women, legal logic assayed, could be best determined and represented, along with those of the entire household, by her husband.[4]

These legal restrictions pertained not to women in general but to married women, who occupied a particular, peculiar status. *Femes soles,* however—those women who were *not wives*—had less complicated legal relationships, and yet more nuanced cultural relationships, to their families, communities, and polities. The legal status of a single woman, whether because she was widowed or had never married, was unambiguous. She could make contracts, own and devise property, and head a household. In short, she possessed the same legal capacity as any man.

<hr/>

sexuality, see Sarah Hanley, "Engendering the State: Family Formation and State Building in Early Modern France," *French Historical Studies* 16 (Spring 1989): 4–27.

4. William Blackstone wrote that "the very being or legal existence of the woman is suspended during marriage, or at least is incorporated and consolidated into that of the husband, under whose wing, protection, and *cover*, she performs every thing." William Blackstone, *Commentaries on the Laws of England* (Oxford, 1765–69), vol. 1, p.430. A compilation of laws relating to women in early modern England can be found in the excerpts of *The Law's Resolutions of Women's Rights* (London, 1632), reproduced in Joan Larsen Klein, ed., *Daughters, Wives, and Widows: Writings by Men about Women and Marriage in England* (Urbana, Ill., 1992), 31–61.

Widowhood was no doubt a time of grief and uncertainty for women.[5] But it also represented a fundamental change in women's status. An early English tract, *The Law's Resolutions of Women's Rights*, urged widows to appreciate their new capacity: "Why mourn you so, you that be widows? Consider how long you have been in subjection under the predominance of parents, of your husbands; now you be free in liberty, and free . . . at your own law."[6]

As wives, women could certainly take part in many kinds of economic and social activities, but as femes soles, their opportunities were greatly expanded. To see opportunity in singleness is not to ignore the economic, social, and cultural problems associated with that status. It is not to suggest either that widows did not mourn the loss of their partners or that most widows did not feel acutely the burdens of having to provide for a family after the death of a wage-earning husband. It is a recognition that a woman's fundamental responsibilities, however she chose to view them, changed dramatically with her marital status. Contemporaries appreciated this point, as a case in Philadelphia clearly illustrates. In 1766 William Thorne, a scrivener, wrote to the coexecutors of the estate of William Plumstead, the late mayor of Philadelphia, to explain why he had not yet settled his account. Thorne had often prepared work for Plumstead, and their association must have occasioned a friendly relationship, for in 1761 Thorne's wife "enter'd into Shop-keeping," encouraged by Plumstead to "Suit herself with Rum, Sugar & c." from his supplies. She did so after Plumstead said that in lieu of immediate payment, he would "take it out with [Thorne] in writing." On several subsequent occasions Plumstead enjoined Thorne not to worry over the debt, and after a partial payment, he instructed his partner not to trouble with it any further. After Plumstead died, however, with Thorne still owing him almost £30 (plus interest), Mrs. Plumstead pursued the matter. Explained Thorne, "I have lately been spoken to twice by a Clerk of Mrs. Plumsted's concerning an Acct standing against me in the late Mr. Plumsted's Books." He endeavored to explain the lapse in payment and promised to "discharge it . . . . as Soon as Possible."[7] Thorne's relationship to Mrs. Plumstead, through his wife's debt to her husband, illuminates the legal and financial intricacies of a feme covert's business activities. William Thorne, not his shopkeeper wife, was responsible for the debt

5. On grief and widowhood, see Lisa Wilson, *Life After Death: Widows in Pennsylvania, 1750–1850* (Philadelphia, 1991), 11–23.

6. *The Law's Resolutions of Women's Rights: or, The Law's Provision for Women* as quoted in Klein, ed., *Daughters, Wives and Widows*, 29.

7. William Thorne to [executors], Philadelphia, February 11, 1766, Plumstead Papers, HSP.

to Mr. Plumstead. This example of a feme sole's (the newly widowed Mrs. Plumstead) and a feme covert's (Mrs. Thorne's) involvement in one debt transaction shows how a woman's legal status could be reinforced, if not by coercive means, then by persuasive reminders that unmarried women could and did freely do what married women could not, or at least not without major complications. From this perspective, the status of unmarried women was much more straightforward than that of their married sisters. Unmarried women participated in the workings of society without legal hindrance.

Yet unmarried women posed a significant cultural contradiction: they lacked what Parliament asserted that the civil war petitioners, and by implication all other women, must have—a male intercessor. Unmarried women existed in a liminal state between what was understood to be masculine (independent, economic, political) and what was clearly feminine (dependent and domestic). More than other liminal subjects (male servants, for example), unmarried women embodied the contradictions of their status. Their bodies made them female, which in the contemporary model of femininity connoted weakness and passivity, but their actions automatically challenged these characterizations. In concrete terms, poor and unmarried women's bodies were the vessels of cultural challenge when they became pregnant and bore their children at public expense.

Certainly unmarried women's public activities highlighted this challenge to cultural ideals of gender. Working for their families without the nominal direction of a husband, engaging in contractual arrangements, whether for significant property or for their own labor, and representing themselves in public forums rather than being represented by men made the public presence of unmarried women quite striking. In the early modern era ideas about what constituted the public and the domestic differed dramatically from our own notions and from those of the nineteenth century. In the sixteenth through eighteenth centuries, public and private were not constituted as exclusively physical spaces (as, for example, in the nineteenth century when domestic space became ideologically feminized and the public world of work and politics masculinized), but rather as realms of activity in which both men and women participated. Men had specific domestic concerns and business, which included provisions and arrangements for family and household. Particularly in an urban environment, where the household as a place of production was not quite as isolated or insular as in rural, agricultural regions, women naturally and of necessity participated in highly public activities. Unmarried women, however, participated in the public worlds of economics and politics both more frequently and more visibly than married women did. Their own authority over household and self gave their public appearance and actions a different meaning. Living outside a marital relationship, unmarried women defied the presumption of masculine authority over women that was embedded in Anglo-American culture.

WOMEN, MARRIAGE, AND THE HISTORICAL LITERATURE

Not All Wives engages the historical problem of detangling the history of women from the history of women in marriage. As Joan Landes has written, "How difficult it is to uncouple women from domestic life."[8] This was true for contemporaries of the eighteenth century, and it has been true for historians. Although the fragmentary work on widows and spinsters in early modern Europe and America has revealed the statistical and social significance of these groups, broader inclusion of these women's experiences and the conclusions of these studies into the larger literature has not occurred. One reason this has been the case is that many scholars, following the example of the people and cultures they study, have chosen to emphasize the "normative" aspects of women's lives. In 1974 Alexander Keyssar described widowhood in eighteenth-century Massachusetts as "a problem in the history of the family" because the issues raised by the lengthy, regular experiences of widowhood did not conform to prevailing interpretations of family life in the Bay Colony.[9] Determining social "norms"—for both contemporaries and later analysts—is less an objective measure of experience than a culturally bound process, in which power plays a significant part, of ascribing roles and ideals.[10] Once marriage and motherhood take center stage as normative,

8. Joan Landes, *Women and the Public Sphere in the Age of the French Revolution* (Ithaca, 1988), 1.
9. Alexander Keyssar, "Widowhood in Eighteenth-Century Massachusetts: A Problem in the History of the Family," *Perspectives in American History* 8 (1974): 83–119. For another comment on unmarried women as a lacuna in the literature, see Richard Wall, "Woman Alone in English Society," *Annales de démographie historique* 17 (1981): 141.
10. The cultural process of creating and rigidly enforcing binary categories, as well as the resultant product of the "natural" category of the universal heterosexual "female," is discussed in Judith Butler, *Gender Trouble: Feminism and the Subversion of Identity* (New York, 1990). As Butler points out, gender and sexual identity is encoded not only in language, but also in the performance of such identities. By this logic, the failure to "perform" femininity by failing to marry or to remarry would challenge the naturalness and universality of the naturalized, universalized female—the wife. Thus, the hostility to unmarried women often marked the extent of a particular culture's concern with the fragility of that universal or normative identity. See also Carolyn Heilbrun, *Writing a Woman's Life* (New York, 1988). Cathy Davidson addressed this phenomenon from another perspective, arguing for the role of novels in a complex discourse "privileging the feme covert." Davidson, *Revolution and the Word: The Rise of the Novel in America* (New York, 1986), esp. 118–25.

the experiences of women outside marriage look marginal, unusual, and deviant and are so defined. As historian of eighteenth-century England Margaret Hunt has argued, "Functionalist and biologistic assumptions about the nature of women's 'role' have diverted attention from women who did not marry, as well as those women who did not have children. It has also led historians to overlook the copious evidence existing for this period of women who sought to escape or modify the constraints of the nuclear family."[11]

The essentializing of marriage and its impact on the history of women can be measured in part by the very conundrum posed by writing "women's history." Although a few intrepid scholars have undertaken an archaeology of men's history, for the most part women's history remains a particularized field, while men's experiences are assumed to be covered in any field of historical analysis. This is true in part; histories until very recently have recounted the events and domains of politics, warfare, and economics in which men have been understood to be the principal actors. At the same time, little history until recently (even in the field of family history) has accommodated the daily or life cycle experiences of men— including sexuality, marriage, fatherhood, relationships, and aging— while women's history has often been bound to pay at least some attention to these topics.[12]

For these reasons, little effort has been made to incorporate unmarried women into the larger literature, even in places and times when unmarried women were a significant proportion of the population. Examining the construction of the unmarried woman as marginal can also be highly revealing. This book aims to expose the ways and means—particularly the ideological and cultural work—through which such women's experiences were being defined as marginal even if that experience was quite common. For example, a number of historians of America in the modern period have effectively explored the means by which a cultural narrative about gender rendered female sexuality and female economic authority mutually problematic.[13] Single mothers supporting their children and women simply on their own needed work. At the same time,

11. Margaret Hunt, *The Middling Sort: Commerce, Gender and the Family in England, 1680–1780* (Berkeley, 1996), 137.
12. For an exception that also draws attention to this pattern, see Ann M. Little, "'Men on Top': The Farmer, the Minister, and Marriage in Early New England," *Pennsylvania History* 64 (Summer 1997): 123–50.
13. See, for example, Mary E. Odem, *Delinquent Daughters: Protecting and Policing Adolescent Female Sexuality in the United States, 1885–1920* (Chapel Hill, 1995); Joanne J. Meyerowitz, "Sexual Geography and Gender Economy: The Furnished-Room Districts of Chicago, 1890–1930," *Gender and History* 2 (Fall 1990); Rickie Solinger, *Wake Up Little Susie: Single Pregnancy and Race Before Roe v. Wade* (New York, 1992).

women's independent economic pursuits were depicted as evidence of sexual promiscuity. And the practices that regularly deprived women of employment opportunities sometimes meant that women turned to sex work for financial support. Thus the woman outside the normative experience of marriage and domesticity faced both an ideological injunction against her existence as well as the practical problems created by that ideology.

Historians of early modern Europe have paid some attention to the important population of widows and spinsters, providing essential interpretive direction but few synthetic accounts. Because of the concentration of Catholic convents in Europe, for example, studies of cloistered women have yielded significant insights into alternative female communities. Looking at issues ranging from the exercise of nuns' authority within bishoprics to the power of female prophets, to the cultural expressions cultivated by cloistered women, it is clear that these communities provided some unmarried women with an important viable alternative to marriage.[14] But aside from these analyses of single women's religious communities and demographic studies of marriage and remarriage patterns, much of this literature has focused on issues of the economic and political conditions of unmarried women's lives. In regimes as different as late eighteenth-century Ireland and seventeenth-century France, and from the Netherlands to Spain, scholars have discovered the depth of economic difficulty that single women, especially widows, faced.[15] They have also uncovered the important means by which women negotiated social, legal, and economic space and authority for themselves within even the most strictly patriarchal cultures.[16]

From these various strands, one can discern key strategies for exploring the significance of unmarried women. Within the parameters of

14. Some examples include Jodi Bilinkoff, *The Avila of St. Theresa* (Ithaca, N.Y., 1989); Judith Brown, *Immodest Acts: The Life of a Lesbian Nun in Renaissance Italy* (New York, 1986); Craig A. Monson, *Disembodied Voices: Music and Culture in an Early Modern Italian Convent* (Berkeley, 1995).

15. On widows and the economy, see Hufton, "Women Without Men"; Anne McCants, "The Not-So-Merry Widows of Amsterdam, 1740–1782" (paper presented to the Washington Area Economic History Workshop, April 1997); Mary Elizabeth Perry, *Gender and Disorder in Early Modern Seville* (Princeton, N.J., 1990), 172–76; Mary Prior, "Women and the Urban Economy: Oxford, 1500–1800," in Mary Prior, ed., *Women in English Society, 1500–1800* (London, 1985), 93–117.

16. For important accounts of the potential and limits of female agency, see Julie Hardwick, "Widowhood and Patriarchy in Seventeenth-Century France," *Journal of Social History* 26 (Fall 1992): 133–48, and "Women Working the Law." Others who have emphasized widows' capacity to shape their circumstances have mostly looked at elites. See, for example, Susan Staves, *Married Women's Separate Property in England, 1660–1833* (Cambridge, 1990); Robert J. Kalas, *Sixteenth Century Journal* (1992).

their individual class, religion, and specific historical and geographical context, unmarried women were poorer than married women. They attracted significant negative attention during times of upheaval, they gravitated to urban areas, and they cultivated communities of kin and other women to alleviate some of these stresses. These studies suggest two key avenues of further inquiry. First, variables of culture, especially religion, economic conditions, and legal structure, must be addressed. Second, unmarried women were a nexus for cultural tensions and thus provide a prism through which vital connections among politics, economics, and gender are refracted.

While scholars of the modern period are more attuned to the cultural and political issues involved in unmarried women's experiences in America, and historians of early modern Europe have begun to explore the cultural impact of this significant population, historians of early America have been slower to examine either the cultures of marriage or the experiences and impact of the unmarried. Kathleen Brown's recent work on the cultural and economic consolidation of Virginia elites through marriage demonstrates the importance of the performance of gender roles inscribed through marriage to the elaboration of planter identity, but most other considerations of marriage have not considered its cultural specificity and relevance.[17] In part this gap can be attributed to an intensive scholarly focus on early New England and the more recent attention paid to the early Chesapeake. In the seventeenth century these places were demographic and cultural extremes, the experiences of which encouraged Mary Beth Norton, in a major 1984 review of the literature on early American women, to draw a sharp distinction between women in early modern England and British North America. Demographic conditions in England such as late marriages and long widowhoods, she contended, meant that English women "spent as much of their adult lives outside a marital household as inside one." By contrast, Norton concluded, "few American women had similar experiences: demographic conditions precluded long-term, independent lives in the colonies."[18] Similarly, Laurel Thatcher Ulrich argued in her elegant and influential *Good Wives: Image and Reality in the Lives of Women in Northern New England, 1650–1750* that the words *woman* and *wife* were "virtually"

17. Kathleen M. Brown, *Good Wives, Nasty Wenches, and Anxious Patriarchs: Gender, Race, and Power in Colonial Virginia* (Chapel Hill, 1996), 247–82. Mary Beth Norton takes up the issue of widows' relative cultural authority within the seventeenth-century New England and Chesapeake colonies in *Founding Mothers and Fathers: Gendered Power and the Forming of American Society* (New York, 1996), esp. 138–80.
18. Mary Beth Norton, "The Evolution of White Women's Experience in Early America," *American Historical Review* 89 (June 1984): 600.

synonymous.[19] Women's extra-household actions were sanctioned only by the notion that they acted as "Deputy Husbands." Both Norton and Ulrich, therefore, described women's lives primarily as the lives of women within marriages and within households headed by men.[20]

There have been a couple of significant exceptions to this pattern. Two books published in the mid-1980s tackled the issues of female autonomy and the question of marriage. Rather than looking to either of the two more intensely studied regions, the Chesapeake and New England, and to the seventeenth century, both Joan Jensen, in *Loosening the Bonds: Mid-Atlantic Farm Women, 1750–1850,* and Lee Virginia Chambers-Schiller, in *Liberty a Better Husband. Single Women in America: The Generations of 1780–1840,* focused on the eighteenth and early nineteenth centuries and made the mid-Atlantic a major target of their investigations. Jensen opened up questions about women's autonomous ambitions and ambivalence about marriage, particularly their future as farm wives, and Chambers-Schiller uncovered a host of evidence to refute the long-accepted notion that a sex ratio imbalance had left too many women without the possibility of marriage. Instead, she found that many single women, especially in nineteenth-century New England, actively sought the means to protect a life that they termed "single blessedness." Although both books addressed issues of enormous importance for scholars of women's history and the early national period generally, for historians of rural America and educational development, neither work has been well incorporated into those larger literatures[21]

Not All Wives demonstrates that in the earlier period, the urban economy and the culture of Philadelphia provided unmarried women many of the same spaces and opportunities available to the nineteenth century women studied by Jensen and Chambers-Schiller. More important, *Not All Wives* explores the development of urban culture in dynamic tension

19. Laurel Thatcher Ulrich, *Good Wives: Image and Reality in the Lives of Women in Northern New England* (New York, 1980), 6.

20. Wilson's *Life After Death,* on widows in late eighteenth- and early nineteenth-century Philadelphia and its hinterland, emphasized widowhood as an extension of the marriage relationship, the conditions of which were shaped by men and women as part of an overall family economic strategy. For a different reading, see Vivian Bruce Conger, "'If Widow, Both Housewife and Husband May Be': Widows' Testamentary Freedom in Colonial Massachusetts and Maryland," in Larry D. Eldridge, ed., *Women and Freedom in Early America* (New York, 1997), esp. 248–49.

21. Joan M. Jensen, *Loosening the Bonds: Mid-Atlantic Farm Women, 1750–1850* (New Haven, 1986); Lee Virginia Chambers-Schiller, *Liberty a Better Husband. Single Women in America: The Generations of 1780–1840* (New Haven, 1984), esp. 29–30. See also Suzanne Lebsock, *The Free Women of Petersburg: Status and Culture in a Southern Town, 1784–1860* (New York, 1984); and Merril Smith, *Breaking the Bonds: Marital Discord in Pennsylvania, 1730–1830* (New York, 1991).

with the city's population of unmarried women. Rather than look exclusively at how such women fitted into their communities and culture, this book also examines the ways that those communities and that culture developed because of the presence and contributions of those women. Two goals are served by this approach: the experiences of the large population of unmarried women in Philadelphia can be narrated, and the broader features of the city's economy, society, and culture can be explored in new ways. Both the lives of unmarried women, whose importance in early modern cities is clear, and the incorporation of those women's lives into the larger context can be appreciated. This approach also puts women's marital status into play as an important category of historical analysis. New studies in the history of women and gender in the colonial period have opened up questions about the emergence of categories of identity such as race and class. Like race, class, and sexuality, marital status was a basic legal and cultural aspect of female identity. Historians must scrutinize the impact of marital status on women's lives and the impact of women's marital status on their families and communities. Through a heightened attention to the category of marital status, to the experiences and representations of unmarried women, we can see more clearly the regional cultures of gender and marriage in colonial British America.

AUNT BEK'S ODDITY: SITUATING UNMARRIED WOMEN IN URBAN AND REGIONAL CULTURES

The usual story of spinsterhood in early America is a bleak one. Women who never married, we are told, spent their lives regretting that they had missed the essential female experiences of marriage and motherhood.[22] An oft-quoted spinster from Hatfield, Massachusetts, Rebecca Dickinson, called "Aunt Bek," mourned "that others and all the world was in Possession of children and friends and a hous[e] and homes while I was so od[d] as to sit here alone."[23] But Aunt Bek's oddity was not typical of colonial spinsters. Her expressions and historians' reliance on them point up the importance of setting unmarried women's experi-

22. Terri L. Premo, *Winter Friends: Women Growing Old in the New Republic* (Urbana, Ill., 1990), 38, 45.
23. Diary of Rebecca Dickinson, quoted in Daniel White Wells and Reuben Field Wells, *A History of Hatfield Massachusetts* (Springfield, 1910), 206–7. Dickinson is quoted in many places, among them Chambers-Schiller, *Liberty a Better Husband*, 14; Premo, *Winter Friends*, 38, 43–44, 131, 135, 162, 168; Mary Beth Norton, *Liberty's Daughters: The Revolutionary Experience of American Women, 1750–1800* (Boston, 1980) 42, 142; and June Sprigg, *Domestick Beings* (New York, 1984), 8 and various.

ences within a specific temporal, spatial, and regional context. Unmarried women were common in most early modern populations, although they were more concentrated in some places and times than in others. Living in rural Hatfield, Dickinson was far more likely to feel "odd" than an unmarried woman living in an urban environment like Philadelphia.

This study is set in colonial Philadelphia in large measure to take advantage of the city's heterogeneous population and culture. The city's size and Quaker character also make it an attractive site for a study of unmarried women. Founded by William Penn with approximately two thousand English and Welsh Quaker émigrés in 1682, by 1775 it was the largest city in the British colonies, surpassed in England itself only by London and Bristol. Although the initial Quaker population's statistical predominance ended fairly quickly, Quakers continued to be a strong cultural and demographic force in the city. The impact of what Allan Tully has called "civil Quakerism" on Philadelphia's development, and on the culture of gender in the city, was profound.[24] English practices were just as evident in Philadelphia as elsewhere—in law, for example, where Quakers never thought of doing away with coverture—but they were filtered through a Quaker ethic. Unlike other British colonial cities, a military culture did not flourish in Philadelphia until the Revolutionary era. What constituted a major form of Anglo-American public culture and galvanized public culture around an explicitly masculine exercise was thus absent for most of the colonial period. In Philadelphia, women's public speaking also took on a different cast. As long as female Quaker ministers were among the most respected visitors and residents, the clashes over women's speech that occurred in other colonies and in England were not in evidence. Although many features of the city's public life would change with the arrival of war, militias, and the retreat of Quakers from political life in the late part of the colonial era, Quakerism heavily influenced the way that gender operated in the colonial city.

Like other early modern cities, Philadelphia abounded with unmarried women. The rates of marriage varied widely by ethnic, religious, and class group. Among Germans, for example, marriage was almost universal. Among Quakers and the elite, a much higher percentage—especially women—never married. And as in many other places around the early modern world, widowers remarried much more frequently than did widows: at about twice the rate, in fact.[25] Thus the urban dynamic included an important population of unmarried women. Carole Shammas

24. Allan Tully, *Forming American Politics: Ideals, Interests, and Institutions in Colonial New York and Pennsylvania* (Baltimore, 1994), 296, 285–309.
25. Susan E. Klepp, "Philadelphia in Transition: A Demographic History of the City and Its Occupational Groups" (Ph.D. diss., University of Pennsylvania, 1980), 120.

has pointed out that "most women were *not* mistresses of a household supported by male income,"[26] that is, wives of male household heads. Many unmarried women lived within male-headed households, but were unmarried daughters or other female kin, servants, or slaves. And, analyses show that women headed up to 20 percent of Philadelphia households in the late colonial period.

Unmarried women formed a significant proportion of the population in early modern Europe and America for three reasons. First, marriage was not universal. In the seventeenth century, the imperatives of new settlement and a strong religious proscription combined to make marriage and remarriage nearly universal, but studies of both New England and the Delaware Valley show a strong trend toward lower marriage rates beginning in the mid-eighteenth century; some specific religious and class groups demonstrated high rates of celibacy much earlier.[27] For example, Barry Levy's study of Quakers in the Welsh Tract bordering Philadelphia revealed that between 1681 and 1735, over 7 percent of men and 14 percent of women never married. That pattern of high rates of singleness among women especially seems to have been exaggerated in the later eighteenth century, as a study of Quakers in two New Jersey meetings showed that over 23 percent of Quaker women had not married by the age of fifty.[28] Moreover, the rates of marriage seem to have dropped considerably over the eighteenth and especially into the nineteenth centuries. By the mid-nineteenth century in cities as varied in culture as Boston and Charleston, over one-third of the adult free women were single.[29]

Second, marriage was only one stage in the life cycle of most women. Women experienced extended periods of singleness, sometimes as long

26. Carole Shammas, "The Female Social Structure of Philadelphia in 1775," *PMHB* 107 (January 1983): 72. A comparative study of female householding in the 1790s is Daniel Scott Smith, "Female Householding in Late Eighteenth-Century America and the Problem of Poverty," *Journal of Social History* 27 (Fall 1994): 83–107.

27. Lois Green Carr and Lorena S. Walsh, "The Planter's Wife: The Experience of White Women in Seventeenth-Century Maryland," *WMQ* 34 (October 1977): 542–71; Lorena S. Walsh, "'Till Death Do Us Part': Marriage and Family in Charles County, Maryland, 1658–1705," in Thad W. Tate and David L. Ammerman, eds., *The Chesapeake in the Seventeenth Century: Essays on Anglo-American Society* (Chapel Hill, 1979); Keyssar, "Widowhood in Eighteenth-Century Massachusetts."

28. See also studies by Susan Klepp and Robert Wells, all summarized in Klepp, "Fragmented Knowledge: Questions in Regional Demographic History," *Proceedings of the American Philosophical Society* 133 (1989): 232. For a comparison with marriage rates in early modern England and France, see Olwen Hufton, *The Prospect Before Her: A History of Women in Western Europe, 1500–1800* (New York, 1996), 256; and "Women Without Men: Widows and Spinsters in Britain and France in the Eighteenth Century," *Journal of Family History* 9 (1984): 355–76.

29. According to an 1845 census examined by Jane H. Pease and William H. Pease, *Ladies, Women, and Wenches: Choice and Constraint in Antebellum Charleston and Boston*

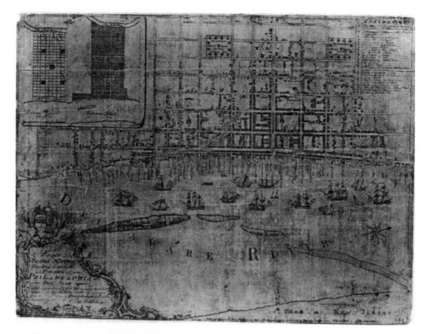

1. This 1762 map of Philadelphia shows streets, alleys, and buildings. Courtesy of The Library Company of Philadelphia.

as or longer than periods of marriage. In almost every historical setting that historians and demographers have studied, widows remarried much less often and much less quickly than did widowers.[30] In colonial America alone, one study shows that the remarriage rate for widows dropped by half from the seventeenth to the eighteenth centuries. This trend also seems to have intensified over time.[31] Among widows in early nineteenth-century Philadelphia, for example, only 17 percent ever remarried.[32]

Third, the population of unmarried women was much higher in urban

(Chapel Hill, 1990), 10–11. On the transition in New England from almost universal marriage to high rates of spinsterhood, see Chambers-Schiller, *Liberty a Better Husband*, 5.

30. A review of the literature on remarriage in early modern Europe is found in Hufton, *The Prospect Before Her*, 221–32.

31. Conger, "'If Widow, Both Housewife and Husband May Be,'" 265 n.23.

32. From the research of Susan Klepp, as cited in Wilson, *Life After Death*, 2, 172, 210 (n. 6). On changing rates of marriage and economic considerations, see Guido Ruggiero, *The Boundaries of Eros: Sex, Crime and Sexuality in Renaissance Venice* (New York, 1985), 13–15; Philip J. Greven, "Family Structure in Seventeenth-Century Andover, Massachusetts," *WMQ* 23 (1966): 234–56. On marriage decisions in England, see Jeremy Boulton, "London Widowhood Revisited: The Decline of Female Remarriage in the Seventeenth and Eighteenth Centuries," *Continuity and Change* 5 (1990): 323–55; Peter Earle, "The Female

areas, reaching extraordinary proportions in early modern cities from Boston to Philadelphia, London to Venice. Unmarried women appeared in large numbers as household domestics, they clustered together in households, and they headed households. As Olwen Hufton reports in her recent survey of women in early modern Europe, even without accounting for spinsters or widows living within other households or even clustered together in households, that "it was usual, throughout Europe, for widows to constitute about 12 percent of the heads of urban families."[33] In areas of pre-Revolutionary Philadelphia, over 20 percent of households were headed by women. Other cities were "widow-rich" even if widows did not head their own families. Widows constituted a major presence in Boston, for example, especially after the Seven Years War, when their numbers reached as high as 25 percent of household heads, and presumably an even larger proportion of household inmates.[34] In cities of southern Europe, a combination of an unbalanced sex ratio and widows' strategies of reclaiming their dowry portions from their rural families created substantial communities of unmarried female renters.[35] These women's presence in the labor force, public culture, and urban life generally helped shaped the character of the early modern city.

Unmarried women were either drawn to the urban environment for economic opportunity or originated in these cities and decided, for whatever reasons, not to marry or remarry. The striking contrast of urban and rural patterns of singleness, marriage, and remarriage suggests that the nature of the urban economy was largely responsible for making such decisions tenable. Unlike the rural household economy, the urban economy could absorb, and in fact demanded, the labor of unmarried women.[36] High demand for domestic labor as well as service and retail labor in cities produced occupational opportunities for women that, although

Labour Market in London in the Late-Seventeenth and Early-Eighteenth Centuries," *Economic History Review* 42 (1989): 328–53.

33. Hufton, *The Prospect Before Her*, 249.

34. Alfred Young, "The Women of Boston: 'Persons of Consequence' in the Making of the American Revolution, 1765–76," in Harriet B. Applewhite and Darlene G. Levy, eds., *Women and Politics in the Age of the Democratic Revolutions* (Ann Arbor, 1990), 184.

35. Hufton, *The Prospect Before Her*, 249–50, on Spanish and Italian cities, especially Roman widows clustered around the Piazza Novona, where over a third of the households were headed by widows.

36. Recent research on the Delaware Valley and New England has demonstrated the extent to which unmarried women were employed as farm labor and in rural households. This kind of work arrangement usually represented a moment in young women's life cycle before they were expected to marry. See, for example, Lucy Simler, "The Landless Worker: An Index of Economic and Social Change in Chester County, Pennsylvania, 1750–1850," *PMHB* 114 (April 1990): 163–99; Laurel Thatcher Ulrich, "Martha Ballard and Her Girls: Women's Work in Eighteenth-Century Maine," in Stephen Innes, ed., *Work and Labor in Early America* (Chapel Hill, 1988).

always more limited than men's, were vastly more abundant and more varied than in the countryside.[37]

A combination of factors, including sex ratios, individual choice, cultural priorities, and economic opportunities, could produce transitions in the rates of marriage and remarriage in a specific setting. The economics of singleness came in a variety of forms, and although singleness or marriage could mean more or less income or economic capital, in different historical settings marriage or singleness could also mean more or less cultural capital, opportunity, or independence. The value placed on each might vary significantly from one place and time to another. Broad cultural changes contributed to changes in the population of spinsters and widows. The rise of a sentimental model of marriage, in which affection and free choice were to be valued over the creation of an economic partnership, worked in some cases to make marriages more difficult to achieve.[38] Remaining single might prove preferable to making the wrong marriage. Expanding opportunities for women, in an economic, legal, or social sense, also contributed to declining rates of marriage and remarriage in a variety of historical contexts.[39] In early nineteenth-century America, expanding educational opportunities combined with new opportunities in teaching and reform vocations, as well as emerging market conditions in which families prized unmarried women's labor, encouraged a generation of American women to embrace spinsterhood.[40]

Some women chose to avoid marriage altogether for the simple reason that they felt disinclined toward such a relationship. As Philadelphian Hannah Griffitts wrote to a married cousin, "There are many of you weded ones who I believe are Placed in your Proper Sphere and I sincerely wish you encrease of Hapiness in it—without envying you one atom." Her own life, she continued, would be different by choice: "Everyone is not fitted for the single life—nor was I ever moulded for The weded one."[41]

37. Christine Stansell's pathbreaking work in gender and urban history, *City of Women: Sex and Class in New York, 1789–1860* (Urbana, Ill., 1982), illuminated the culture of urban women in early nineteenth-century New York.

38. See Susan E. Klepp and Karin Wulf, "Cultural Crosscurrents: Quaker Marriage and Constrained Sensibility in the Eighteenth-Century Delaware Valley" (paper presented to the Philadelphia Center for Early American Studies Seminar, May 16, 1997).

39. Barbara Todd, "The Remarrying Widow: A Stereotype Reconsidered," in Mary Prior, ed., *Women in English Society, 1500–1800* (London, 1985), 54–83. See also Boulton's refutation of what he calls this "liberation ideology" of spinsterhood and widowhood, "London Widowhood Revisited," 325–26, and Todd's response to Boulton in "Demographic Determinism and Female Agency: The Remarrying Widow Reconsidered . . . Again," *Continuity and Change* 9 (1994).

40. Chambers-Schiller, *Liberty a Better Husband*, 29–46.

41. Hannah Griffitts to "My Dear Cousin," n.d., Edward Wanton Smith Collection, QC.

Unmarried women's prominence in cities demonstrates one important context of their experiences and is mirrored by the distinctions among colonial regions. Variations in legal practices, demography, labor patterns (including the overwhelming significance of slavery in both the Chesapeake and Lower South), religious culture, and economic conditions (including those affected by warfare in the late seventeenth and eighteenth centuries) affected many aspects of regional culture, including gender. From these variations and their impact on the ideals and practices of gender emerged distinct cultures of marriage and singleness. Although much work in this field has focused on early New England and the Chesapeake, and much less scholarship is available for the mid-Atlantic and Lower South, some comparative features of distinctive regional cultures of marriage can be discerned from the existing literature. By the mid-eighteenth century an Anglo-American elite, drawn to metropolitan culture, had begun to share an assimilated view of marriage and, by default, singleness. But in the seventeenth and early eighteenth centuries, each region experienced its own distinctive culture of marriage and singleness. Perhaps even more important, the metropolitan culture of elite Anglo-Americans had much less impact on the vast majority of colonials—many of them in servitude or bound in slavery—for whom marriage represented a very different kind of achievement or arrangement.

New England's culture of marriage was most distinctive in the seventeenth century, when the Puritan legal and cultural regime was dominant. Early New Englanders generally viewed spinsters with suspicion and hostility. The ideology and practice of Puritanism depended on a strict construction of gender, which placed women as wives and mothers within patriarchal households. Ideally, "woman" and "wife" were synonymous in meaning and unanimous in obedience to God and husband.[42] As a Boston bookseller commented in 1686, "An old (or Superannuated) Maid . . . is thought such a curse as nothing can exceed it, and look'd on as a dismal Spectacle."[43] In the eighteenth century, as Puritan patriarchy waned, another patriarchal system took its place, but it was no more tolerant of the spinster or widow. A lingering skepticism about singleness combined with a harsh economic climate for women to keep

42. Ulrich, *Good Wives*, 6–7. On changing patriarchal forms in New England, see Cornelia Hughes Dayton, *Women Before the Bar: Gender, Law, and Society in Connecticut, 1639–1789* (Chapel Hill, 1996).

43. Quoted in Lyle Koehler, *A Search for Power: The "Weaker Sex" in Seventeenth-Century New England* (Urbana, Ill., 1980). On the connections of Puritan theology, household order, and attacks on (especially female) celibacy, see Erik R. Seeman, "'It is Better to Marry Than to Burn': Anglo-American Attitudes toward Celibacy, 1600–1800," *Journal of Family History* (forthcoming).

the status—legal, cultural, and economic—of unmarried women quite low. This status changed somewhat in the late eighteenth and early nineteenth centuries, as economic and educational opportunities for women provoked a slightly more tolerant climate for singleness, just as women began to assert more control over the timing of marriage and fertility.[44]

The culture of marriage in the Chesapeake was profoundly affected by two demographic phenomena that became interpolated with cultural meaning: the early sex ratio imbalance among European immigrants and the importation and enslavement of Africans. In the first years of Chesapeake settlement, demographic conditions seemed to favor widows economically compared to their sisters in England or other parts of the nascent empire. Because so many women were widowed at a young age and had dependent children, for example, they received larger shares of their husband's estates than women in some other regions.[45] Widows' economic power posed little challenge to that of men, but the phenomenon was so marked among contemporaries that one early writer called "Rich Widows . . . the Best Commodity this Country Affords."[46] This invested marriage with even more capacity to make or cement ambitions; to succeed in the early Chesapeake, men looked to marry, and to marry well. Any advantages widows might have discerned in the mid-seventeenth century, particularly in legal latitude and a seemingly wide choice of marriage partners, were ultimately considerably reined in. Consolidating class, gender, and race interests, the late seventeenth century saw a vigorous enforcement of patriarchal values in law and in culture.[47]

With the advent of a newly racialized patriarchy, the enforcement of ideals associated with white womanhood became more important. Part of that program involved defining marriage as a white institution, enshrining white womanhood with the mantle of wives and domesticated heterosexuality, and ascribing an opposing, lascivious sexuality to black women.[48] Thus in the Chesapeake and by extension in the Lower South,

44. On women's changing expressions of fertility and the changing cultural construction of fertility, see Susan E. Klepp, "Revolutionary Bodies: Women and the Fertility Transition in the Mid-Atlantic Region, 1760–1820," *JAH* 85 (December 1998): 910–45.

45. Lois Green Carr and Lorena Walsh, "The Planter's Wife: The Experience of White Women in Seventeenth-Century Maryland," *WMQ* 34 (October 1977): 542–71.

46. From Terri Lynn Snyder, "'Rich Widows Are the Best Commodity This Country Affords': Gender Relations and the Rehabilitation of Patriarchy in Virginia, 1669–1700" (Ph.D. diss., University of Iowa, 1992).

47. Brown, *Good Wives, Nasty Wenches, and Anxious Patriarchs*, 287–91; Snyder, "'Rich Widows Are the Best Commodity,'" passim.

48. On the imbrication of gender, race, and sexuality in slaveholding societies, see especially Brown, *Good Wives, Nasty Wenches, and Anxious Patriarchs*; and Deborah Gray White, *Ar'n't I a Woman: Female Slaves in the Plantation South* (New York, 1985).

[18]

marriage became a signifier for gender, race, and sexuality.[49] Laws preventing interracial unions and ultimately forbidding (or simply not recognizing) marriage between enslaved people consolidated the status and practice of marriage as the privilege of whites. Often harshly demanding in the late seventeenth and eighteenth century, the language that described marriage and its connections to patriarchal order grew more sentimental and reflective in the late eighteenth century. Virginia's "big men" described their wives and families as part of a consensual union whose centrifugal force was not power but love.[50] However they described it, women's sexuality, and by explicit extension their marital status was a key component in the construction of southern racial and gender hierarchy. As Kirsten Fischer has recently demonstrated, slanderous charges of interracial sex were extremely dangerous to women who were unmarried and who were therefore vulnerable by the very nature of their suspect marital status.[51]

By virtue of their heterogeneous European population, their urbanity, their economic structure, and their religious diversity, the middle colonies of New York, New Jersey, and Pennsylvania sharply contrasted with both New England and the South. The hegemony of Anglo-American culture was contested (at times fiercely) by the prevalence of Dutch and German values. Dutch property laws, for example, gave women more control over property and thus more voice in public matters.[52] The varieties of Protestantism, particularly dissenting groups, made the imposition of any dominant theological system impossible. If any religious

49. Brown, *Good Wives, Nasty Wenches, and Anxious Patriarchs*, 125–28, discusses the distinct opportunities and meanings of marriage for whites and blacks in late seventeenth-century Virginia. For an example of similar efforts to use marriage as a way of implementing specific ideologies of race and gender in a colonial society, see Ramon Gutierrez, *When Jesus Came the Corn Mothers Went Away: Marriage, Sexuality and Power in New Mexico, 1500–1846* (Stanford, 1991).

50. In a telling elision of the ways that slave marriages were not recognized by law and that planters regularly ignored voluntary unions when it served their interests, Robert Bolling argued in 1760 that only consent made a marriage valid. In a fit of pique over Anne Miller's rejection of him, Bolling argued that their verbal commitments to one another made her his wife. J. A. Leo Lemay, *Robert Bolling Woos Anne Miller: Love and Courtship in Colonial Virginia, 1760* (Charlottesville, Va., 1990), 10. The language of affective unions is explored in Jan Lewis, *The Pursuit of Happiness: Family and Values in Jefferson's Virginia* (Cambridge, 1983).

51. Kirsten Fischer, "'False, Feigned, and Scandalous Words': Sexual Slander and Racial Ideology in Colonial North Carolina," in Catherine Clinton and Michele Gillespie, *The Devil's Lane: Sex and Race in the Early South* (New York, 1997), 142–43. See also the case of Anne Tayloe, discussed in Brown, *Good Wives, Nasty Wenches, and Anxious Patriarchs*, 306–18.

52. David E. Narrett, "Men's Wills and Women's Property Rights in Colonial New York," in Ronald Hoffman and Peter J. Albert, eds., *Women in the Age of the American Revolution* (Charlottesville, Va., 1989), 91–133.

group before the Revolution was able to assert its culture, it was the Quakers, whose influences were most strongly felt in the Delaware Valley. The proximity of the two largest cities in the colonies, New York and Philadelphia, added a component of cultural diversity. And the economic diversity of the middle colonies would not permit the development of a cultural system as bound to one economic form as was that of the southern colonies.

This remarkable diversity in the mid-Atlantic created a much less coherent culture of gender than in the other regions. By extension, the cultures of marriage and singleness in this region were also less coherent. For example, while Quakers exhibited some of the highest rates of celibacy of any group in the colonies, the heavily German population of Germantown, just outside Philadelphia, seems to have exhibited some of the lowest.[53] And yet there was remarkable diversity within the German population itself. Moravians and other radical pietists maintained spiritual communities of single persons and a religious ideal of marriage far different from that of English Protestants. Out of this diversity of experience emerged a popular culture that accommodated differences to a greater extent than other places. The dominance of Anglo-American gender hierarchy was clear, but its iteration was different from other regions of British America.

On Sources and Methods

This study draws on a wide array of sources to illuminate the lives and the importance of unmarried women. While a comparatively greater body of material has survived that speaks to the interests and experiences of wealthier women, a range of sources nevertheless allows working and poor women to be the focus of much of the text. I analyzed publicly and privately generated records with several goals in mind: to create a prosopography of unmarried women for periods in which overlapping records are extant, to generate portraits of individual women's lives, and to recover the urban culture that these women helped shape and were simultaneously shaped by.

I systematically reviewed public records such as tax records, Constable's Returns (a kind of census), court dockets, and the minutes and accounts of public poor relief officials to help construct a portrait of un-

---

53. Stephanie Grauman Wolf, *Urban Village: Population, Community, and Family Structure in Germantown, Pennsylvania, 1683–1800* (Princeton, 1986), 254.

married women's economic status. Although only a fraction of these materials are extant, enough survive to depict significant periods, and in all cases I have used these records to re-create eighteenth-century conditions and culture. For example, I have relied heavily on tax assessments for Philadelphia City and County. Many historians have outlined the problems inherent in using these tax lists, arguing that the assessments underestimate the concentration of wealth in upper brackets because important sources of wealth, such as book debts, the contents of warehouses, and other merchant paraphernalia, were not taxable. Other problems with using tax assessments include suspicions of chronic undercounting, the accuracy of the assessors, and the slippery and often inexplicable assessors' estimates of occupational value and situations requiring informal abatements.[54] I have chosen to view the tax assessments and other public documents not as perfect or even flawed reports of an individual's actual and relative wealth, but as culturally informed representations of economic condition.

A full range of private records, including account books, commonplace books, correspondence, diaries, and school materials, proved vital in fleshing out the ideologies of gender, marriage, and singleness that permeated Philadelphia at this time. A crucial set of printed sources, especially almanacs and literary magazines, provided the material for an examination of the cultural forum for those ideas. In eighteenth-century Philadelphia, access to printed materials from Europe was very good, and several local printers kept busy supplying the demands of a reading public. At the high end of the scale, elites perused a wide range of literary materials from abroad, primarily from England.[55] Elite Philadelphians also subscribed to the locally produced literary magazines, which reprinted European material as well as the work of local authors. These magazines were passed through circles of friends and family and enjoyed a relatively wide readership among men and women of the middling and upper sort.[56] Ordinary folk became acquainted with some of the same ma-

54. Gary B. Nash, "Urban Wealth and Poverty in Pre Revolutionary Philadelphia," *Journal of Interdisciplinary History* 6 (1976): 547–48. See also Billy G. Smith, *The "Lower Sort": Philadelphia's Laboring People, 1750–1800* (Ithaca, N.Y., 1990), 224–29.

55. The libraries of individual Philadelphians, as well as the lending libraries, the Library Company of Philadelphia, the Union Library, and school libraries, are discussed in Edwin Wolf II, *The Book Culture of a Colonial American City: Philadelphia Books, Bookmen, and Booksellers* (Oxford, 1988), 1–34.

56. Pattie Cowell, "Colonial Poets and the Magazine Trade, 1741–1775," *Early American Literature* 24 (1989): 112–19, provides some information on publishers, authors, and readers (or subscribers) of literary magazines. Philadelphia figured prominently in this business, sustaining several magazines for relatively long periods during the colonial era. Other works that suggest regional literary cultures include Richard Beale Davis, *A Colo-*

terial through newspapers that reprinted poetry, but especially through almanacs.[57] As the most popular venue for literature in the colonies, almanacs over the eighteenth century contained increasing amounts of diversionary material.[58] This "usable fiction" translated moral lessons and observations into palatable, recognizable forms.[59]

THIS INTRODUCTION HAS stressed the significance of unmarried women as a population in early modern Europe and America, particularly in cities. It has emphasized as well the importance of this group as a site of inquiry, because of the intersections of cultural norms and expressions about gender, marriage, the nature of authority, and the dynamic of urban culture that their presence and their impact reveal. The book examines several locations where these intersections appear most vividly, beginning with the most intimate realms of social interaction and proceeding to more communal and public realms. The first chapter, "Martha Cooper's Choice: Literature and Mentality," argues that a counterdiscourse of marital resistance flourished in the Delaware Valley. In materials as widely varied as almanacs and private commonplace books, women considered the potentially tyrannical nature of marriage. Chapter 2, on religion and self, explores the development of a feminine model of individualism based on corporeal possession and spiritual independence, as opposed to the developing masculine notion of materially based individualism. It delineates how some women, especially Quakers but also some German sectarians, began to see marriage as a threat to

nial Southern Bookshelf: Reading in the Eighteenth Century (Athens, Ga., 1979), and William J. Gilmore, Reading Becomes a Necessity of Life: Material and Cultural Life in Rural New England, 1780–1835 (Knoxville, Tenn., 1989). Rosalind Remer examines the growing commercialization and thus expansion of literary culture in Printers and Men of Capital: Philadelphia Book Publishers in the New Republic (Philadelphia, 1996).

57. David Jaffe, "The Village Enlightenment in New England, 1760–1820," WMQ 47 (1990): 331. Jaffe estimates, based on the work of Marion Bareber Stowell and others, that almanacs in colonial New England could reach a readership of sixty thousand. David Hall concludes that almanacs were "widely available" and includes them, with a limited number of other books such as Bibles, psalmbooks, and primers, in a category of books most colonials would have come into contact with, if not owned themselves. Hall, "The Uses of Literacy in New England, 1600–1850," 24. Many studies of readership use estate inventories, but the most common forms of popular literature, almanacs and chapbooks, would not have been inventoried; they were worth too little. Similarly, they rarely appeared in booksellers' ads because they were so cheap. Margaret Spufford, Small Books and Pleasant Histories: Popular Fiction and Its Readership in Seventeenth-Century England (Athens, Ga., 1982), 48.

58. See, for example, the difference between the Ephemeris for the Year 1721 by "John Jerman" and Father Abraham's Almanack for 1770, both at the LCP.

59. I am using a definition of "usable fiction" provided by Sarah Emily Newton, "Wise and Foolish Virgins: 'Usable Fiction' and the Early American Conduct Tradition," Early American Literature 25 (1990): 139–67.

their achievement of a satisfactorily independent spiritual relationship with God.

The next two chapters move into the communal realms of the household and the urban neighborhood. Chapter 3 focuses on the place and role of single women within households, as residents of other marital households, as heads of their own households (either with children or with other unmarried women), and as dependents such as domestic servants. Chapter 4 links unmarried women's work to the process of community formation. Through networks of association, in which unmarried women were important participants, urban community developed in Philadelphia neighborhoods. This chapter also takes up the important question of what kinds of work women did, and how much, and how women acquired wealth.

The last two chapters deal with the developing public world through an examination of public poor relief policies and political culture. Chapter 5 looks in detail at the lives of poor women, their experiences with poor relief, and the implications for women of the late colonial transition to institutional poor relief. Chapter 6 explores the drive to equate masculinity with independence and femininity with dependence, and the impact on political culture. Examining the actions of propertied unmarried women and their access to certain kinds of local political authority as property owners, this chapter then examines these women's experiences during the transition from property to masculinity as the prerequisite for political authority. It argues that by the close of the colonial period, the connections among gender, conceptions of marriage, and women's marital status were fundamental aspects of the transition in political culture.

We begin by meeting Martha Cooper and her father, David Cooper, both engaged with the issue of Martha's impending maturity and the possibility of an eventual marriage. Imbedded deep in the Coopers' Anglo-American heritage was an array of cultural ideals of masculinity and femininity about the significance of hierarchy and the kinds of authority that men should wield over wives and parents over children, and the function of marriage as a form of property consolidation. Layered over these presumptions were a set of Quakerly ethics of equality and partnership, a disavowal of certain forms of hierarchy, including the exercise of spousal and parental power, and a commitment to marriages made by choice and the guidance of God's light. An urban- and class-based aesthetic topped this cultural layer cake, leading both Coopers to express their deepest desires and emotions in the discursive forms of the educated elite. For each of the Coopers, quite apart from the cultural strata on which they perched, the problem of marriage was very personal indeed.

[23]

[1]

Martha Cooper's Choice: Literature and Mentality

Many a father worried over his daughter's future. David Cooper, raising his children alone after the death of his wife in 1759, was especially concerned about his eldest daughter, Martha. Was she prepared for adulthood? Had he done everything he could to help prepare her? He was not sure. Martha's successes and failures would be the test of David Cooper's parenting skills, and, for better or for worse, she would be a role model for her younger brothers and sisters. Cooper was an expressive man, given to directing his thoughts and emotions through the nub of a pen. So when Martha Cooper began to look less like a girl and more like a young woman to her father, he sat down to write to her of his love and concern.

"My Daughter Martha," he began, "Thou art now drawing near the State of a Woman, the Journey of Life, lies before thee, now is the Critical Stage."[1] In her father's eyes, the most treacherous part of Martha's "Journey" was the decision to marry. "When thee comes to know the World," he warned, "thee will admire to find how few are happy in a married life." The worst marriages were marked by a painful inequity, and Cooper brooded over the possibility that Martha would suffer this kind of unhappiness. It was not his role to make decisions for her, for he had determined that "thee shall be thy own Chooser," but he wanted to make sure she understood the ramifications of a poor choice:.

> Oh how would it afflict me, what unhappiness would it intail on the remainder of my days, should I live to see thee disagreeably married, tyed for Life to a Man not worthy of thee, & who after he had thee fast would disregard thee & make thee a Slave that himself might be a GentleMan—

1. David Cooper to Martha Cooper, n.d., Allinson Collection, QC.

Avoid a Man Bold, & Full of himself [for they make] Insolent & Overrule-ing Husbands & treat their Wives with disregard.

Rather than risk this fate, Cooper encouraged his daughter to take the counsel of her parent, to pray for additional guidance, to exercise caution in evaluating young men, and, above all else, to wait rather than rush-ing into marriage. Martha's independence in the absence of her mother made her, David Cooper felt, particularly vulnerable to attention. After all, "young people beginning to keep company are exceeding apt" to fall for their first flirtation. "Thy being my Housekeeper, & [your] prudent management at this age, occations thee to be much talk'd of," and per-haps the object of a particular suitor's attentions. But her father wanted her to "Think not of Marrying my Child, till thee has seen enough of the World, & attain[ed] years of maturity, & experience sufficient, to enable thee to Judge, & Choose for thyself." David Cooper's extraordinary letter expressed his devotion to his daughter and his anxieties about his par-enting and her future, as well as a particular cultural perspective on marriage.[2]

Perhaps it is no wonder that David Cooper's daughter also chose written expression to communicate her most intimate concerns. Like many other young women in late colonial Philadelphia, Martha Cooper copied favorite, meaningful poems into a commonplace book. A Quaker, Cooper followed the example of the many educated women in her social and kinship group who kept commonplace books to collect special pieces of poetry and prose.[3] These works derived from a variety of sources. Copyists often exchanged and copied from one another's books. Some-times they copied directly from English or American literary magazines or even from current almanacs, one of the most widely read materials after the Bible. Copying was also a school activity, as schoolteachers regularly presented their students with poetry to copy. Not surprisingly given her father's concerns, one of the poems Cooper copied into her book was titled "Choice of a Companion."[4] She may have found this poem in the widely circulated commonplace book of a friend, but it also

2. For a similar sentiment, see John Gregory's *A Father's Legacy to His Daughters* (Lon-don: reprinted Philadelphia, John Dunlap, 1775), esp. 104–10. Gregory, like Cooper, claimed to wish only a happy marriage for his daughters, for "Heaven forbid you should ever relinquish the ease and independence of a single life, to become the slaves of a fool or a tyrant's caprice." (Gregory, 109–10). I am grateful to Ruth Wallis Herndon for this reference.
3. See Catherine La Courreye and Karin A. Wulf, eds., *Milcah Martha Moore's Book: A Commonplace Book of Early American Literature* (State College, Pa., 1997).
4. Martha Cooper Allinson Commonplace Book, c. 1770, QC.

appeared in the Philadelphia publication of *Father Abraham's Almanack* for 1771 under the title "The Maiden's Choice."[5]

The poem "Choice of a Companion" addressed the anxieties attendant on choosing a marriage partner, opening with a prayerful plea for God's assistance in making such an important decision. "If e'er I'm doomed the marriage chain to wear," Cooper carefully copied, "Propitious Heaven attend my Virgin prayer." The poem then listed desirable qualities in a prospective mate, such as an "Unblemish'd . . . character" and an "easy but not great" fortune. It also indicated the author's preference for a marriage of companions rather than a hierarchically ordered marriage. The husband in question, Cooper wrote, should not be tyrannical, but should "kindly govern with a gentle sway." Although she was surely not the original author of this poem, Martha Cooper nonetheless signed her name to it in her commonplace book, signifying, even beyond the commitment to copy it in the first place, her sympathy with its sentiments.

Part of a much larger discourse on marriage in colonial society, these verses articulated through popular literature the anxieties and problems associated with both the public and domestic aspects of marital relationships.[6] This poem about "Choice" also raised important questions about not just whom to marry, but whether to marry at all.[7] If no potential husband had the desired qualities, the "Maiden's Choice" was to remain single. The prayerful quality of the poem continues through the last stanza: "Be this my fate if e'er I'm made a wife,/ Or keep me happy in a single Life."

The anonymous poet's, and perhaps by extension Martha Cooper's, insistence on either a good marriage or no marriage, and Cooper's father's

5. *Father Abraham's Almanack for . . . 1771* (Philadelphia, 1770). This poem was also printed in the *Halifax Gazette* in 1765, according to J. A. Leo Lemay, *A Calendar of American Poetry in the Colonial Newspapers and Magazines and in the Major English Magazines Through 1765* (Worcester, Mass., 1972), 286. For other analyses of the "choice" genre, see David Shields, "Happiness in Society: The Development of an Eighteenth-Century American Poetic Ideal," *American Literature* 55 (December 1983): 541–559; and Margaret Ezell, *The Patriarch's Wife: Literary Evidence and the History of the Family* (Chapel Hill, N.C., 1987), 101–107.

6. I use the term "popular literature" to refer to broadly circulated material (through publication, borrowing, or reading aloud) or to literature intended for a broad audience. For helpful definitions, see the Introduction to Daniel Cohen, *Pillars of Salt, Monuments of Grace: New England Crime Literature and the Origins of American Popular Culture, 1674–1860* (New York, 1993), and David Hall, "Readers and Reading in America: Historical and Critical Perspectives," *Proceedings of the American Antiquarian Society* 103 (1993): 340–47.

7. A number of scholars have noted the late eighteenth-century fascination with the themes of Hannah Webster Foster's *The Coquette* (1797), which centered on a disastrous marriage choice. See, for example, Cathy Davidson, *Revolution and the Word: The Rise of the Novel in Early America* (Chapel Hill, N.C., 1986), and Carroll Smith-Rosenberg, "Domesticating Virtue: Coquettes and Revolutionaries in Young America," in Elaine Scarry, ed., *Literature and the Body: Essays on Populations and Persons*, (Baltimore, 1988), 160–84.

contention that good marriages were rare, were part of a public barrage of marital critique. In letters, diaries, and commonplace books as well as in popular literature appearing in colonial newspapers, literary magazines, and almanacs, Philadelphians reiterated their concerns that marriage and freedom were diametrically and unacceptably opposed, particularly for women. Literary depictions of the specters of the tyrannical spouse and the financially motivated match gave rise to alternative portraits of marriage and the single woman. The typically cranky spinster was replaced in some contexts by the virtuous virgin who defied social pressures and chose not to marry.

Traditionally, Anglo-American law and custom dictated a woman's submission in marriage to her husband, the patriarch and head of their household. The notion of a natural hierarchy of men over women was first articulated in religious terms. Scripture and doctrine provided Christians with a wealth of evidence that men's authority over women was part of God's plan and that it was in the household of a conjugal couple that this plan was enacted.

But such arrangements did not sit comfortably for many women (and some men). A variety of countering discourses and ideologies, including Protestant theology, rational thinking, and the emerging political language that emphasized the importance of liberty, challenged social and cultural hierarchies. The assumptions of privilege bestowed by birthright and by property were challenged in the name of individual equalities. In most cases these challenges were launched on behalf of men of little property, whose possession of masculinity but not much else was to give them new access to politics and governance. But as traditional social ordering was challenged and old assumptions about appropriate social relationships were eyed more critically, even the hierarchy of gender that composed the very center of colonial households—and thus colonial society itself—was questioned.

Neither Protestantism nor the Enlightenment could completely overturn these assumptions, but challengers became increasingly vociferous.[8] One of the most important topics around which debate circled was marriage, especially the function of hierarchy within it. Writers were already assailing the notion of marriage as an economic arrangement and were instead pressing the view that the best marriages were those in which true affection reigned. At the same time, writers debated the relationship between affection and authority within marriage. In British America,

8. A good introduction to the ensuing debates, culminating in the post-Revolutionary writings of English, American, and French women on the subject of women and democracy is Susan Groag Bell and Karen M. Offen, eds., *Women, the Family and Freedom: The Debate in Documents* (Stanford, Calif., 1983), pt. 1.

2. "Choice of a Companion," from Martha Cooper's commonplace book. Courtesy of the Haverford College Library, Quaker Collection.

colonists drew on English literary traditions, and, often, English authors to represent the identification of marriage and family with a particular kind of civil society.[9] Some writers argued that men would naturally rule and women would most happily obey in matches motivated by love. Others argued that such rigid patterns of power and authority were unnecessary; a loving marriage would be marked by the lack of hierarchy.

The figure of the unmarried woman constantly shadowed this debate. Widows and spinsters had long entertained the popular imagination, alternately appearing as objects of scorn, pity, or antagonism. In early modern Europe and America, the strong association of witchcraft with unmarried, independent women was just one example of the ways in which widows and spinsters were vilified.[10] The most infamous examples of American colonists' commentary on spinsterhood come from New England, where spinsters were looked on as "a dismal spectacle."[11] Widows, spinsters, and young virgins also populated literature, from the almanacs carried by thousands to the commonplace books compiled by women like Martha Cooper. In these varied forms, unmarried women were regularly used to depict the significance of marriage. Elaborate descriptions of the unhappy, perilous existence of unmarried women caricatured spinsters as alternately sluttish or prudish, arrogantly picky or ridiculously unwise about selecting a mate. Widows often appeared as poor and helpless to support their children.

In many poetry and prose depictions, the figure of an unmarried woman was used as a form of intellectual and cultural discipline; women who did not marry, or were no longer married would be subject to the kinds of ridicule or misfortune that befell the women in the stories. But unmarried women could also represent the counter-argument. Valiant widows, reasonable spinsters, and virtuous virgins challenged the hegemony of marriage and argued for its irrationality, arduousness, and potential for misery. Although much of the debate about marriage and gen-

9. Marriage was often used as a political metaphor. See, for example, Jay Fliegelman, *Prodigals and Pilgrims: The American Revolution Against Patriarchal Authority* (Cambridge, 1982), and Jan Lewis, "The Republican Wife: Virtue and Seduction in the Early Republic," *WMQ* 44 (October 1987): 689–721.

10. On the connections among gender, marital status, and witchcraft accusations, see Carol Karlsen, *Devil in the Shape of a Woman: Witchcraft in Colonial New England* (New York, 1987), and Anne Llewellyn Barstow, *Witchcraze: A New History of the European Witch Hunts: Our Legacy of Violence Against Women* (San Francisco, 1994).

11. A Boston bookseller, 1686, quoted in Lyle Keohler, *A Search for Power: The "Weaker Sex" in Seventeenth-Century New England* (Urbana, Ill., 1980), 44. See also the characterization of spinsters in Mary Beth Norton, *Liberty's Daughters: The Revolutionary Experience of American Women, 1750–1800* (Boston, Little, Brown, 1980), 42, 142; and Terri L. Premo, *Winter Friends: Women Growing Old in the New Republic* (Urbana, Ill., 1990), 38, 45.

der was carried out in satires and comedies, the regular appearance of unmarried women demonstrates its wide limits.

The ways in which unmarried women and marriage itself were represented, however, varied by region. In some cultural milieus, the eighteenth century produced intensely misogynistic literature; in others, more variety and more tolerance was the norm.[12] In Philadelphia, the literary evaluation of marriage was carried out within a culture that legitimated singleness in important ways. Popular literature from colonial magazines, targeted primarily at elite audiences, to almanacs, read by a much wider range of Philadelphians, reflected a cultural awareness of marriage as potentially problematic and of marriage as only one possible choice. Some writers and other cultural purveyors identified and promoted paragons of singleness; these women were referred to as positive "patterns" for youth. This literature, reflected in the commonplace books, letters, and diaries of contemporary women, conveyed a broader range of options and ideals for women outside of marriage than generally has been recognized. Spinsterhood (and to a lesser extent bachelorhood) was not only accepted as an alternative life course for women (and men), but in some cases celebrated. In the minds of colonial Philadelphians, and on the pages they read, singleness could be a respectable choice.

Perhaps most important, critiques of marriage and discussions of singleness allowed Philadelphians to imagine women's lives outside of marriage. The relationship between popular literary representations of marriage and women's relationship to marriage was not causal, but was nonetheless significant.[13] Marital critique and a discourse on singleness developed within the context of English social and political upheaval and was reproduced in a colonial environment in which a Quaker young woman like Martha Cooper could reiterate a common concern with finding a compatible marriage partner and assert a willingness to forgo marriage entirely if that partner could not be found. Martha Cooper married Samuel Allinson in 1773. Their letters evince a loving partnership. Allinson at least suited worried father David Cooper very well indeed,

12. More work needs to be undertaken on the regional cultures of gender and popular literature, particularly for the eighteenth century. Cornelia Hughes Dayton has suggested that relatively benign aspects of seventeenth-century New England patriarchy were reflected in the popular literature of that era, in stark contrast to the misogyny of the next century. Dayton, "Satire and Sensationalism: Emergence of Misogyny in Mid-Eighteenth Century New England Newspapers and Almanacs," (paper presented to the New England Seminar at the American Antiquarian Society, November 15, 1991).

13. On the relationship between print culture and sociopolitical developments, see Roger Chartier, *The Cultural Origins of the French Revolution*, trans. Lydia G. Cochrane (Durham, N.C., 1991), esp. 67–91.

for the two had been close friends for a decade or more before the marriage.[14] A crucial development, however, was the articulation of marital "choice" in an almanac poem, and Martha Cooper's reiteration of that sentiment. Even if she did not remain single, she knew women who did, and she both read and wrote about singleness as an option. Produced in one cultural moment, the poem she called "Choice of a Companion" resonated in another through a commonplace book entry. It then reverberated beyond the individual writer and reader into a broader social and cultural context.

This chapter looks at the ways in which marriage was critiqued and spinsters lauded in the Philadelphia's popular literature. It also examines the transmission of these ideas through schools, and by way of women's manuscript circulation.

REPRESENTATIONS OF MARRIAGE: TYRANTS AND VIRGINS

The contemporary problems of marriage are suggested by the regularity with which marriage and marital status were topics of literary representation in the most accessible publications, almanacs, and literary magazines. Although literacy was common, particularly by the eighteenth century and particularly for men, most early American families owned little more than a Bible.[15] But the availability of print material was another hallmark of the urban seaport. Elite Philadelphians not only purchased books from abroad, but also subscribed to locally produced literary magazines, which reprinted European material as well as published the work of local authors. Philadelphians of all ranks used the many almanacs published locally. These small booklets printed the monthly calendar with a wealth of meteorological and astronomical information and other important information, such as court and fair dates.[16] Existing copies show intensive use by both men and women. Carrying the slim volume in a coat pocket or bag, the almanac user scribbled notes and

14. *Dictionary of Quaker Biography,* Haverford College. Letters between Samuel Allinson and David Cooper dating from 1764 which demonstrate their closeness can be found in the Allinson Collection, QC.
15. David Hall, "The Uses of Literacy in New England, 1600–1850," *Printing and Society in Early America* in William Joyce et al., eds., *Printing and Society in Early America* (Worcester, Mass., 1983), 24. Edwin Wolf II, *The Book Culture of a Colonial American City: Philadelphia Books, Bookmen, and Booksellers* (Oxford, 1988), provides an excellent overview of the kinds and numbers of books, primarily Bibles, psalmists, and schoolbooks, that circulated in colonial Philadelphia.
16. David Jaffe, "The Village Enlightenment in New England, 1760–1820," *WMQ* 47 (1990): 331; Hall, "The Uses of Literacy in New England, 1600–1850," 24.

calculated sums on the pages of months past. Mary Attmore claimed her almanac by inscribing it, "Mary Attmore her almanac for 1769," and figured sums on the backs of pages.[17] Beyond their inarguable utility, almanacs also provided entertainment. As the most popular venue for literature in the colonies, eighteenth-century almanacs contained increasing amounts of diversionary material, including poems to accompany the months, essays on popular subjects, and satirical or funny stories.[18] The kinds of literary devices and figures that populated the literary magazines were often common to the almanacs. The stories, essays, and poems that appeared as popular literature in the magazines and almanacs were also didactic, translating moral lessons and observations into palatable, recognizable forms. Readers could shake their heads at the foolish antics of such stock figures as the lovelorn, the spendthrift, and the grouch, and nod approvingly at the conduct of the wise, the penitent, and the cheerful. Many of the literary conventions reproduced in American publications came directly from English popular literature.

What almanacs and literary magazines had in common, besides their mutual debt to English traditions, was an interest in the topics of courtship, marriage, and singleness.[19] Marriage and the role of women within and without households had been the subjects of intense debate in seventeenth-century and eighteenth-century England.[20] By the eighteenth century, American purveyors and consumers of literary culture had a very recent tradition of writings on these subjects upon which to draw. Men and women who read or heard this popular literature understood the representations of gender and the contests of gendered power played out on the pages. Although depictions of marriage relations or of individual figures were not expected to represent particular household realities, the characterizations evoked familiar situations. Humor and satire were especially reliant on the receptivity of the audience or the audience's sympathy or at least familiarity with the conditions portrayed in an essay or a poem.

17. Almanac of Mary Attmore, *The Pennsylvania Town and Countryman's Almanac for . . . 1769* (Wilmington, Del., 1768).

18. See, for example, the difference between the *Ephemeris for the Year 1721 . . .*, by "John Jerman," with two short poems, and *Father Abraham's Almanack for 1770 . . .*, which included more than a dozen essays and poems.

19. For this study fifty-nine Philadelphia almanacs published between 1720 and 1780, various almanacs from Burlington, Pennsylvania, and New York, and the extant volumes of seven literary magazines published in the Delaware Valley between 1740 and 1780 were analyzed.

20. For selections and analyses of the pamphlet wars in England, see Katherine Usher Henderson and Barbara F. McManus, eds., *Half Humankind: Contexts and Texts of the Controversy About Women in England, 1540–1640* (Urbana, Ill., 1985).

Even conventional prescriptive literature was ambiguous on the subject of marriage. A poem that appeared in the *Pennsylvania Gazette* in 1731, "Few Happy Matches," expressed a sense of discontent and even desperation with the difficulty of establishing satisfying marriages. The poet concludes, after a litany of examples of poor marital prospects, including bad reasons to marry and mismatched characters, that "Two kindest Souls alone must meet; Tis Friendship makes the Bondage sweet." The net effect was to suggest that marriage itself was a difficult institution, that the "bondage" it represented could be made palatable, even enjoyable, only by a very few, perfectly matched pairs. In a work of belles lettres owned by a Philadelphia spinster, Eliza Stedman, a poet caustically noted that "The Happiest Day of Marriage" was also the last. "In Marriage are two Things allow'd, / a Wife in Wedding Sheets, and in a Shroud: / How can a married State then be a-Curst,/ Since the last Day's as Happy as the First?"[21]

The primary criticisms of marriage concerned the original terms of courtship and engagement and the happiness of the marriage once underway. Many poems and essays expressed anxiety about the flattery, trickery, insincere intentions, and false representations or claims by either partner during courtship.[22] Writers also focused on the contrast between courtship behavior and married behavior. In these works, the problems of the tyrannical husband and the demanding wife figured prominently. A serialized conversation between Lady Lurewell and Lady Loveless, purporting to be a translation of a Latin work by Erasmus, appeared in a 1767 almanac. Its conclusion appeared the next year.[23] Titled "The Female Council: Or, The Moot-Point of Matrimony Fairly argued," Lurewell and Loveless's discussion covered many of the points other contemporary writers were making about the troublesome nature of marriage. They debated the roles of money and love, but dwelled primarily on the function of male authority and female submissiveness in making marriages successful or at least acceptable to both parties. Women and men clearly understood that husbands, like other governors, had to balance their use of power with the cultivation of authority. Tyranny, or the abuse of power by husbands, thus occasioned a great deal

21. "Few Happy Matches," *PG*, February 2–9, 1731; [Anonymous], *The Second Volume of Familiar Letters of Love, Gallantry and Several Occasions, By the Wits of That Last and Present Age.* (London, 1718), 358. The copy at the LCP is inscribed "Eliza Stedman."

22. A male perspective on courtship among the eighteenth-century Virginia gentry is J. A. Leo Lemay, ed., *Robert Bolling Woos Anne Miller: Love and Courtship in Colonial Virginia, 1760* (Charlottesville, Va., 1990).

23. *Father Abraham's Almanac for . . . 1766* (Philadelphia, 1765); "Continuation of the Female Council or the Moot-Point of Matrimony Fairly argued," *Father Abraham's Almanac for . . . 1768* (Philadelphia, 1767).

of commentary. Law was structured around the assumption that patriarchal households would function best when men did rule "gently," as Martha Cooper wished, and when women submitted to this government graciously. But neither was a sure thing. Lurewell and Loveless, like many other fictional commentators, examined and criticized the behavior of tyrannical husbands.[24]

Tyrannical behavior could take many forms, violence chief among them. Loveless's husband, she reported, had returned home drunk and "brandish'd his Cane, and threatened me most violently." A fear of violence was not an uncommon problem in the popular literature. A 1758 tale about a grocer whose wife was too proud to do grocer's work concluded with his publicly beating her while customers observed and debated the merits of each spouse's perspective.[25] Loveless also complained that her husband's tyranny extended to the meanness of his purse. "Lavishing enough abroad," he left her little money with which to buy clothing. "Is this a Dress for a lady?" she asked her friend. "Every tradesman's Daughter makes a better figure." [26]

Just as tyrannical husbands came in for severe critique, so did overly assertive or willful wives.[27] While Loveless complained about her husband's bad behavior, Lurewell assessed blame elsewhere. First she inquired whether Loveless needlessly berated her husband when he returned from his nightly binges. "And what Reception do you give him when he comes home in this Disguise?" she wondered. Answering her own query, she concluded, "You scold, I presume." Lurewell relished the telling, "Ay you may depend on't. He finds I have not lost my tongue." This was exactly what her friend suspected, who pronounced, "Loveless, there is no Conduct in this." Lurewell then proceeded to explain that it

24. In Mary Flower's commonplace book, an anonymous "Matron" advised that young women guard against a flattering suitor, arguing that "for truth your golden days are gone / the moment that you marry / in courtship we are all divine / and vows and prayers ensnare us." If women did not make a judicious choice of marriage partner, the result could be disastrous; once married, "the Goddess sinks to housewife Moll / And they reign Tyrants 'oer us." "Advice From a Matron to a Young Lady Concerning Wedlock," Mary Flower Commonplace Book, QC. See also "On the Occasion of unhappy Marriages," *Father Abraham's Almanac for . . . 1770* (Philadelphia, 1769), LCP), following April. This author posited that marriages were unhappy largely because during courtship, men would put on "a Behavior like a Holiday Suit, which is to last no longer than till he is settled in possession of his Mistress." Then a new wife would find that "the most abject *Flatterers* degenerate into the greatest *Tyrants.*"

25. *New American Magazine* (October 1758).

26. "Continuation of the Female Council."

27. On the figure of the scold, see David Underdown, "The Taming of the Scold: The Enforcement of Patriarchal Authority in Early Modern England," in Anthony Fletcher and John Stevenson, eds., *Order and Disorder in Early Modern England,* (Cambridge, 1985), 116–36; and Susan Amussen, *An Ordered Society: Gender and Class in Early Modern England* (London, 1988).

was Loveless's obligation as a wife to be obedient, patient, and submissive, and she cited St. Paul's praise of Sarah, "a perfect Pattern of obedience." Lurewell's objection to this line of reasoning is instructive. She questioned why she should behave as a good wife, when her husband was acting so inappropriately: "While he ceases to act as a Man, I shall never be persuaded to regard him as a Husband." Lurewell pressed her point, however, arguing that women's submission would compel men's appropriate use of their authority. Ultimately, then, women's submission, and not men's assertion of authority, marked a good, workable marriage.

Writers often prescribed women's submissiveness and obedience as the solution to marital problems. The narrator of the story about the grocer's wife concluded that if she had just done what she was told in the first place, she could have avoided such harsh disciplinary action. Women observing this scene, however, objected. A customer laughed and promptly got into a fight with his wife. As the author noted caustically, "Your true vixen will, for no man / Forbear defending of a woman; / And, Let the cause be bad or good, / fights tooth and nail for sisterhood." Women were often depicted as objecting to the necessity for obedience, even as they resigned themselves to it.[28] The English author Mrs. Deverel, whose letters were reprinted in American publications, explained to her sister:

> To be a wife, Maria, such as I could wish you, requires more care, more temper, more conduct and solidity, than young women usually pretend to; therefore, to become a wife, it were necessary to become a new woman, in the most esential parts of her conduct. The very great difference between the obsequiousness of a lover, and the authority of a husband, will set this in a proper light. To the moment of your marriage it is your reign; your lover is proud to oblige you, watches your smiles, is obedent to your commands, anxious to please you, and careful to avoid everything you disapprove; but you have no sooner pronounced that harsh word *obey*, than you give up the reins, and it is his turn to rule so long as you live.[29]

28. For example, in her essay "Woman Not Inferior to Man," the anonymous Sophia (London, 1739) complained of the arbitrary nature of gendered hierarchy and disputed its basis in anatomy. She also, however, concluded that her sole purpose was not to "stir up any of my own sex to revolt against the *Men*, or to invert the present order of things, with regard to *government* and *authority* . . . . I only mean to shew my sex, that they are not so despicable as Men wou'd have them believe themselves." In Bell and Offen, *Women, the Family and Freedom*, 13–41. Sophia's essay, a male rejoinder on male superiority, and her response, were reprinted many times. A fascinating Pennsylvania example is Elizabeth Magawley's contribution to the *American Weekly Mercury* of January 5, 1731, reprinted with a poem she wrote satirizing the male poets of the region, in Sharon Harris, ed., *American Women Writers to 1800* (New York, 1996), 137–140.

29. *The Ladies Literary Companion; or, a Collection of Essays Adapted for the . . . Instruction and Amusement of the Female Sex* (Burlington, N.J., 1792), 1–97.

Marriage was particularly fertile ground for satire and comedy, which derided the institution and pointed out its flawed foundation. If marriage was dependent on men being good husbands and women being good wives, clearly marriage was an exceedingly fragile creature. As one writer concluded, "Marriage is a Lottery, in which there are many Blanks to one Prize."[30] Humorous and satirical depictions suggested that even at its most fundamental moments, including the sexual union of husband and wife, each partner's motives and intentions were suspect.

Many satirical and comedic treatments appeared in serialized form, giving character and identity to the critics of marriage. Commentaries, advice, and answers to letters appeared from "The Old Bachelor" in the *Pennsylvania Magazine or American Monthly Museum*, beginning in March 1775. In his first number, the author poked fun at himself for not having married by the age of sixty-five. It pained him to see happily married couples, because it reminded him of his unmarried state. But, he added, "I ought to be hanged for not being married before; but I ought to be hung in chains if I get married now." In later installments, he lamented the lack of a mistress for his household; she would have saved him from the whims of his servants and their odd desires for such household items as new linens. Yet the Old Bachelor quickly turned to his good fortune in remaining single. Correspondents reassured him that he could easily have been "as unhappy even in the desirable matrimonial state." And he devoted an entire number to "Reflections on Unhappy Marriages." He observed that one of the most fundamental problems in a marriage developed out of the unnatural assertion of authority by women and the unnatural unwillingness of men to exercise it: "A governing woman is never truly happy, nor a submitting husband perfectly reconciled." Finally in his sixth installment, the Old Bachelor concluded that, for these reasons and more, "I hug myself in my solitary state, and bless stars, that I did not marry."[31]

Discussions such as these prompted a serious defense of marriage. In the same publication as "The Old Bachelor," an author who styled himself "Epiminondas" began a series titled "Reflections upon the married state" in which he rebuked comics, satirists, and "those who turn matri-

30. "Thoughts upon Love and Marriage, by the Honourable Robert Boyle, Esq.," in *The Universal American Almanac . . . for . . . 1764* (Philadelphia, 1763). See also "A-La-Mode," *New American Magazine*, (January 1758): 14.

31. "The Old Bachelor #1," (March 1775); "The Old Bachelor No. III," (May 1775); "Consolation for the Old Bachelor," (June 1775); "The Old Bachelor No. 5," (July 1775); "The Old Bachelor No. 6," (October 1775): all in *Pennsylvania Magazine or American Monthly Museum*.

mony into ridicule."[32] Epiminondas reminded his readers of the "absolute necessity of marriage for the service of the state, and the solid advantages that arise from it to domestic comfort, in ordinary cases." While critics railed against the hypocrisies of courtship and the failures of marriage, Epiminondas countered that these writers always pointed to the extraordinary cases. Those writers also seemed to extol extraordinarily happy and fortunate marriages, whereas Epiminondas argued that in marriage, there was "not so much happiness as young lovers dream of, nor is there by far so much unhappiness, as loose authors universally suppose."[33] Other writers undertook a defense of marriage in poetry and prose pieces that promoted the institution, but Epiminondas emphasized both the civic responsibility to marry and the domestic comforts of marriage, while most writers chose to focus only on the latter.[34]

Defenses of marriage could also appear as attacks on the unmarried, particularly women. Spinsters were regularly depicted as women who had somehow failed at courtship; if they had behaved differently, they would have married. These chastisements served both a male and a female audience. Men were warned about such women and were encouraged to believe that women who refused them were acting under mistaken presumptions of their own value. Women, on the other hand, were warned not to be too selective about their mates, lest they find themselves the objects of scorn or ridicule.

Popular notions about women's sexuality informed these cautionary tales. Women's sexuality was addressed quite apart from their mind and spirit. While their bodies should and did impel women to make heterosexual connections, their virtue and modesty demanded that they pro-

32. "Reflections upon Marriage," *Pennsylvania Magazine or American Monthly Museum,* (September 1775), 409.

33. Ibid. See also the sex manual written by "Aristotle," which defended marriage, decrying that "a married State . . . . in the Age we live in, is look'd upon as a most insupportable yoak; nothing being now ridicul'd more than matrimony." *Aristotle's Compleat Master-Piece. In Three Parts. Displaying the Secrets of Nature in the Generation of Man,.* 16th ed. (London (?): Printed and Sold for the Booksellers, 1725), 27, LCP. In this case Aristotle opposed those who promoted the pleasures of extramarital sex, no doubt in search of a little respectability for his book, otherwise viewed as quite sensational.

34. "Of Marriage," *The Burlington Almanac for . . . 1772* (Burlington, 1771). See also "Poem in Praise of the Married State," *Father Abraham's Almanac for . . . 1770* (Philadelphia, 1769). Benjamin Franklin's views on marriage varied in his publications, probably reflecting the entertainment value of the subject material. In one letter he referred to an unmarried man as "the odd Half of a Pair of Scissars," and insisted that marriage was the only proper state for adults. Leonard W. Labaree, ed., *The Papers of Benjamin Franklin* (New Haven, Conn., 1961), 3: 30–31. See also the *PG* issue of 1735, with one contribution mocking marriage (in verse) and the next defending it. Labaree, *Papers of Benjamin Franklin,* 2: 21–26. A widely circulated publications on marriage was Jonathan Swift's *Reflections on Courtship and Marriage: In Two Letters to a Friend* (1747), printed and sold by Franklin at least once; [Evans Collection, microfilm at LCP].

ceed more slowly. Virginity was something women wanted to dispose of, and they were encouraged to do so within the bounds of marriage before neglect of their sexuality produced a bitterness and discontent that made them less likely to marry. Women who indulged their sexuality outside of marriage lost their virtue and their reputation, if not their virginity in fact. For these reasons women should look to marry as soon as possible. They should not be too overly selective or too concerned with the fortune of their suitors. In an almanac's verses titled "The unfortunate Delay," Kitty, the subject of the verse, considered all kinds of men but could not settle on a single suitor as her spouse. Eventually no one would marry her, for "none dare to single to himself / Whom all in common claim."[35] In other words, because she belonged to no individual man, she was understood to belong to all men. Without the legitimate focus for her attention that one man would have provided, her behavior toward all men was scrutinized and found inappropriate. By implication, she was a whore.[36]

While women's sexuality needed to be carefully handled, their virtue and morality were to be protected—carefully guarded and only cautiously bestowed on a male guardian. As a consequence of this binary construction of femininity, prescriptive writers considered the control of women's bodies (and their questing sexuality) immediate and essential, while at the same time promoting the careful evaluation of marriage partners as a positive sign of a woman's virtue.

An essay in the 1772 edition of Philadelphia's *Father Abraham's Almanac* explained "the reasons why Miss Jenny Tinderbox, Miss Squeeze, Miss Betty Tempest, and the sagacious Sophronia remains [*sic*] unmarried."[37] These four proved the archetypal spinsters. One was too picky, the next too greedy, another too flirtatious, and the last too learned. All refused to settle for any man who did not meet their outrageous standards of position, fortune, and education. Jenny Tinderbox's sister had married "a man of quality," thus upping the ante for Jenny. Unwilling to consider honest tradesmen, an attitude that dismayed her social superiors, she found herself acting as "tutoress" for her sister's children. Thus employed, she performed "the drudgery of three servants without receiving the wages of one." Miss Squeeze was a pawnbroker's daughter, and thus highly sensitive to the value of things. Keen on getting immediate

35. "The unfortunate Delay; or the Unfortunate Fair One," *Father Abraham's Almanac . . . 1777* (Philadelphia, 1776), opposite November.
36. See also "Epigram on an Old Maid, who married her Servant," *Pennsylvania Magazine or American Monthly Museum* (April 1776), 180. Plenty of other popular pieces connected women's unmarried status with a licentious or a frigid sexuality. See, for example, the letter and then paraphrased verses in the January 1759 *New American Magazine*, 323–324 ; and *Aristotle's Compleat Masterpiece*, 32–33.
37. "The reasons why . . . ," *Father Abraham's Almanac for . . . 1772* (Philadelphia, 1771).

value in her marriage, she refused longer-term investment in men "who wanted to better themselves." Unfortunately, she should have considered condition upon sale. "Being pale, and marked with the smallpox," she priced herself out of the marriage market. Miss Squeeze "grew old and ill-natured, without ever considering that she should have made an abatement in her pretensions." Where the first two women were lacking, Miss Betty Tempest had it all: beauty, family, and fortune. Inclined to read novels, from which she learned that "a plain man of common sense was no better than a fool," she "sighed only for the gay, giddy, inconstant and thoughtless." She refused those who would be suitable, and chased after those who would never have her. She became "company only for her aunts and cousins," and was so reviled that she had to partner chairs or stools at local dances. Sophronia, like Betty, read too much. But whereas Betty's downfall was the romantic novel, full of miscast heroes and misled heroines, Sophronia "was taught to love Greek, and hate the men from her very infancy." This summation of her education explained why she "rejected fine gentlemen because they were not pedants, and pedants because they were not fine gentlemen." Like the others, Sophronia paid for her foolishness. "Now, without one good feature in her face, she talks incessantly of the beauties of the mind."[38]

"The reasons why" each of the four remained unmarried were distinct and yet interconnected. Although a desire for status, money, character, or education distinguished their preferences, each woman insisted that her suitors meet the ideal she had individually determined. Rather than follow custom or, as it was articulated, simple common sense, each allowed some base aspect of the culture to shape her ideas about marriage prospects. Pride, profit, sentimental fiction, and women's education all came in for the author's rebuke. The essay implied that women were no longer satisfied to make solid matches and to accept a future as wives and mothers among the middling, respectable sort. Instead, through a new set of values associated with the market and with emerging sensibilities most fully articulated in fiction, these women demanded access to marriages that they determined to be worthwhile. The essay thus criticized young women's foolishness, as well as their exposure to and influence by the social and economic pretensions of the era. Society and their parents were to blame, but each woman paid for her indulgences by becoming a pariah. Unwelcome by any except those whose kinship obligated them, they lived out old age unhappy, unattractive, and impoverished.

Arguments about the value and structure of marriage were reflected in many literary depictions of unmarried women. Miss Kitty, Jenny Tinder-

38. Ibid.

box, and the others were exaggerated portraits, but th
sterhood as dangerous also reinforced the attractiver
Despite these characterizations of unmarried women, (
tions of unmarried women would challenge the noti
would be poor, socially outcast, or morally corrupted wi

COUNTER-CLAIMS: LIBERATED SPINSTERS

In a teasing poem to a young friend, the first stanza of which reads, "I've neither reserve nor aversion to man, (I assure you Sophronia in Jingle) / But to keep my dear Liberty, long as I can, Is the reason I chuse to live single," Hannah Griffitts, a confirmed spinster, identified the loss of personal independence as chief among the reasons she avoided matrimony.[39] It was not men, she averred, but the restrictions that marriage imposed. Griffitts explained to a married cousin, "There are many of you weded ones who I believe are Placed in your Proper sphere," but she was not among them. "Everyone is not fitted for the single life," Griffitts asserted, "nor was I ever moulded for The weded one."[40]

Griffitts's views found space for expression in Philadelphia's popular literature. The familiarity of stereotypes about bitter spinsters and widowed hags is a potent reminder of the cultural coerciveness of gender ideals and the cultural emphasis on heterosexual marriage as the only reasonable means for women to attain those ideals. In colonial Philadelphia, however, such images of women and marriage were contested within the same popular literature that promoted them. Beyond using stock figures to tap cultural resonances about independent women, popular literary stylists also betrayed a familiarity with the complexity of unmarried women's situations and deep knowledge of the ambivalence with which many men and women regarded marriage. Writers and printers drew on stereotypical notions of the wretched spinster for satire and comedy, but the more serious considerations of marriage granted women considerable leeway in debating the benefits and drawbacks of marriage. Spinsters appeared in colonial magazines and almanacs as figures of sympathy as well as scorn, and as thoughtful participants in the debate about marriage and gender. A discourse about women's rational objections to marriage and about the pleasures and rewards they

39. Hannah Griffitts, "To Sophronia. In answer to some Lines she directed to be wrote on my fan 1769," in Blecki and Wulf, ed., *Milcah Martha Moore's Book,* 173–74.
40. Hannah Griffitts to [Milcah Martha Moore], n.d., Edward Wanton Smith Collection, QC.

ght find outside of marriage countered and challenged hackneyed depictions of crones and withered old maids.

The poem on the "choice" to marry, reprinted in several places and copied by Martha Cooper and doubtless many others, was just one of a number of verses on the theme of marital choice. Some poems emphasized the "choice" as one between potential spouses rather than between marriage and singleness, whereas the one Cooper copied was quite explicit in seeing marriage as an option rather than an absolute.[41] Similarly, "The Maiden's Best Adorning," a poem copied by Catharine Haines in the 1770s, also stressed women's discretion in choosing whether to marry. As Haines copied, one should acquire a husband with a listed set of desirable characteristics, but only "if thou resolve to change a single Life / and has a purpose to become a Wife."[42] These pieces implied that women took considerable care in deciding to assume the status of wife.

Even after they had determined to marry, women questioned the costs of marriage. In particular they repeatedly mourned the loss of personal freedom that marriage entailed. "The Maid's Soliloquy," reprinted from an English magazine in the New Jersey *New American Magazine* for February 1758 and again in a Philadelphia almanac for 1773, addressed the poet John Milton's riddle about God's exhortation to human increase and the corollary evil, the devilish attachment to abstinence.[43] This poem is full of contradiction. In this soliloquy, the "Maid" discovers why she feels an inclination to marriage even though she rationally shrinks from the loss of freedom and demands of obedience that marriage entails for women. Surely, she thinks aloud, "*Milton* thou reason'st well." Nature and God must explicitly promote marriage. Why else "this secret dread and inward horror / of dying unespoused?" This association of God with marriage and the devil with its opposite made some sense, particularly as this maid explained her compulsion to marry despite its many disadvantages. From a rational standpoint, marriage created innumerable

41. See, for example, the pair of poems, "The Female Choice—A Poem" and "The Bachelor's Supplication," in the *Burlington Almanac* for 1771 (Burlington, 1770). Both stress that if the man or woman speaking through the verses is to marry, he or she wishes to find a partner with a particular set of virtues. Each begins with the qualification "if," as in the "Female Choice,"—"If marriage ever be my lot in life / and I by fate am destin'd for a wife,"—but this construction implies much less authority and discretion on the part of the woman than does Martha Cooper's "Choice" or "the Maiden's Best Adorning." See also "The Lady's Choice: An Ode," in *PG*, February 28, 1749.

42. Commonplace book of Catherine Haines, c. 1775, QC. Haines's copybook includes a dire warning about the trickery and flattery of suitors in "Verses on the Death of the Unfortunate Mary Blandy who was executed for Poisoning her Father."

43. "The Maid's Soliloquy," *New American Magazine* (February 1758): 39–40; "The Maid's Soliloquy," *Philo Copernicus ... The American Calendar ... 1773* (Philadelphia, 1772).

problems for a woman, not the least of which was her obligation to obey her husband. To marry, then, was to sublimate reason to nature, and to accept a natural happiness through an unnatural obedience. Women had to acknowledge these prospects as intimately connected, despite or perhaps because of their inherent contradictions. As the maid observed, "Bondage and pleasure meet my tho'ts at once." And then, "I wed! My liberty is gone forever." [44]

In this piece, marriage is simultaneously promoted and discouraged. The woman determines to marry, but she complains about the loss of her personal liberty. An ideal patriarchal family would be marked by a woman's contentment in her subordinate position. This woman submits but is discontent or suspicious. Further, the language suggests that she recognized that her "inward horror of dying unespoused" could be the product of cultural as well as religious pressure. Perhaps it is not only God who compels her to submit to marriage. Like "The Maid's Soliloquy," "The Wedding-Ring" emphasized the contrasting "alternatives of joy and pain" present in marriage, as well as women's ambivalence about their obligations as wives, describing that "little but too powerful tie" as the "Bane of female liberty." "Now we bless the pleasing yoke; / Now we wish the bond were broke; / Virgins sigh to wear the chain; / Wives wou'd fain be free again." [45]

Some young women appeared in print as resolute spinsters. For Amelia Gray, the subject of a 1775 *Pennsylvania Magazine* essay, singleness was not only personally rewarding but also socially responsible. Amelia Gray was an orphan, raised by her grandfather and other relations who made Amelia's education a priority "from a motive of religion, and zeal for my advancement in the sciences." With a decent fortune and a good education, Amelia attracted any number of suitors. She considered and then declined all her "real and pretended admirers from various quarters." She reported, "as I consider the matrimonial engagement as a matter of the utmost moment to *me*, I have hitherto treated the flattery of coxcombs with indifference or disdain, the offers of more serious men with caution, and remain the mistress of my own affections." Rather than dedicate herself entirely to the domestic realm, Amelia could appreciate nature, God, and art and extend care to the needy among her community:

I consider myself capable, in my present situation, of passing through life with pleasure to myself and benefit to others. I find myself at leisure to

---

44. "The Maid's Soliloquy," 40.
45. "The Wedding-Ring," *New American Magazine* (September 1758).

range in the flowery fields of literature, and to contemplate the wondrous works of the celestial architect, so finely displayed around me; and also for the *social* duties of administering comfort to the widow and the fatherless; of visiting the sick, and of affording relief to the indigent of various classes. From employments of this kind I derive a secret satisfaction, which far exceeds my ideas of the happiness of some married women, whose fortunes were the principal objects of their husbands addresses. They have infinitely more charms for me, than the constituents of modern granduer, the glitter of assemblies, the pomp of equipage, and the decorations of the palace. The one I consider as a constant source of wonder and delight, the other of perpetual inquietude and satiety.[46]

Amelia Gray's worthy and noble spinsterhood was contrasted with the frivolity of marriage, particularly among women of the elite. Amelia eschewed society pleasures for "*social* duties."[47]

The actual as well as fictional lives of unmarried women were models for the rest of the community. In 1759, for example, eighteen-year-old Hannah Callender recorded in her diary a conversation among friends "on the married and the single states." They concluded that "both [were] eligible when well conducted thro life," and noted that "History as well as our own time furnishes many Instances, of worthy Single Women."[48] Callender then pointed to notable single women, including the Quaker minister Elizabeth Smith of Burlington, who "always has been and still remains to be of use in the Creation by reason of a Prudent Conduct."[49] For Callender, both women she read about and women she knew effectively modelled singleness.

Popular literature highly critical of marriage recognized and explored women's discontents with the institution. Although in many cases the female characters in the prose and poetry that debated marriage did marry, heightened attention to women's objections to patriarchal hierarchy provided space for a legitimate discussion of the alternatives. A positive illustration of singleness followed the implication that marriage was not a natural, simple, or reflexive commitment on women's part.[50]

46. "History of Amelia Gray," *Pennsylvania Magazine or American Monthly Museum* (January 1775): 22–24.
47. For another example of an unmarried woman's life dedicated to others, see "The Way to be W[torn, illeg.]," [*Burlington Almanac*] (Burlington, 1775).
48. Diary of Hannah Callender, 11th month, 1759, APS.
49. Ibid., 3rd month, 1758.
50. The seventeenth-century English feminist writers Mary Astell, Katherine Phillips, Jane Barker, and Anne Finch all critiqued marriage and supported spinsterhood to varying degrees. Donoghue, *Passions Between Women*, 121–130; N. H. Keeble, *The Cultural Identity of Eighteenth-Century Woman: A Reader* (London, 1994), 255–263.

READING, WRITING, AND LEARNING SINGLENESS

Hannah Callender's invocation of Elizabeth Smith and Hannah Griffitts's defense of her "liberty" demonstrate the strong connection between literary representations of singleness and a community of women readers and writers. The circulation of manuscript writings played a key role in women's reading, writing, and education. The impact of unmarried women, particularly spinsters, as teachers, authors, circulators, copyists, and readers of manuscript literature was profound and combined to create both readership and authorship among a wide range of class and religious groups. The literary culture that developed owed much to their interests and perspectives.

Many of the most prominent women writers in the Philadelphia region were unmarried women who wrote about marriage and singleness. Elizabeth Graeme Fergusson (1737–1801), Hannah Griffitts (1727–1817), and Susanna Wright (1696–1785) were among the most respected literary women in the Delaware Valley, and each remained single. (Although Fergusson married in the early 1770s, she lived with her husband for fewer than four years and never saw him after 1779.)[51] Each wrote about marriage and singleness. For example, although most of Wright's poetry was spiritual and meditative in tone, one of her best-known pieces was a versification of a letter from Anne Boleyn to Henry VIII while she was imprisoned. These verses, with their emphasis on Henry's tyrannical treatment of his wife, were copied by many women, including Mary Flower, Milcah Martha Moore, Deborah Morris, and Hannah Callender.[52] Callender recorded the following stanza of "Susy Wrights translation of Ann Bullens letter into verse":

When Bones sepulchred leave there narrow rooms
And hostile Things rise tumbling from there tomb,
When nor your heart nor mine can bye conceal'd,
But every secret motive stands reveal'd
Stands full reveal'd that God and Man may see,
How fate has err'd, and you have Injured me.[53]

51. Karin Wulf, "Milcah Martha Moore's Book: Documenting Culture and Connection in the Revolutionary Era," in Blecki and Wulf, ed., *Milcah Martha Moore's Book*, 54.

52. Wulf, "Milcah Martha Moore's Book," 11–15. Mary Flower and [Deborah Morris], commonplace books, QC.

53. Diary of Hannah Callender, 10th month, 7 day, 1758, APS.

The implication of Wright's poem was that Henry's treatment of Anne was not simply that of a tyrannical king but of a tyrannical spouse. Indeed Anne is depicted describing herself as an injured "Loyal Wife."

The phenomenon of unmarried women writers and readers reveals important facets of the processes of cultural production and transmission. One way in which ideas about singleness were produced and transmitted was through the circulation of manuscript literature, such as Wright's poem about Ann Boleyn.[54] Manuscripts could reach wide audiences as friends of friends borrowed and lent, read, recommended, and copied commonplace books, diaries, individual manuscript pages of poetry and prose, and letters. Women like Martha Cooper, with whose commonplace book this chapter opened, copied as much material from manuscripts as they did from printed sources.[55]

Friendships, kin networks, religious affiliations, and school settings all worked to generate and circulate these materials and ideas. Individual women wrote poetry for other women, or sent poetry directly to other women. It is tempting to read Hannah Griffitts's defense of liberty, for example, as a verse-letter from one spinster to another. Certainly Griffitts herself never married, and the reference to "Sophronia" as the poem's recipient echoes the use of that name in the almanac essay of 1772 that described Sophronia as having been brought up to "hate men" and "love Greek." The reasons Griffitts listed for her continued singleness support this interpretation. In one of the last stanzas, she seems to reprove women who reserve their adoration for human men rather than for God: "The Men (as a Friend) I prefer, I esteem, / And love them as well as I ought / But to fix all my happiness solely in Him / was never my wish or my thought." Griffitts then makes a reference to her imperviousness to "the satyrical sneers thrown on the single Life" and slyly suggests that Sophronia should "Leave me to enjoy the sweet freedom I love/ And go marry—as soon as you please."[56]

More institutional settings also provided a venue for the circulation of manuscript literature, investing authority in the work of manuscript au-

54. On manuscript circulation, see Margaret Ezell, *The Patriarch's Wife*, 62–100; Harold Love, *Scribal Publication in Seventeenth-Century England* (Oxford, 1993).

55. David S. Shields, "The Manuscript in the British American World of Print," *Proceedings of the American Antiquarian Society* 102 (1992): 403–416. On women's commonplace books, see Blecki and Wulf, eds., *Milcah Martha Moore's Book*; Carla Mulford, "Political Poetics: Annis Boudinot Stockton and Middle Atlantic Women's Culture," *New Jersey History* 111 (1993): 66–110.

56. The note on "satyrical sneers" may be Moore's marginal explanation and not Griffitts's, but it elaborates on Griffitts's reference to "Giants," presumably giant comments. I know of no other copy of this poem, but Griffitts did use marginal notes of explanation on other occasions.

thors. Literature played an important role in teaching about courtship, marriage, and singleness. Thus Hannah Callender concluded after an evening with friends, sewing while listening to a reading from Samuel Richardson's *Clarissa* (1748): "A fallen woman is the more inexcusable as from the cradle the sex is warned against them."[57] Women also learned about these subjects in schools, especially those run by Quaker women and attended by girls from a wide variety of socioeconomic backgrounds, where manuscript literature formed an important source of curricular and cultural instruction.

Teachers such as Rebecca Jones and Hannah Catherall promoted the poetry written by women they knew by assigning it to their students to copy. Although teachers used printed books of miscellanies and other literature, students' surviving school copybooks, as well as other evidence from diaries, shows that generations of girls educated in Quaker schools were introduced to the unpublished poetry of spinsters Susanna Wright and Hannah Griffitts.[58] Jones and Catherall, Quaker spinsters who shared a home in Philadelphia for over twenty years, taught school together when they were not travelling in the ministry.[59] In the 1770s, Sarah Sandwith Drinker and Catherine Haines enrolled at Jones and Catherall's school.[60] There the students copied a number of Griffitts's poems, which often lauded unmarried women. These included a memorial to Quaker spinster and minister Sarah Morris.[61] Morris, they copied, was an extraordinary woman of talent and strength.

So flow'd the Powerfull Language of her Tongue
In Soft Persuasion and in reasoning Strong
Her noble faith and Generous Charity
(From Biggots modes and Superstition free)
Fixed her Foundation on a Gospel Plan,
And Grasped the whole creation in her Span.[62]

57. Diary of Hannah Callender, November 17, 1758, APS.

58. Rebecca Birchall may have introduced Hannah Callender and Elizabeth Sandwith Drinker to Wright's work as well. See the mention of Wright's verses on Ann Boleyn in Callender's diary soon after she finished school.

59. "A short account of Rebecca Jones," *The Westonian* (1907); Rebecca Jones Almanack, 1770, Allinson Collection, Box 12, QC. Nancy Rosenberg, "The Sub-textual Religion: Quakers, the Book, and Public Education in Philadelphia, 1682–1800" (Ph.D. diss., University of Michigan, 1991), 342–348, mentions Jones and Catherall's student population.

60. Elaine Crane, ed., *The Diary of Elizabeth Drinker* (Boston, 1991), 115, 383.

61. These also included an exchange between Griffitts and a male member of Susanna James's family after her death and a poem on the death of Margaret Mason. Sarah Sandwith Drinker's copybook (1775), HSP; Catherine Haines's copybook (1775), QC.

62. Fidelia [Hannah Griffitts], "To the Memory of Respected Friend Sarah Morris," in Sarah Drinker's copybook, HSP; Catherine Haines's copybook, 108–111; Blecki and Wulf, ed., *Milcah Martha Moore's Book*, 253–255.

Griffitts taught through her memorial that Sarah Morris—spinster and minister—was a worthy model. The "powerful Language of her Tongue," her "[strong] Reasoning," as well as commitment to "the gospel plan" marked Morris as a curious counterpoint to fictional heroines such as Clarissa or Pamela from Richardson's eponymous novels of the 1740s. Jones and Catherall, like poet Griffitts whose work the girls copied, and Morris, the subject of her poem, stood before the students as models of the single life.

Schools like Jones's and Catherall's did more than provide manuscript literature for the Quaker elite. The reach of these schools was much broader. The Quaker school system employed a large number of women over the eighteenth century, and educated a large number of poor female students. An accounting in 1765, for example, found that the Quaker Overseers of the Public School were supporting the tuition and other expenses of 128 children in twelve different school settings. Six male-headed and six female-headed schools were then operating within this system. More men taught boys, and more women taught girls, although this was not an exclusively sex-segregated arrangement. Almost 30 percent of the students with female teachers were boys, and 16 percent of the students in male-headed schools were girls. This last group was dominated by the ten girls in an all-female academy taught by the reformer and abolitionist Anthony Benezet. The majority (56 percent) of the students were Quakers, but a significant percentage of Anglicans (27 percent) and adherents of other religions (17 percent, including eight Catholic children) were also represented. [63]

Many of these students stayed in the same institution for a number of years, something of a feat considering their economic background. Of those students on the 1765 roster for whom the overseers had recorded an entrance date, one third had been enrolled for four or more consecutive years; just over half the students had been enrolled for three or more years. Poorer students' families made a significant financial commitment to keeping them in school and out of service. One family exemplifies this experience. Martha Stackhouse's husband, James, was a plasterer, a skilled artisan whose business probably profited from Philadelphia's mid-century housing boom.[64] He died in the late 1750s or early 1760s,

63. "List of the Scholars now in the several Schools at Philada at the Expense of the Overseers of the Public School," August 23, 1765, William Penn Charter School Archives, Box 14, QC.

64. William Wade Hinshaw, *Encyclopedia of Quaker Genealogy*, Vol. 2 (Baltimore, 1969); 1756 tax lists show that James Stackhouse was rated at a middling £20. For skilled workers and housing construction cycles, see Billy G. Smith, *"The Lower Sort": Philadelphia's Laboring People, 1750–1800* (Ithaca, N.Y., 1990), 81–83.

leaving his widow with five young children to raise. In 1765 the children's ages ranged from six to thirteen. Although Martha Stackhouse's occupation is unknown, she must have worked to support her family. She was regularly rated for taxation among the lowest group of Philadelphians, most likely signifying that she was a working widow with some income and with children who needed her care. Martha Stackhouse started sending her children to school at a young age and kept them in school for a comparatively long time. The eldest boy, Hastings, was enrolled in Moles Patterson's school in 1758 and was still there in 1765. The eldest girl, Margaret, was enrolled in Rebecca Jones and Hannah Catherall's school in 1760. She stopped attending in 1764, but her younger sister Mary was there from 1760 until 1769.[65]

Poor, working students and their parents, like the Stackhouse family, had to make a commitment to education. Not only did parents have to keep their children out of permanent service (although some students clearly worked part of the time), but the children had to attend school faithfully. It seems that most were quite diligent. Sometimes they and their parents decided to switch schools, perhaps looking to benefit from one teacher's specialties and then another's.[66] A number of students switched schools involuntarily. For example, when Rebecca Birchall, the beloved schoolmistress who had taught Elizabeth Sandwith Drinker, Hannah Callender, and other daughters of the Quaker elite, died in March of 1763, her students were placed with other teachers. Ann Patterson took in seven of Birchall's "Poor Childrin," and Rebecca Jones and Hannah Catherall took in five.[67] Teacher Jane Loftus took the unusual step of keeping the schools' overseers informed about the progress of her students and their reasons for leaving. Loftus's accounts clearly show the obstacles to education for children from poor families, but they also show the depth and breadth of the Quaker schools' reach. In 1759, for example, Loftus reported that Elizabeth Henchman would not be returning to school because she had been bound out, and that "I believe Sarah Callahan will be bound out soon for she is upon triall and seems to like the place very much."[68] Six months later Loftus reported that "Hannah Berry

65. "List of the Scholars...," August 23, 1765; Records of Jones and Catherall in Teachers' Accounts, William Penn Charter School Archives, Box 7, QC.

66. See, for example, the note on Hannah and Sarah Webb, who transferred from Jane Loftus's school, to that of Rebecca Birchall. "Jane Loftus her Accot dated 24 3 mo. 1762," Jane Loftus Accounts, William Penn Charter School Archives, Box 8, QC.

67. Crane, ed., Diary of Elizabeth Drinker, 1: 99; Trustees Account with [estate of] Rebecca Birchall, June 23, 1763, Teachers' Accounts, William Penn Charter School Archives, Box 7, QC; Teachers' Accounts, William Penn Charter School Archives Box 7, QC.

68. "Jane Loftus her accot of Schooling 16 poor Children to 6 mo: 1759," Accounts of Jane Loftus, William Penn Charter School Archives, Box 8, QC.

is bound out her father being Dead and so is Mary Price. . . . Margaret Henchman is bound out in the country."[69] Clearly the desire for literacy was in competition with families' needs for the income children could provide, or at least the financial relief their indenture could bring. One report makes this struggle plain. Sarah Keys first enrolled in Jane Loftus's school in 1757. But by 1763 Keys's family needed the resources her labor could provide, and she was expecting to have to leave school: "She thought She could not be spared . . . but her mother let her come [to school] another Quarter afterward She is now put out" to service.[70] Poor girls had other claims upon their time, too. Margaret Craft, for example, was sometimes "oblidge[d] to keep at home to help her father her mother not being capable of it at all times she is sometimes out of her sences."[71] Education was clearly desirable for the children of poor families, but it had to be balanced against the harsh realities of their economic circumstances.

The number of poor female students who were educated within the free Quaker school system indicates a broad, diverse audience for manuscript literature. The implication of teachers such as Jones and Catherall in the circulation of manuscript poetry suggests that the institutional bases of literary culture were not confined to the nascent middle class. Young women like the Stackhouse sisters, or those girls who went from school into domestic service, were part of a literate culture that both produced and consumed popular material in almanacs, newspapers, and beyond.

CONCLUSION

Through printed and manuscript sources, from authors and printers to purchasers or borrowers, from friends and family or teachers to target audiences, ideas about the problems of marriage and the value of singleness challenged the cultural dominance of marriage. A range of concerns about locating appropriate partners and the prospect of disharmony or, worse, tyrannical inequity was expressed in popular literature. These

69. "The Overseers of the Friends Publick School to Jane Loftus the 28 of the 11 mo 1759," Jane Loftus Accounts, William Penn Charter School Archives, Box 8, QC. Other accounts by Loftus in this folder confirm the same patterns of sickness, family needs, and indentures among poor school children.

70. "The 26th 7 mo 1764 The Overseers of Friends Publick Schools to Jane Loftus," Jane Loftus Accounts, William Penn Charter School Archives, Box 8, QC.

71. "The Overseers of the Friends Publick Schools to Jane Loftus the 20th the 2 mo. 1761," Jane Loftus Accounts, William Penn Charter School Archives, Box 8, QC.

reflections of cultural anxieties would be further disseminated as women like Martha Cooper copied the literary articulations of their concerns.

There is no doubt that ideas about marriage and singleness were mediated by religion and class. For many women marriage was an economic necessity. Philadelphia's socioeconomic elite had the highest percentage of women who never married. Yet, economics are not the best measure of the appeal of singleness. For Quaker women more than others, education and ministerial work could provide an avenue of opportunity that made marriage much less attractive. Rebecca Jones, for example, whose students' copybooks as well as other evidence demonstrated her commitment to singleness, came from a very poor background and never made much money. Her example and her teaching served to generate, reproduce, and circulate a cultural perspective on spinsterhood. The broad dissemination of ideas that countered the traditional view of women's place within marriage also suggests that the elite and well-educated may not have been the exclusive focus or audience for these views. The appearance of this material in almanacs in particular argues for the much broader circulation, appeal, and reception of the notion that singleness could constitute a legitimate alternative to marriage.

The production and transmission of these materials have significant implications for our understanding of gender and social structure in early America. Although we know that marriage was normative and that the legal prescription for marriage was a gender hierarchy, it has been unclear how women faced and understood that arrangement. Abigail Abbott Bailey's moving late eighteenth-century account of domestic violence in New England is a reminder that not all women could gracefully accept the secondary role assigned to them.[72] Although her husband abused her and raped their daughter, Bailey struggled with a theology and a culture that assured her that patriarchy would be absolute but benign. In Bailey's case it was neither. For most women, marriage posed none of the devastating problems faced by Bailey, but for many women it was risky, and for all women it was fundamentally transforming. The popular literature makes clear that although most women chose to marry, they did not do so uncritically. Both women and men understood that the hierarchy inherent in marriage was one of its most difficult aspects, and negotiating daily life within that structure was a cause for concern among women.

The popular literature on marriage and singleness also provides evi-

72. Ann Taves, ed., *Religion and Domestic Violence in Early New England: The Memoirs of Abigail Abbot Bailey* (Bloomington, Ind., 1989).

dence of a growing awareness of singleness as conceivable for women. The identification of "liberty" with singleness implied not only an awareness of the boundaries of married life but also an appreciation of possibility for female action outside marriage. Literature in print and manuscript helped popularize the notion that the unmarried could be, as Hannah Callender called them, "Worthy Single women." Although most of the literature critiquing marriage addressed spinsters and the choices inherent in first marriages, by contesting the dominance of the wife as the principal female social role, the literature on singleness could also speak to widowed women. The numerical preponderance of widows, for whom remarriage was often a possibility but seldom a reality, suggests that their unmarried status was validated by the culture. As we will see in the next chapter, these ideas about women's choice for independence from marriage could have special resonance within some theologies.

[2]

Elizabeth Norris's Reign: Religion and Self

Elizabeth Norris was descended from one of the most privileged families in colonial Pennsylvania. Her father, Isaac Norris, Sr., was extraordinarily wealthy, having capitalized on his family connections with Quaker merchants in England and the West Indies to market Philadelphia trade goods. Her mother, Mary Lloyd Norris, was the daughter of Thomas Lloyd, the colony's lieutenant governor and a close advisor of William Penn. A more distinguished Quaker lineage was hard to find. The wealthy Norris and Lloyd families had both converted to Quakerism in the seventeenth century.[1] Born in 1703, Elizabeth Norris died in 1775 as one of the wealthiest women in the colony. Two of her three sisters married men from similarly prominent families. Elizabeth and her sister Deborah, however, never married.

Elizabeth set about creating a very different life for herself from that of most other women of her generation. From quite early in her adulthood, she expressed a resistance to contemporary patterns of gender hierarchy, provoking a reaction in her father similar to John Adams's deliberate misunderstanding and dismissal of his wife's admonitions that the Revolutionary government "Remember the Ladies." In 1731, when Elizabeth was in her mid-twenties, her father reported from Philadelphia to his niece Prudence Moore in the West Indies that the family had just passed a pleasant evening reading aloud from Moore's letters. Elizabeth, he wrote, was so full of admiration for this cousin that she intended to make Moore "Patroness by a Dedication" in a "Learn'd peice" she and her sister Hannah Harrison were writing "to shew the Injustice of mens Assuming so great Superiority over the Women."[2] Isaac Norris claimed

1. Genealogical information on the Lloyd and Norris families is included in entries for Thomas Lloyd and Isaac Norris I in Craig Horle et al., eds., *Lawmaking and Legislators in Pennsylvania: A Biographical Dictionary*, 2 vols. (Philadelphia, 1991).
2. Isaac Norris, Sr., to Prudence Moore, December 8, 1731, Isaac Norris Copybook, HSP.

to have seen "some sheets of the work" and wondered whether he would be allowed "to write a preface—as there may phaps be need to say something wch may take off the jelousy the world might have on publication, Least they shoud: be Thought to Intend or mean Domination instead of the pretended Equallity."[3] Norris's attempt to defuse the message of his daughters' writing did not blunt the significance of their act: two women of an eminent Quaker family, one married and the other an avowed spinster, critiqued the behavior and the religiosity of the men around them. Their father's pique was manifested in a rejoinder not uncommon to his and later eras; he implied that when women objected to the gender hierarchy of their society, they meant to reverse rather than eliminate unequal power relations.[4] The perversity of female domination would have been clear to any of his contemporaries.

The discomfort that Elizabeth Norris caused was enhanced by strong theological support for her view that men's dominance of women was wrong. Unlike those who followed the Calvinist tradition, Quaker women could turn to the teachings of their founder to encourage their equalitarian leanings. Quaker ideas about gender and marriage were quite radical, and although New World Quakers often seemed comfortable with conventional behaviors, some insisted that the subversive implications of Quaker theology be acknowledged.

At the family estate of Fairhill, north of Philadelphia, Elizabeth Norris created a sort of religious retreat for Quaker women, where she particularly welcomed her sisters in singleness. She invited three spinster cousins to join her home, and one of them later cared for Norris in her old age. Friends in need of solitude and ministers looking to break their journey or recuperate from a mission abroad stopped at Fairhill for rest and spiritual sustenance. Praise from visitors included a lengthy poem from the pen of the accomplished Susanna Wright, who heralded Norris as valiantly resisting secular patterns of marriage and gender hierarchy. Praise from her family included imitation: niece Hannah Griffitts, Norris's confidante, companion, and executor, became just as ardent a defender of singleness as her aunt, writing her own poems and prose in favor of what she called "My Dear Liberty."

Elizabeth Norris's extraordinary life might seem only that—extraordinary—were it not for the culture in which she lived and flourished. Her wealth and status gained her both audience and tolerance, but

3. Isaac Norris, Sr. to Prudence Moore, 1731, Isaac Norris Letterbooks, Norris Family Letters, HSP.
4. The classic treatment of early modern anxiety about female dominance is Natalie Davis's "Women on Top," in her *Society and Culture in Early Modern France* (Stanford, Calif., 1975).

she seemingly needed neither to lead a single life. Her message of a theologically inspired singleness, and her life centered on other single women, brought not opprobrium but praise. Little if any invective was aimed at her flouting of what historians have assumed to be the unchallenged foundation of Anglo-American society: the married couple, with a patriarchal husband and a submissive wife. Even those who have studied Quaker marriage patterns have suggested that although patriarchy was muted by Quaker teachings, submissiveness in women was still expected. And yet Norris tolerated none of this. By Susanna Wright's account, she openly disputed what she saw as backsliding from the original tenets of Quaker faith, including the equality of the sexes and a prelapsarian vision of gender relations unhampered by biblical stories of Eve's transgressions and women's subsequent portrayal as simultaneously seductive and deceived.

Norris's life challenges many of our understandings of early American women's approach to marriage, religion, and the intimate connection between them. John Milton wrote that the appropriate, indeed divine, order of things was "He for God, she for God in him." Protestantism asked men to eschew the intercession of priests in their relationship with God, but it continued to prescribe that women's relationship with God be directed through the voice and the authority of their husbands. Historians of women have largely accepted this premise, seeing in religion an opportunity for fleeting moments of independent spiritual experience or authority, primarily through mysticism.[5] Yet some theologies, primarily those of Quakerism and of the German Pietist sects, challenged Milton's formulation and directed women to experience God independently. Thus, in the same way that popular literature allowed some challenge to the essentializing and universalizing claims of marriage, some religions also explicitly challenged the notion that marriage did or should dominate women's lives.

In Chapter 1, we saw how popular literature allowed a discourse of marital critique, as well as a discourse on the benefits of singleness, to counter the hegemony of matrimony. In Pennsylvania, women also had diverse models for a religiously inspired conception of self. They could

5. The literature on women and religion in early modern Europe is very rich; that in early America is much less extensive. Among those works that treat the spiritual authority that extraordinary women could attain as mystics or prophets, especially in marginal religions, but also that appropriated by lay women within mainstream Protestantism and Catholicism, see Jodi Bilinkoff, *The Avila of St. Theresa* (Ithaca, N.Y., 1989), and "A Spanish Prophetess and her Patrons: The Case of Maria de Santo Domingo," *Sixteenth Century Journal* 23 (1992): 21–34; Natalie Davis, "City Women and Religious Change," in *Society and Culture in Early Modern France* (Stanford, Calif., 1965), 88–95; Phyllis Mack, *Visionary Women: Ecstatic Prophecy in Seventeenth-Century England* (Berkeley, 1992).

look to denominations such as Quakerism (mainstream in Pennsylvania, but of course not elsewhere in the colonies, even by the eighteenth century). They could also look to more radical sects such as the Moravians or the Ephrata collective, which espoused the doctrine and practice of celibacy. Philadelphians often travelled to Ephrata and Bethlehem to see and learn more about these different folk and their beliefs. The German Pietists also reinforced some aspects of Quaker and radical Protestant thought on the essential equality of souls and the practice of some forms of gender equity.'

This chapter explores the development of a feminine individualism based on theological ideals of spirituality and corporeality. This female individual self is contrasted with the traditional relational self of the wife and with the masculine models of materialistic individualism that became prominent in the eighteenth century. This chapter also looks at the models or "patterns" of single piety provided by Quakers and other groups in and around Philadelphia. The city's urban culture fostered the development of these ideas and practices, in part because of the dense web of Quaker female ministers, many of whom were single, and in part because—as we have already seen—these ideas could be expressed and communicated in the urban media of manuscript, print, and discourse.

QUAKER CULTURE AND A FEMALE SELF

Elizabeth Norris and other women of her acquaintance expressed the idea that rejecting marriage and its attendant gender hierarchy was a spiritual obligation. This idea resonated with fundamental features of Quakerism. Quaker religious teachings, from founder George Fox and others of the mid-seventeenth century to the Quaker reformers of the mid-eighteenth century, supported an attack on hierarchy in many forms, including gender hierarchy. Within that critique, and embodied in the foundations of Quaker communal order, was a re-visioning of the family around an equalitarian marriage. A defense and even promotion of female ministers, many of whom either never married or placed their marriage second to their religious callings, was also related to the critique of hierarchy. These two phenomena came together in the Delaware Valley in a potent form, as New World Quakers attempted to deal with the secular seductions of material success and a turn toward "worldliness," including social hierarchy. The large and prominent female ministry, the Quaker reform movement, and the ability of wealthy Quaker women such as Elizabeth Norris to create a private retreat for Quaker spinsters all made Philadelphia a proving ground for discussions of marriage, religion, and a female self.

More than any other branch of early modern Protestantism, Quaker theology emphasized bodily experience and feminine spiritual independence. The core of the Quaker belief system was a faith in the Inner Light of Christ.[6] While radical Protestants shared an emphasis on God's saving grace, the (potential) equality of souls, the authority of the Bible, and the importance of an individual, unmediated relationship with God, Quakers took all these concepts much further. They believed not only that all souls were equal but also that all persons could open themselves to experience God intimately. This experience of "the "inner light" could include revelations beyond scripture, making the personal, individual relationship to God superior to any other experience of worship, such as liturgy and sermonizing. The emphasis upon the body as a vessel of the spirit and the individual's intimate knowledge of God made Quakerism intensely corporeal. The name "Quaker" itself was derived from the ecstatic physical movements of some early Friends.

Women were among the most active of early Quaker prophets, and the intensity of their ecstasy was widely known. In part, as Phyllis Mack has argued, this intensity flowed from women's ability to access both their culture's (usually derogatory) notions of the open, moist, absorbing qualities of the female body and their own capacity for self-transcendence. Each of these qualities allowed women to open themselves to religious ecstasy and to explain their ecstasy in uniquely feminine terms.[7] For Quaker women, their ability to become open—to transcend their gender, their bodies, their selves—not only made the feminine ecstatic model seem appropriate but also justified women's public prophesying. As mere women, they could not act, but because they were women, they had a unique capacity for passive reception of the spirit and thus for public prophesy. "From the Quakers' own perspective," Mack observed, "their altering of the popular meaning of womanhood, holding to it as a negative abstraction while rejecting its descriptive power for individual, sanctified women, must have seemed a very effective argument . . . that could justify the public authority of female prophets in a patriarchal world."[8]

Social as well as spiritual relations had to accommodate this radical

6. A good introduction to Quaker beliefs is Chapter One, "The Dry Bones of Quaker Theology," in J. William Frost, *The Quaker Family in Colonial America* (New York, 1973), chap. 1. See also Hugh Barbour, *The Quakers in Puritan England* (New Haven, Conn., 1964).
7. Mack, *Visionary Women*, 15–44, 127–211.
8. *Ibid.*, 177.

perspective on the roles and capacities of women. For Quakers, the significance of the light within went beyond the individual experience to reach into the home and the community. Believing a prelapsarian state of gender relations divine and a gender hierarchy indicative of humanity's fall from grace, Quakers sought to reinstate the "helpsmeet" model of marriage. Man and woman, husband and wife, such "restorationists" argued, should be equal and mutual companions. As George Fox wrote:

> And some men may say, ye man must have ye power and superiority over ye woman, because God says, ye man must Rule over his wife, and yt man is not of ye woman, but ye woman is of ye Man: Indeed, after man fell yt command was; but before man fell, there was noe such Command, ffor they was both meett helpes, and they was both to have Dominion over all that God made.[9]

Fox's vision of the restoration of a prelapsarian world where men and women would be equal, and not tainted by the evils of hierarchy, was an important source of authority for Quaker women. In the late 1670s Sarah Fell, daughter of Margaret Fell, the Quaker leader who married George Fox, wrote an epistle from the Lancashire Friends Meeting to Quaker meetings in England and across the Atlantic on the subject of women's spiritual authority and women's separate meetings. "As Christ saith," Fell wrote, "that which he made them in the beginning made them male and female, & c. they were both in the work of God in the beginning, and so in the restoration." The whole notion of male superiority and domination was a punishment upon both sexes alike; to try to recall God's kingdom on earth, believers would have to resist that pattern of relations. Fell cautioned that "if the work of the old serpent, put them out of the work of god, and as he did the beginning tempt them to sinne and transgression, and disobedience, so he would still keep them there." The consequences, and the symptoms, of such "sinne and transgression" would be clear. There would be "a superiority one over another, that Christ the head should not rule in male and female alike: and so keep them in bondage, and slavery, and in difference and dissension one with another, and then they are fit for his temptations."[10]

Implementing this Edenic vision of sexual equality involved rethinking women's relationship not only to their church (the meeting, that is)

9. George Fox, quoted in Bonnelyn Young Kunze, *Margaret Fell and the Rise of Quakerism* (Stanford, Calif., 1994), 153.

10. [Sarah Fell], "From our Country Women's meeting in Lancashire to be Dispersed abroad, among the Women's meetings every where," (1675–1680), Milton D. Speizman and Jane Kronick, transc., "A Seventeenth-Century Quaker Women's Declaration," *Signs* 1 (1975): 236.

but to their families as well. The re-visioned marriage, based in a prelapsarian theology of gender equality, was at the center of this radical social agenda. In what Barry Levy has called the "radical spiritualization of all household emotions," George Fox moved to make families the centrifugal center of Quaker morality. Women were to play an essential role as the equal spiritual partners of their husbands and as co-parents of their children. Marriages would be contracted between two persons who had thought and prayed about their suitability, and whose commitment the Quaker meeting had deemed worthy of acknowledging. Parents would focus, not, as other Protestants did, on the innate sinfulness of the child, but on their own extensive responsibilities for the nurturance of a spiritual child. Levy has termed this familial model of authoritative wives, loving marriages, and child-centered households "Quaker Domesticity," but the enforcement of domesticity reached far beyond the boundaries of the home.[11] Separate women's meetings would be the arbiters of issues touching the family, including the investigation of couples intending to marry. The establishment of these separate meetings was opposed by some Quakers, particularly Quaker men, who rightly saw that both church and familial government would then be the equal province of women.[12]

George Fox and Margaret Fell's own marriage was the conscious, contemporary model of Quaker marriage partnership.[13] The two Quaker leaders waited for a leading from the Inner Light; they confirmed their commitment's rightness through announcement of their intentions to multiple meetings; finally they claimed each other in a ceremony unique to Quakers of the time, in which neither partner was given by parents or another figure of authority, and in which women did not promise to obey their husbands. Rather, both spouses declared themselves to be married to each other in their own words. Fox made doubly sure that no earthly motivation could mar his marriage by renouncing any claim to Fell's considerable wealth and by securing the inheritance of her children by Thomas Fell.[14]

11. Barry Levy, *Quakers and the American Family: British Settlement in the Delaware Valley* (New York, 1988), esp. 70–80.

12. Discussions of the debate surrounding the establishment of the separate women's meetings can be found in Mack, *Visionary Women*, 264–304; Kunze, *Margaret Fell and the Rise of Quakerism*, 143–168; and Speizman and Kronick, "A Seventeenth-Century Quaker Woman's Declaration."

13. Jacques Tual, "Sexual Equality and Conjugal Harmony: The Way to Celestial Bliss: A View of Early Quaker Matrimony," *The Journal of the Friends' Historical Society* 55 (1988): esp. 168. See also Barbara Ritter Dailey, "The Husbands of Margaret Fell: An Essay on Religious Metaphor and Social Change," *The Seventeenth Century* 2 (1987): 65; Mack, *Visionary Women*, 226–232.

14. Daily, "The Husbands of Margaret Fell," 63–64; Mack, *Visionary Women*, 226–227.

The radical version of marriage relations was clearly central to and consistent with other Quaker teachings, but it must have been virtually impossible to achieve. Even, or perhaps especially, ministers who were women had trouble sustaining the delicate balance between the Quaker ideal and predominant contemporary notions about gender. In account after account, women on both sides of the Atlantic described husbands who not only failed to act as "helpmeet" but actively opposed their wife's ministry.[15] Perhaps more tellingly, other women ministers postponed or avoided marriage altogether because of its potential competition with their spiritual calling.[16] The ideal Quaker partnership placed God above all else, as the English Quaker Eleanor Haydock remembered her marriage to another minister: "My dear husband often expressing his great love to me, above all visibles, as the best of enjoyment he had in this world; yet would say, I was not too dear to give up to serve the truth."[17] For men this path was clear, but the normative view of women as subject to husband and household responsibilities made a ministerial vocation more problematic, and vice versa.[18]

The equalitarian marriage was particularly elusive as Quakers migrated to America and as eighteenth-century Quakers moved away from their religion's radical roots. A strong reform movement, beginning in earnest in the mid-eighteenth century, agitated for change and for a recommitment to the original tenets of the faith. Reformers argued against aspects of Quaker culture, including materialism, complacency, the notion of "birthright" membership, laxity in marriage disciplines, and slaveholding, which they saw as signs of a turn toward permissiveness and secular values. One of the areas that most concerned them was marriage. Central features of the Quaker marriage ideal, such as the injunction to marry endogamously, the ban on consanguinity, and the prescribed format for a couple's multiple appearances before the meeting to declare their intentions and to receive "clearance" for their marriage from the women's meeting, had all been relaxed or ignored. After midcentury, reformers instituted a much stricter regime. The difference can be seen in just one family. A pair of cousins who married in 1739 apolo-

---

15. Mack, *Visionary Women*, 379. See also the account of Elizabeth Ashbridge in William L. Andrews et al., *Journeys in New Worlds: Early American Women's Narratives* (Madison, Wisc., 1990), and the introduction by Daniel Shea, esp. 128–130, 154–158.

16. Catherine Peyton Phillips described the "restrictions" she felt regarding marriage because of her ministry and the long delay in her marriage because of these concerns. *Memoirs of the Life of Catherine Phillips: To Which are Added Some of her Epistles* (London, 1797), 206–17.

17. As quoted in Mack, *Visionary Women*, 381.

18. Ibid., 379–386.

gized to the meeting for their multiple infractions (not only consanguinity, but also their failure to get their marriage cleared or approved) and were forgiven. A pair of cousins in the same family, married in 1767, also attempted apology, but they were completely rebuffed and disowned until the death of one partner, more than thirty years later, left the other free to rejoin the meeting.[19] The reformers' energy in this regard was extraordinary. Between 1761 and 1776, the Society of Friends disowned close to fifteen hundred members of the Philadelphia Yearly Meeting for marriage infractions.[20]

While the Quaker reformers, led by such figures as John Woolman and Anthony Benezet, organized ways to counter the declension of American Quaker marriage by attention to the process of marriage formation, individual Quaker women also critiqued secularizing patterns in marital relationships. The reality of daily life in an intimate relationship, especially the ramifications of adherence to or disregard of equalitarianism in principle and practice, was their primary concern.

Compelling evidence of lay Quaker women's ambivalence about marriage comes from their own writings. Although letters and a few journals sometimes flesh out the context in which this criticism was launched, poetry provided the venue for sustained meditation on the subject. This kind of poetry, often written for an audience of friends and kin and not meant for general circulation or publication, is a unique place in which to locate women's sentiments. One poet very explicitly invoked Quaker theology to celebrate a wedding, and express hope for the marriage. This poem, in celebration of a specific marriage, wished that the young Quaker couple: "not know the Name of Strife / and drive domestic Jarrs away; / That the whole Tenor of their Life / May seem to them a nuptial day." The poet also reminded readers (or listeners) of the source from which marriage drew its purpose, strength, and inspiration: "Marriage in Eden first began / Ordained and blessed by heavenly powers / The greatest Bliss attending Man / Unless the guilty fault be ours." The author thus connected "bliss" to the "ordained" state of marriage, which was the prelapsarian, equalitarian, or "helpsmeet" marriage. Only through humanity's "guilty fault" was that "bliss" endangered. Atten-

19. The cases of Hannah Hill Moore (who married cousin Samuel Preston Moore in 1739) and her sister Milcah Martha Hill Moore (who married Samuel's brother, Charles Moore, in 1767) are discussed in Catherine Blecki and Karin Wulf, eds., *Milcah Martha Moore's Book: A Commonplace Book from Revolutionary America* (University Park, Pa., 1997), 14–18.

20. Jack Marietta, *The Reformation of American Quakerism: 1748–1783* (Philadelphia, 1984), 67.

tion to the principles of the Edenic model would provide the surest hope of "Love & Peace . . . smiling Joys & sweet Delight."[21]

A circle of Quaker women in the mid-eighteenth century most forcefully articulated a striking combination of a theological critique of contemporary disregard for the equalitarian marital ideal and a defense of spinsterhood as a form of resistance to gender hierarchy. The most explicit of these writers was Susanna Wright, a poet of considerable talent who lived in Lancaster County but corresponded and visited with a wide variety of people from the Delaware Valley. Her intellectual gifts were widely appreciated in her era. In addition to writing poetry, she was a botanist, experimented with silk production (her samples of finished cloth graced British royalty), offered medical advice, acted as a diplomat, and served as a county magistrate in the stead of a sick friend. Wright was called the "bluestocking of the Susquehanna," for her intellectual pursuits and her friendships with such prominent figures as Benjamin Franklin and James Logan, the colony's foremost publisher and bookman. When she died in 1784, she was remembered by Benjamin Rush as "the famous Suzey Wright, a lady who has been celebrated above half a century for her wit, good sense and valuable improvement of mind."[22]

Wright's family was prominent in Quaker and political circles. Her father and brother both served in the Pennsylvania Assembly and were important actors in the boundary dispute between Pennsylvania and Maryland that involved an area very close to their own properties on the Susquehanna River. Among the family's closest friends and political allies were the Norrises of Philadelphia. The second generation of Wrights and Norrises, particularly Elizabeth Norris and Susanna Wright, remained close friends. It was in a poem celebrating Elizabeth Norris's single status—and by extension her own single state—that Wright articulated her most complete defense of Quaker spinsterhood.

In the poem titled "To Eliza. Norris at Fairhill," Wright celebrated spinsterhood as a form of resistance to the sexual hierarchy she saw as inherent in contemporary marriage.[23] The poem has three distinct parts.

21. "An Epithalamium on the Marriage of E.D. with F. B_d," in Blecki and Wulf, eds., *Milcah Martha Moore's Book*, 193–194.

22. Journal of Benjamin Rush, April 7, 1784, as reprinted in "Benjamin Franklin in Lancaster County," *Journal of the Lancaster County Historical Society* 63 (October 1959): 6. A summary of Wright's life can be found in Barbara Hunsberger, "An Analysis of the Public Life of Susanna Wright" (master's thesis, Pennsylvania State University, 1982). The fullest accounts of the Wright and Blunston families are found in entries for John and Samuel Blunston and John Wright, Sr., and John Wright, Jr., in Horle et al., eds. *Lawmaking and Legislators in Pennsylvania*. I am indebted to Craig Horle for an advance look at the essay on James Wright.

23. Susanna Wright, "To Eliza. Norris at Fairhill," LCP.

In the first, Wright provided a rich and interpretive description of the theological foundations for Quaker equalitarianism. She devoted the second to celebrating Norris's choice of singleness and the contemplative life she led in her country home. She praised the example that Norris set by refusing to "yield obedience" both to individual men and to a conception of marriage that was contrary to Quaker theology. In the third part, Wright sounded a call to arms, suggesting that righteous women should "forbear" marrying and that men's abuse of power within marriage would be punished on Judgement Day.[24]

In this poem and in her other writings about relationships, including a poem on the difficulties of heterosocial friendships and a verse version of a letter from Anne Boleyn to King Henry VIII, three themes are prominent. First, Wright viewed gender equality not only as the soundest foundation for relationships but also as scripturally mandated. She based her assertions on the Quaker reading of Genesis. In Eden, men and women were "helpsmeet" or partners, and neither was subordinate to the other. After the fall from grace, God determined that men "should rule & die."[25] Along with mortality came hierarchy, an equally burdensome departure from the divine plan. Just as people strove for salvation and an afterlife, they should strive for a more Edenic existence on earth.

The second theme in Wright's writings is her critique of humanity's, and usually specifically men's, delinquency in pursuing an Edenic existence. The secular values and vices of ambition, greed, materialism, and desire for dominance caused even Quaker men to stray from the goal of equality. Wright did not find women blameless; she suggested that some women allowed themselves to be tricked into subservience, rather than vigilantly insisting on the Quaker marriage model. But Wright's harshest criticisms were reserved for men. In "To Eliza. Norris" she argued that men peddled gender hierarchy as a "pleasing dictate of Almighty will," although they knew it lacked divine authorization. They were intentionally disregarding the appropriate marital model in order to satisfy their own desire for dominance. For this ambition and adherence to secular values, Wright explicitly blamed the notion of hierarchy introduced through "our first Parents curious crime."[26]

The third main theme is Wright's meditation on the consequences of unequal relationships, in which she invoked the post-Edenic "doom" of

24. A more extensive analysis of this poem appears in Karin Wulf, "'My Dear Liberty': Marriage, Spinsterhood and Conceptions of Female Autonomy in Colonial Philadelphia," in *Women and Freedom in Colonial America*, ed. Larry D. Eldridge (New York, 1997), 83–108.
25. Wright, "To Eliza. Norris at Fairhill."
26. Susanna Wright, untitled, in Blecki and Wulf, eds., *Milcah Martha Moore's Book*, 130–132.

hierarchy to describe men's attempts to "govern womankind." In her versification of a letter of Anne Boleyn to King Henry VIII, Wright angrily described Henry's betrayal and Anne's loyalty.[27] At the end of time Henry's sins would "stand fully reveal'd" before God and man; not only had he condemned Anne to death, but he also had ensured his own damnation. In a similar vein, in the elegy "To Eliza. Norris" Wright predicted that on Judgement Day men would be "strip'd of Power, & placed in equal light." By implication, their judgment for having claimed and enforced superiority would be severe.

One could speculate that Wright's own romantic history was responsible for generating at least part of her heated disavowal of the hierarchy she saw inherent in heterosexual relationships. She herself never married, but she did have a long and intimate friendship with Samuel Blunston, who, on his death, left her a life interest in his home. The nature of the relationship between the two is not known, although many have suggested that it was at least romantic, if not explicitly sexual. Certainly it was the most important relationship in both of their lives. Lore speculates that they had had a falling out, during which time Blunston married a rich widow, but that the two were reconciled after his wife's early death.[28] Blunston's provision of his home for Wright's life use looked astonishingly like a dower portion, to which widows were entitled under English law.[29]

It is possible, although not likely, that Wright's denunciation of the masculine character was connected to some twist in her relationship with Blunston. More likely she was defending the kind of relationship she had come to know and value and then had lost. Even when celebrating the joys of heterosociability, she consistently described gender equality as the strongest foundation for a relationship and remained keenly aware of its rarity. Her belief in gender equality was grounded in theology, and it was God's plan for human relationships that she most wanted to emulate. Thus, even if a friendship was joyous, she worried that it still might interfere with her spiritual life. In a poem "On Friendship" she explained that "as Souls [have] no sexes," she "claim'd a right" to love a male friend. Yet Wright worried that the "refin'd delight" of such a friendship might detract from her reverence for God. She might "grow giddy with

27. Susanna Wright, "Anna Boylens Letter to King Henry the 8th," in Blecki and Wulf, eds., *Milcah Martha Moore's Book*, 121–124. Hannah Callender Sansom specified in her diary that she read this poem by Wright.

28. Mrs. Henry Hiestad, "'I, Samuel Blunston': The Man and the Family," *Journal of Lancaster County Historical Society* 26 (1922): 191–204.

29. This insight is Bernard Herman's, based on his work on the Wright and Blunston homes. Very little documentation of Wright's life is extant.

excess of Love." Even worse, she confided, she might confuse the love of friendship with the devoted love reserved for God. She confessed this directly: "What most of all I fear / Is loving the Creation man more than thee."[30] Thus while criticizing men for violating one tenet of Quaker theology, she admitted that where human relations were concerned, women must also remain vigilant against emotional lapses.

In her elegiac poem, "To Eliza. Norris at Fairhill," Wright drew together her critique of heterosexual relationships with an advocacy of spinsterhood. She praised Norris as a "queen" who refused "to yield obedience" to heterosexual norms. Thus Norris could "in your freedom reign," unshackled by the demands of such relationships, and devote herself to contemplation and worship. "Bless that choice," Wright wrote, "which led your bloom of youth, from forms, & shadows,—to Enlightning truth."[31] Quakers often used the metaphors of "forms" and "shadows" to describe what was illusory, unreal, or ungodly. The world could be distracted from God's light by the illusions of wealth or power.[32] Wright implied that marriage, with its attendant hierarchy, was one of these distractions. Norris's choice of singleness left her free to experience what was most important.

It was within this acclaim for Norris's "choice" of spinsterhood that Wright articulated an interpretation of Quaker theology that drew heavily on both early Quaker notions and a more modern sensibility.[33] Elizabeth Norris's real achievement in resisting marriage, Wright suggested, was in protecting her "self" from the corruptions of a relationship. She concluded the piece by exhorting Norris to "shine your self" as a reproof to less staunch followers of Quaker doctrine. Norris was able to attend more closely to "truth" than could those who married.[34] The message of Wright's verse was that each woman would choose a marital status that could either protect or betray her "self." Quaker teachings on marriage directed that men and women wait for the Inner Light to confirm or deny

---

30. Susanna Wright, "On Friendship," in Blecki and Wulf, eds., *Milcah Martha Moore's Book*, 143–145. Hannah Griffitts referred to the temptation of loving a human too much in "To Sophronia," noting that she loved men only "as well as I ought." Also in Blecki and Wulf, eds., *Milcah Martha Moore's Book*, 173–174. For another Quaker woman's meditation on friendship and its role in spiritual enhancement, see Sarah Morris, "On Friendship," n.d., Pemberton Papers, vol. 3, p. 154, HSP.

31. Susanna Wright, "To Eliza. Norris at Fairhill."

32. See Catherine Blecki, "Reading Moore's Book: Manuscript vs. Print Culture and the Development of Early American Literature," in Blecki and Wulf, eds., *Milcah Martha Moore's Book*, 59–106.

33. Wright's repeated references to "reason" also marked her work as distinctly modern.

34. This idea that human relationships complicated one's primary spiritual relationship also appeared in Wright's other works, such as the poem on friendship in which she worried that she might love her friend with a passion more suited to divine worship.

their choice of a partner. Wright and others seemed to suggest that to encourage the workings of the light within, women must first choose whether or not to marry at all.[35]

From what little is known of Elizabeth Norris, it seems clear that Wright's elegy was quite reflective of its subject's positions, as well as its author's. Norris established a household of spinsters at Fairhill, the Norris family home and one of colonial Philadelphia's premier country residences. While she headed the household, first caring for her aging parents, then acting as housekeeper for her brother, Isaac, Jr., and finally mentoring her young nieces when they inherited the property at Isaac's death, she invited a number of younger, unmarried female relatives to live there.[36] Other Quaker women sought Fairhill as a contemplative refuge. Susanna Wright praised Fairhill's rural environment, which would "enlarge the thought and elevate the heart."[37] The Quaker minister Elizabeth Hudson spent much of 1744 at Fairhill, crediting Elizabeth Norris with aiding her in at least one major spiritual crisis. Hudson wrote that Norris was "affectionately tender to me during my religious exercise in which she was made an Useful Instrument in ye hand of the Lord," and she likened their friendship to that "which subsisted betwixt Jonothen & david whch Strength of love induced me to leave my father's House & spend most of my time wth her."[38] In celebrating Elizabeth Norris's spinsterhood, Wright also celebrated the bonds that had formed among this group of women Friends at Fairhill.

The life that Norris and Wright led and the ideas they espoused challenge some basic assumptions about women in early America and about Quakerism. One of the most influential historical works on American Quakers in the eighteenth century is Barry Levy's *Quakers and the American Family*. Levy argues that Quaker family forms, by emphasizing the role of women in moral development and discipline and by making their households child-centered, presaged the kind of domesticity usually associated with proto-industrial nineteenth-century New England. Levy described Quaker women's social role as "characterologically consistent." "The Quakers," he argued, "melded women's sexuality, spirituality, and maternal authority into a novel feminine mystique that later be-

35. In her poem "The Only True Happiness," Hannah Griffitts emphasized the determinant role of the "self." In the last stanza she wrote: "To no particular lot of life / is Happiness Confin'd / But in ye self-approving heart / and firm, contented mind." Griffitts poetry, LCP.
36. Among the women at Fairhill were Elizabeth Norris's nieces Hannah and Mary Griffitts, and Mary and Sarah Norris, as well as another cousin, Mary Lloyd.
37. Wright, "To Eliza. Norris."
38. Journal of Elizabeth Hudson (later Morris), QC.

came the model for New England advocates of domesticity."[39] In Levy's model, clearly a woman's work as wife and mother was central to her Quaker identity. Yet women's position within eighteenth-century Quakerism cannot be so easily and so definitively attached to their domestic roles.

Although Levy's depiction compellingly and convincingly describes many features of eighteenth-century Quaker domesticity, two factors mediated against the adoption of the single "characterologically consistent social role for women" that he posited. First, so many women never married that one has to wonder how they would have fitted into this new Quaker ideal of purely domestic femininity.[40] These women did not devote their spiritual resources exclusively to the management of others, but like Susanna Wright they concluded that they needed to attend to a self protected from precisely these responsibilities. That is not to say that single women eschewed the obligations and the joys of intense human connections with family and friends. Rather, it is to suggest that some women found the obligation to their own spiritual development an exclusive one. Women were not automatically drawn to a relational existence; some found independence of person and spirit the most natural state. As Hannah Griffitts reminded a married cousin, "There are many of you weded ones who I believe are Placed in your Proper Sphere and I sincerely wish you encrease of Happiness in it—without envying you one atom. Everyone is not fitted for the single life—nor was I ever moulded for The weded one."[41]

Second, the organization of Quakerism itself, from the separation of men's and women's meetings to the prominence of female ministers, was an important and potent force in the Quaker culture of the eighteenth-century Delaware Valley. These two related models offered an alternative to the household, creating a female spiritual community. Rather than base the entire weight of Quakerism's successes and failures on the institution of the family, as George Fox had done, these alternative communities came to foster some of the most intense, reflective, and influential Quakers of the era.

Quaker ministers were at the center of female spiritual community. Other women, particularly those who served the meeting in other formal

39. Levy, *Quakers and the American Family*, 193.

40. Ibid., 193–230. The increase in disciplines for exogamy may have contributed to the rising incidence of spinsterhood. Marietta, *The Reformation of American Quakerism*; Robert V. Wells, "Quaker Marriage Patterns in a Colonial Perspective," *WMQ* 29 (July 1972): 415–442.

41. Hannah Griffitts to [Milcah Martha Moore], n.d., Edward Wanton Smith Collection, QC.

capacities, were also important leaders, but ministers had a special place in Quaker culture. Women ministers were almost as numerous and vocal as men.[42] Most female ministers married.[43] Nonetheless, the significance of unmarried women among the female leadership is remarkable. Sarah Morris was just one of a number of spinsters who became preeminent ministers. Elizabeth Smith of Burlington and Rebecca Jones of Philadelphia were equally distinguished. Hannah Catherall, Jones's longtime partner, was clerk of the Philadelphia Northern District Women's Meeting from 1778 to 1794.[44] Elizabeth Norris was remembered as "a woman of exemplary piety and virtue." Those qualities, together with education and social rank, made her a natural candidate for committee work.[45] The Women's Meeting regularly assigned Norris tasks as varied as transcribing minutes into the official minute book and "deal[ing] with Mary Brown (late Walne) for outgoing in Marriage" (marrying a non-Quaker).[46] Indeed, she was jointly responsible for the Women's Meeting minutes for over twenty years. Norris and Morris several times represented the Women's Meeting, and presented their important resolutions about discipline and other matters to the quarterly business meeting.[47] These examples illustrate that Quaker women's singleness, far from being an aberrant or unacceptable status, was perfectly compatible with leadership in the Quaker community.

Even more than other kinds of service, women's activism in the ministry served as a model of Quaker femininity. Ministerial activity allowed women who felt moved by the spirit to follow that leading. Between 1700 and 1775 a minimum of twenty-four English and Irish women ministers visited the colonies. Twenty-four women from Philadelphia made at least

42. In 1746, forty-eight men spoke at meeting 376 times, and forty women spoke 268 times. Among the four most frequent speakers was Sarah Morris, who spoke thirty-eight times. From the journal of John Smith, as excerpted in J. Thomas Sharf and Thompson Westcott, *History of Philadelphia, 1609–1884*,(Philadelphia, 1884) vol.2, p. 1248.
43. An analysis by Jean Soderlund of women who were active in the Delaware Valley Women's Meetings, including Philadelphia and Chester meetings, reveals that most of those women had married and started families before their meeting activism commenced. Jean Soderlund, "Women's Authority in Pennsylvania and New Jersey Quaker Meetings, 1680–1760," *WMQ* 44 (October 1987): 728–729.
44. Elaine Crane, ed., *The Diary of Elizabeth Drinker* (Boston, 1991), 732, 732n, 882, 2124. Catherall was disciplined for inebriation in 1795 and then reinstated with the meeting in 1797, although she continued to attend meeting and to socialize with her Quaker friends during the two intervening years.
45. Deborah Norris Logan quoted in Charles Stille, *Memoirs of the Historical Society of Pennsylvania* (Philadelphia, 1891–1895), vol. 13, p. 312.
46. Philadelphia Women's Meeting minutes, January 31, 1743, and March 25, 1748, microfilm, FHL.
47. Ibid., January 25, 1765, and October. 30, 1767.

sixty-five trips in their ministry over roughly the same period.[48] Women's active ministry allowed women to see other women as central to the Quaker mission. No one could miss the significance of these women's work: public and private praise and thanksgiving followed the arrival, teaching, and eventual departure of ministers from abroad. The substantial collective of ministers who called the Philadelphia Yearly Meeting home were among the most respected members of their communities. Women's speech, rather than being regarded as peculiar or in need of special defense, as it was in so much of the rest of the early modern Anglo-American world, was regular, expected, and anticipated.[49]

Occasionally a woman could accompany a minister in her travels if another female minister did not feel called to travel at that time or if the experience was deemed important for the non-minister. Deborah Morris, selected to accompany her aunt Sarah Morris to England "on religious service," kept a journal of her travels.[50] Sarah Morris, a renowned minister, had already traveled widely, and preached very regularly. The English minister Catherine Peyton Phillips, whom Morris accompanied to various meetings around Pennsylvania in the 1750s, called her "a truly exemplary woman, and sometimes highly favored in the ministry."[51] Most of Deborah Morris's journal was taken up with observations of her aunt's testimony. In April 1772, for example, Deborah reported that a meeting at Devonshire was very well attended by Friends as well as "many of other societys." "Aunt was the first yt apeard," Morris reported, "& began wt the cry of the prophit, all flesh is Grass & was carried on to admiration, as she Generaly is Most favord in Largest Assemble: So it was then, . . . Concluded it in prayer, the people, tho the meeting held Long were very quiet & attentive."[52] The experience of observing other women's public power could be transforming. For Deborah Morris, herself unmarried, the model of her spinster aunt's effective and famous ministry was sustaining and inspiring.

48. Ministerial visits could be very extensive, as was that of the celebrated Catherine Peyton Phillips, who traveled almost nine thousand miles over three years. Margaret Hope Bacon, *Mothers of Feminism: The Story of Quaker Women in America* (San Francisco, 1986), 24–41; and Bonnelyn Young Kunze, "'vesells fitt for the masters us[e]': A Transatlantic Community of Religious Women, The Quakers 1675–1753," in Kunze and Dwight D. Brautigam, eds., *Court, Country and Culture: Essays on Early Modern British History in Honor of Perez Zagorin* (Rochester, N.Y., 1992), 177–197.

49. See Jane Kamensky, *Governing the Tongue: The Politics of Speech in Early New England* (New York, 1997).

50. Diary of Deborah Morris, 1772, in Philadelphia Yearly Meeting Manuscripts, FHL.

51. *Memoirs of the Life of Catherine Phillips* (London, 1797), 135. On Sarah Morris, see Crane, *Diary of Elizabeth Drinker*, 2188–2189; Joyce Benezet to Sarah Morris, Philadelphia, October 16, 1772, American Friends Letters and Portraits Collection, QC.

52. Diary of Deborah Morris.

In a number of important ways, Quaker culture fostered an appreciation of women's life outside of the household and outside of the traditional roles of wife and mother. From Fox and Fell's model marriage of spiritual and secular partners to the theological implications of radical Quakerism identified and promoted by Susanna Wright and the example of women's ministry, Quaker women in the Delaware Valley could find ample articulation of the significance of unmarried women and of an alternative interpretation of the role of marriage in a woman's life.

MARRIAGE, RELIGION, AND FEMALE INDIVIDUALISM

Ideas expressed by Quaker women challenged connections between secular practices and Christian teachings about the body and sexuality. The deeply gendered ways in which early modern societies understood the significance of women's bodies and the spiritual and secular uses to which female bodies could appropriately be put framed women's understanding and experience of marriage. The common investment of Protestant sects as otherwise dissimilar as Puritans and Quakers in particular orders of marriage and household also help explain why women often found their spiritual calling in conflict with wifely obligations and yet consonant with an emerging notion of bodily possession. Women argued that they could "own" their bodies, and commit them to God, in ways at sharp variance with the ways that their contemporaries were merging religious and social practices of gender, marriage, and family.

To understand fully the cultural chasms that eighteenth-century women had to leap in order to gain access to the increasingly individualistic ethos of their era, we must explore not only the gendered character of individualism, but also its connection to ideas about women, heterosexuality, religion, and marriage. The tight connections within Protestantism between theology and women's social roles made the explication of women's independent spirituality highly problematic. Women, and the men around them, struggled to reconcile their religious obligation to a heterosexual life that elevated their families' needs with the promise of a more individualistic Protestant spirituality.

In a variety of contexts, Christians demanded adherence to specific kinds of marriage ritual and relationship as the only way of confining and directing human sexuality to its Godly purpose, procreation. Protestantism in the early modern period was especially reliant on ideas about gender and sexuality to express fundamental aspects of theology as well as to delineate its difference from Catholicism. Protestants denounced celibacy and instead focused on harnessing sexuality to the formation of what Lyndal Roper has described as the "Holy Household."[53] In this model, female sexuality was accorded special prominence, and its regulation required special attention. Codifying and regulating the confinement of female sexuality to a household order characterized by masculine dominance became a priority for Protestants ranging from sixteenth-century Lutherans in Germany to Puritans in seventeenth-century New England. The dangers of female sexuality expressed outside the bounds of the marriage and the marriage household were such that New England Puritans, for example, expressly forbid unmarried adults from living alone. Unmarried women challenged the Puritan notion of female sexuality by *not* committing their bodies to marriage. As Sally Kitch has argued, "Even in the earliest centuries of Christianity, female celibacy challenged the premises of male dominance by eroding the sexual and reproductive bases of gender difference."[54]

Other traditions, such as Catholicism, had a long history of women's claims to religious authority based on female celibacy or alternative female sexuality. The contest between a purely domestic female socio-religious role and celibate authority was intense, particularly because secular culture was so closely aligned with, and invested in, heterosexual marriage. Thus, when some Protestant groups advanced either celibacy or independent female religious authority, the two often became conflated. Puritans, for example, attacked the Quakers' advocacy of gender equality as dangerous to both social and religious order. The establishment of sex-segregated celibate communities was opposed for similar reasons. Once female sexuality was removed from the obligation of household duty and female spirituality released from the gender hierarchy that governed households and polities, the very foundations of the early modern world seemed shaken.

By the eighteenth century the emergence of enlightened ideas gave new impetus to female religious individualism and tempered the stigma of celibacy. The dyadic intellectual forces at work in Early America were Protestantism and the Enlightenment; they can no more neatly be separated one from the other than Siamese twins can be. Just as magic continued to inform and compete with organized religion in the early modern world, so too did religion inform and compete with enlightened, rational ideas. The tensions between individual and community, between the obli-

53. Lyndal Roper, *The Holy Household: Women and Morals in Reformation Augsburg* (New York, 1989).

54. Sally Kitch, *Chaste Liberation: Celibacy and Female Cultural Status* (Urbana, Ill., 1989), 7. Caroline Walker Bynum also discusses how medieval women used a spiritual commitment to celibacy (as well as ritual fasting) as a way of controlling their marital relations. Bynum, *Holy Feast and Holy Fast: The Religious Significance of Food to Medieval Women* (Berkeley, Calif., 1987), 219–221.

gations to self and to family and society, were often worked out in terms that were at once theologically and rationally informed. The interplay between these two intellectual imperatives bore gendered characteristics.

While most historians have charted the transition from a premodern to a democratic and capitalistic society in the West largely as the rise of individualism, historians of women and gender have been more critical of this lineage, and have worked to understand and expose the gendered nature of these broad changes.[55] Individualism's historical emergence is a profoundly masculine phenomenon. The transition from a corporate, communal set of values and purposes to what Robert Calhoon has described as the "personal and civic celebration of the potentiality, creativity, and psychic wholeness of the autonomous self" was bound in part to the development of private property.[56] For Anglo-Americans, the possession of private property, and the legal rights and protections of that possession, were definitive structural antecedents to a full-blown culture of individualism.[57] In the eighteenth century the notion of individualism became attached to the idea of "independence," or self-possession. American notions of individualism in the nineteenth century increasingly referred to the notion of the "self-made man," a creature whose dependence on the material wealth and labor of many sacrificing women (and other family members) is ironic only in hindsight.[58] Women's notions of an individual self, particularly during the early modern period, developed out of a different tradition and had very different sources of authority than did men's. This difference was partly a result of the legal and cultural prescriptions that separated women from property and law, the principal agents of individualism; it was also due to the relational nature of cultural ideals of woman, which informed law and politics and which had a lingering tenacity even while individual, independent masculinity came to be celebrated as the highest achievement of the Enlightened man.

While men were regularly seen as independent, individual actors, or as acting on behalf of others in their households, early modern people

---

55. The long list of feminist scholars who have explored the gendered dimensions of the Enlightenment and the democratic movements of the eighteenth century includes Joan Landes, *Women and the Public Sphere in the Age of the French Revolution* (Ithaca, N.Y., 1988); Linda K. Kerber, "Can a Woman Be an Individual? The Discourse of Self Reliance," in Richard O. Curry and Lawrence B. Goodheart, eds., *American Chameleon: Individualism in Trans-National Context* (Kent, Ohio, 1991), 151–166.

56. Robert M. Calhoon, "Religion and Individualism in Early America," in Curry and Goodheart, eds., *American Chameleon*, 44.

57. On England and the concept of private property, see Alan Macfarlane, *The Origins of English Individualism: The Family, Property, and Social Transition* (New York, 1978).

58. Kerber, "Can a Woman Be an Individual?" 158–160.

regularly conceived of women only in relational terms. Women were understood primarily through their relationship to men and to children. Thus, to be "a man" had some cultural and linguistic resonance; "a woman" was a less potent category of identity. Women were characterized as wives and mothers; men were seldom characterized as husbands and fathers. Politicians and theologians alike used the model of the wife as the perfect example of the willing subordinate.[59] Women in marriage were the ultimate analogue of the submissive posture. Transformed by the nature of the institution, wives became permanently relational figures, rarely, if ever, independent.[60]

In a thoughtful consideration of the issue of women and individualism, Linda Kerber has laid out three possible routes by which women historically could have come to a sense of an individual self. Focusing on the early Republic, Kerber finds that although evangelical religion, mysticism, and republican motherhood could have served as a first step, women were almost entirely ineligible to participate in the highly materialistic, explicitly masculine notion of American individualism.[61] She does point to religion as a potential source of power and individualistic ethos for women in the colonial era. Although scholars too often look to women's extra-religious motives for seeking religious authority, rather than taking their spiritual needs and desires seriously, it is also true that women in the early modern period quite often counter-posed the demands of the spirit with those of the household. Many women found in religion not just a source of authority but a reason for authority; their theology demanded of them more than their society was willing to let them have. Many radical religions in particular asked women *as individuals* to undertake commitments and actions that would have been unthinkable in any other context. Indeed, to consider women's individual needs or desires in any other context was, literally, unimaginable. But once women's individualism was imagined, it could be sought.

The intensely independent, personal, and individual nature of women's spiritual commitment can be seen in the testimony of the Quaker minister Elizabeth Smith. During a severe illness in 1771, Smith narrated

59. On the use of bridal and marital imagery to explain men's willing submission to God, see Michael Winship, "Behold the Bridegroom Cometh! Marital Imagery in Massachusetts Preaching, 1630–1730," *Early American Literature* 27 (1992): 170–184.

60. Kerber, "Can a Woman Be an Individual?" 151–154. On the use of marriage as the model for benevolent or beneficial hierarchy in both polity and religion, see Mary Lyndon Shanley, "Marriage Contract and Social Contract in Seventeenth-Century English Political Thought," in Jean Bethke Elshtain, ed., *The Family in Political Thought* (Amherst, Mass., 1982), 80–95.

61. Kerber, "Can a Woman Be an Individual?"

an account of her awakening as a Christian and as a minister. Her narrative placed great emphasis on the significance of her bodily afflictions, the resignation of her body to God, and the personal, intimate relationship with God that she experienced. Smith described her relationship with God in terms of a traditionally scripted heterosexual courtship: he beckoning, she following, he offering commitment and new status for her, she adoring and accepting. When she was twenty-one years old, she became aware of her potential future as a minister. "I delighted much to wait often on the Lord," she wrote, "to feel his living presence near." She could "but admire and secretly adore that hand of Power, and canopy of Heavenly Regard that covered my spirit by Day, and by night." Finally, God revealed to her, through "a Sight and Sense, that he would commit a gift of the Ministry to my Trust, in which if I was faithful untill Death, he would give me a Crown of Life." She recounted how "I enter'd into solemn covenant," similar to marriage: if he would agree to "indeed be my God," then "I would obey." Once she accepted this offer, she found her "mouth was open'd" to tell others of her experience and to invite them, too, to "come, taste, & see for themselves how go[o]d the Lord is."[62]

Smith's relationship with God and her Quaker ministry precluded marriage. "By the secret and yet Powerful Draughts of renewed love extended to my soul," God had "let me see it was his pleasure to wean me from the Inordinate love of all fading and transitory things, and to make me a Chosen vessel for his use." Sacrificing earthly goods and relations, she had to "give up all to his requirings." She would be free to become "just what he would have me to be if he would but be with me all my life long."[63] For Elizabeth Smith, as for other Quaker women, religion promised personal salvation that was a uniquely individual, independent experience. Smith's relationship with God was the principal relationship of her life; it shaped her daily existence as well as her life-long goals, and it determined her marital status.

Quakerism emphasized women's individual experience of the spirit and salvation and, unique among Protestantisms, matched that with an equalitarian social order. While in many early modern Protestant communities, women's obligations to religion were matched with a social role that was purely relational, as wife or mother, and often embedded in a social hierarchy that subordinated women, in Quakerism women's social and religious roles were more analogous. When they found that Quaker marriages did not meet this ideal, Elizabeth Norris and women like her

62. "The Under writing I took down from my Cousin Eliza: Smiths mouth at her Request this 24th of ye 9 mo 1771 E Barker," Smith manuscripts, F101, LCP.
63. Ibid.

drew on a long tradition of connecting female sexuality with household obligation, and the rejection of marriage—at least in theory a rejection of heterosexuality and an embrace of celibacy—with a clearer commitment to God and to their own individual spiritual path.

SINGLENESS AND RADICAL RELIGIOUS COMMUNITY IN PENNSYLVANIA

Philadelphia women could look to other models of female religious individualism. Sectarians in Pennsylvania, such as the Moravians and the Ephratans, attempted to make women's secular status conform to their spiritual status, rather than the other way around. Both groups celebrated female celibacy and established separate living quarters for the large numbers of single women in their midst. The significance of radical Pietist women's marital status and communal living was profound in a region where most Protestants, even Quakers, hewed to a more conventional social and sexual organization. Women who either visited or read about the Moravian Single Sisters or the Ephrata collective discovered a model of female piety that explicitly disavowed marriage.

Philadelphia's religious culture was a polyglot of Protestantisms, and most Protestant groups had a quite conventional approach to gender and marriage. Although there were several hundred Catholics who might have offered a celibate model to counter the Protestant emphasis on marriage, and a handful of Jews living in and around Philadelphia by mid-century, Protestants, primarily of English origin, dominated the city.[64] Quakers, Anglicans, Presbyterians, and Baptists mingled with Swedish and German Lutherans in the city; various other German denominations and sects, including the Dunkers and Mennonites, had congregations in the outlying townships, most prominently Germantown. All of these religious groups espoused a theology of the equality of souls, yet few translated that spiritual equality into either a position for women in church governance or a change in women's traditionally subordinate secular role.[65]

64. The best study of Delaware Valley Protestantism remains Jon Butler, "Power, Authority, and the Origins of American Denominational Order: The English Churches in the Delaware Valley, 1680–1730," *Transactions of the American Philosophical Society* 68, 2 (1978): 5–81.

65. As Janet Lindman has argued, "Whatever the specific task, congregations carefully distinguished between episodic exercises of power by women, such as the selection of a new minister, and the ongoing, structured authority that came with office holding and participation in church policy formation." Lindman, "Wise Virgins and Pious Mothers: Spiritual Community Among Baptist Women of the Delaware Valley," in Eldridge, ed., *Women and Freedom in Colonial America*, 130.

For Philadelphians, the most important examples of unmarried women's spiritual communities were the Moravians at Bethlehem and in other settlements around the province, and the Ephrata collective. Founded in 1744, the Moravian settlement at Bethlehem (and smaller settlements, such as Lititz) was an attraction for travelling Philadelphians. The communal style of life, the unfamiliar forms of sex segregation, and the beauty of Moravian artistry in such products as needlework and music all drew Philadelphians to visit.[66] The architecture of Moravian communal life reflected a powerful commitment to individual spiritual growth. Believing that individuals drew strength and inspiration from others of their same sex and status, the Moravians carefully segregated men from women and married from unmarried persons. These groups were known as "choirs," and the members of each choir ate, slept, worked, and worshipped together. Segregation fostered an unimpeded commitment to religion, which was regarded as especially important for women. Moravians believed that individual familial relationships required so much time and attention that they detracted from one's spiritual needs.[67]

Beverly Smaby's carefully constructed profile of Bethlehem, Pennsylvania, in its first forty years demonstrates the importance of single women to the community and the attraction of singleness for Moravian women. The number of women—of a variety of European, Native American, and African backgrounds—who chose to join the church in America was astonishing to the founders. And once they joined as Single Sisters, many were reluctant to leave the choir to marry. Unmarried women usually comprised a significant majority of Bethlehem's sizeable female population. Between 1764 and 1773, for example, when many Philadelphians were visiting, 62 percent of the town's residents were female. And the majority of Bethlehem's population was single: 57 percent of women and 51 percent of men had not married. Including widows and widowers, 67 percent of Moravian women were unmarried, and 57 percent of men were unmarried.[68]

For Moravian women, the process of selecting and approving a mar-

66. Beverly Smaby, *The Transformation of Moravian Bethlehem: From Communal Mission to Family Economy* (Philadelphia, 1988), 3–9, 45; Sharf and Westcott, *History of Philadelphia*, 2: 1320–1331.

67. Smaby, *Transformation of Moravian Bethlehem*, 10.

68. This paragraph is drawn from ibid., 54–56, 60–61; and Smaby, "Transplanting the Communal Life: Establishing the Single Sisters Choir in Bethlehem," unpublished paper, courtesy of the author. Smaby notes that, over time, singleness became more attractive for women. In the first decade of settlement, 38 percent of the women were single (not counting widows and widowers). By the third decade, 57 percent of women were single. This trend continued until the turn of the nineteenth century, when marriage became more preferable for both men and women, although twice as many women as men remained single.

riage partner was quite complex.[69] Once chosen or matched to one another, a married couple had a difficult spiritual row to hoe. The challenge of keeping her relationship with God stable was difficult enough for a single woman. Now she had to learn to make that relationship primary even after she was married. Married persons carried greater practical as well as spiritual burdens. Only married men could be ministers (which may explain men's increasing and disproportionate interest in marrying), and only married persons could hold certain church and community offices. While unmarried women derived their status and positions within their choirs from their own spiritual achievements, married women derived their status from their husbands. When a woman was widowed, she had to retire from the offices she had held as a married person. Furthermore, Moravians treated single sisters as less likely to fall by the spiritual wayside; men were seen as prone to depravity of the body and senses, while women were seen as likely to be influenced by others. In sum, the status of a single sister was more stable, predictable, and dependent on herself, than that of a married woman. For one German Moravian woman, who eventually married, "I was happy to go to America, but to enter into marriage! That cost me dear."[70]

The unique features of Moravian life made Bethlehem a favorite spot for tourists from Philadelphia, who found the two-day trip very appealing. For Hannah Callender, Elizabeth Drinker, and Hannah Smith, who visited Bethlehem in the 1760s and 1770s, the Single Sisters' house and the sisters themselves were a particular attraction of the community. These visitors commented on the artistry of the Moravian women, the paintings of Moravians by John Valentine Haidt, and the arrangement of the community's settlement. The commonalities in their accounts suggest that women were especially intrigued by the lives of Moravian women.

The extensive connections that individual Philadelphia Quakers had to the Moravian community probably whetted their appetite for such tours. The family experience of Anthony Benezet, a famous Quaker abolitionist, reformer, and teacher, suggests the close theological connections some people found between the two religions. Benezet's French Huguenot parents migrated to Philadelphia in 1731. Although Anthony Benezet became a Quaker, a significant portion of his family, including his father, a brother, and three sisters, had converted to Moravianism by the mid-1740s.[71] In fact, the three Benezet daughters were among

69. Smaby, *The Transformation of Moravian Bethlehem*, 160–161.

70. Anna Seidel, quoted in Katherine M. Faull, ed., *Moravian Women's Memoirs: Their Related Lives, 1750–1820* (Syracuse, N.Y., 1997), 126.

71. George S. Brooks, *Friend Anthony Benezet* (Philadelphia, 1937), 13–21; *Abstract of the Philadelphia Monthly Meeting Records (1730–1785)*, vol. 33, p. 115, GSP.

the first members of the Single Sisters' choir, formed in the summer of 1742.[72] While Anthony Benezet was acclaimed in his own time as a Quaker teacher and leading reformer, his family continued to be largely Moravian, and thus he maintained close connections with the community at Bethlehem.[73] Other Philadelphians had friends who decamped for the Moravian communal life. Diarists Hannah Callender and Elizabeth Drinker had both been school fellows of Mary (Polly) Penry, a Welsh immigrant who was converted to the Moravian faith in the 1750s.[74] Drinker and Penry visited and corresponded very regularly over the next five decades.[75] The ongoing intimacy between this elite Quaker matron and a committed member of the Moravians' Single Sisters collective suggests that these two faiths—and perhaps these two conceptions of women's life course—were not so very far apart after all.

Hannah Callender, Mary Penry's other school chum, actually met with Penry at Bethlehem. As Callender reported, she knew the history of [Penry's] unfortunate life" (Penry's family had immigrated to Philadelphia amid difficult circumstances) and the two old friends were "greatly affected at seeing each other." In addition to Penry, Callender had known another of the Moravian sisters at school, and she spent time getting to know a third woman, Sister Becky Langley, with whom "Polly" Penry "enjoy[ed] a strict friendship." These three women gave Callender a unique, intensely personal account of their lives, and a valuable perspective on the appeal of Moravianism's emphasis on the communal life of single women. Callender, Langley, and Penry walked together along a stream, and at one point Callender pulled out a cup she had in her pocket

72. On the Benezet daughters as original members of the Single Sisters choir, see Faull, ed., *Moravian Women's Memoirs*, 3. On their marriages, all in late 1742, see Clarence E. Beckel, ed., "Marriage Records of the Bethlehem Moravian Congregation," vol. 1, registers 1–4 (1742–1854), GSP.
73. See, for example, the will of Judith Benezet, in which Anthony Benezet was named one of his mother's executors and a trustee for his three sisters' share of her estate. Will of Judith Benezet, W217, 1765 (microfilm, HSP). See also the discussion in Faull, ed., *Moravian Women's Memoirs*, 77, of Benezet's connection to Philadelphia Recorder of Deeds Charles Brockden, who manumitted an enslaved woman, Magdalene Beulah Brockden, and commended her to the community at Bethlehem.
74. A letter from John Jordan of the HSP to George Vaux, dated September 1, 1888, and laid in the Hannah Callender diary, suggests that a letter, possibly no longer extant, written by Mary Penry states that her family immigrated to Pennsylvania in 1744. Other biographical data on Penry comes from page 16 of the "Bethlehem Catalogue of Single Sisters & Older Girls" c. 1744–1835, very generously provided to me (along with a translation from the German) by Beverly Smaby.
75. When Penry died in 1804, Drinker expressed shock. Crane, *Diary of Elizabeth Drinker*, 1745. Penry is listed in the index to the Drinker diary eighty-six times. For examples of the regularity of the Drinker-Penry correspondence between 1790 and 1795, see pp. 161–161, 452, 455, 483, 550, 628, 648, 681.

(probably a wise accessory for an eighteenth-century traveler) and the three "drank peace & tranquility to each other." Penry then "named it Leanders Stream, in rememberance of those white moments." After dinner Callender joined her new intimates in the traditional Moravian "love feast," a sex-segregated ritual of sharing bread and coffee or chocolate and exchanging the kiss of peace.[76]

Both male and female visitors were intrigued by the facets of Moravian life that altered traditional relationships between the sexes. Some found these features appealing to themselves and to their Moravian hosts. While Hannah Callender's visit to the single sisters was marked by the personal connections she made and already had among the choir, Hannah Smith was struck by the order that communal life among the single sisters provided. She noted when visiting their house in 1773 that "these Innocent Communicants seem to be an Industrious Tribe." At the evening worship service, the sisters entered with "a striking order and regularity." "So many neat Headdresses together look very pretty."[77] The attractions of the Moravian life were known to contemporaries and even served as a source of teasing amusement. Before Smith's preparations for the trip to Bethlehem, a cousin teased that she hoped Smith would not "deprive the world of so good an Ornament as to take up thy residence with the Single Sisters."[78]

Other visitors examining the Single Sisters' lives were convinced that the Moravians must surely suffer from such unnatural arrangements. In the early 1790s one visitor wondered why women would choose to live in such a "confind situation." The women exhibited a "pensive melancholy upon most of their Countenances & a complection that indicates declining Health." And yet the sisters seemed content: "They appear'd pleas'd to see us and answer'd many questions, indeed their Sentiments were more liberal than what I had an idea of." This was so surprising, in fact, that:

> I should have had no objection to hearing some of their reasons for such a seclusion from the World for if any judgment could be form'd from the external appearance of several of them, I should suppose they possess'd

76. All quotations are from the diary of Hannah Callender, August 30, 1761, APS. The Love feast is described in Smaby, *The Transformation of Moravian Bethlehem*, 17. Twelve years after Hannah Callender's visit to Bethlehem, Hannah Smith described Becky Langley as "one of the Chief Sisters." Hannah Smith to Rachel Pemberton, nd [1773], Pemberton Papers, vol. 25, pp. 100b–101b, HSP.

77. Hannah Smith to Rachel Pemberton, Bethlehem, n.d. [1773], Pemberton Papers, vol. 25, pp. 100b–101b, HSP.

78. Rachel Pemberton to Hannah Smith, n.d. [1773], Pemberton Papers, vol. 25, p. 165a, HSP.

endowments requisite for social society—but that was a freedom I did not take and consequently my Curiosity remain'd unsatisfied.[79]

In other words, nothing other than the style of life itself, so at odds with mainstream culture, could have convinced these women to remain among the single sisters. That fact alone seemed disturbing.

For Alexander Mackraby, visiting Bethlehem in 1768, it was not only disconcerting that women lived with other single women rather than in marital households, and thus displayed none of the attributes associated with traditional female roles, but it was peculiar that men were prevented from exercising the privileges and requirements of masculinity as he understood them. In a letter to his brother in England, Mackraby reported that the Moravians' schools, language, religion, and music were all evidence that "so far, [the] state is a natural one." "But," he continued, "the poor devils have no [private] property." The communal economy meant that the "labors of each individual [were] being dedicated to the general advantages of the community," and that "each had his portion of necessary comforts (not excepting their wives) allotted according to the pleasure of the directing fathers."[80] A man's inability to work for his own individual benefits, and thus to provide for his own family, made him a "poor devil"; the lack of private property and the undermining of traditional household arrangements so distorted Anglo-American notions of gender that men were emasculated.

Explaining the peculiarity of Moravian sex segregation, then, was essential for tourists; in particular, casting the Moravian single state as unnatural or unreasonable was an important way of asserting the normative, central, universal quality of Anglo-American heterosexuality. Another male visitor commented in 1773 that he could not understand the unnatural separation of men and women among the Moravians. This state was especially odd for young women, for "sure it never was the design of the Wise disposer of all things, that the Loveliest part of the Creation should thus be Cloistered up, as they were no doubt given to smooth the rugged path of Life, and to soften the turbulent temper of the other Sex: to be without their agreeable company is not to live!"[81]

To the contrary, Moravian theology held that women could do some of their most important spiritual work only while they were single and thus undistracted by the consummate, ordained heterosexual union: marriage. Surely men could not live without women, the writer averred;

79. "Journal of a Tour from Philadelphia to Bethlehem, 1791," AM 202, 1773, HSP.
80. Alexander Mackraby to [brother], Philadelphia, August 17, 1768, reprinted in *PMHB* 11 (1887): 285.
81. "A Summer Jaunt in 1773," reprinted in the *PMHB* 10 (1886): 209.

surely it was *more* difficult for men and women to live together, Moravian practice asserted. Thus Bethlehem, and particularly the Single Sisters Choir, served as a kind of proving ground for heterosexuality and Anglo-American gender norms.

The Ephrata Cloister, located about ten miles northeast of Lancaster and sixty miles northwest of Philadelphia, shared some features with the Moravian town of Bethlehem. Both groups drew upon a Pietist theological tradition, both communities strictly observed sex segregation and a communal lifestyle, and both settlements were closed to outsider residence but open to outside visitors. Perhaps most significantly, both places attracted visitors who used the community to evaluate the norms of their own communities. In "Saron," the house remodelled to accommodate the single sisters, Ann Kirschner has demonstrated the significance of architectural features that reflected the sisters' isolation and commitment to what they called their "virginal discipline."[82] There visitors found the sisters at work, "engaged in spinning, sewing, writing, drawing, singing and other things." Just seven of the most spiritually advanced of their company were permitted to deal with outsiders; the others, it was felt, were still too spiritually fragile and could be tempted by worldliness, including relationships with men. The only door of Saron through which the sisters regularly passed led into the worship hall. In Ephrata, as in Bethlehem, the sisters had to overcome the willfulness of the worldly "self" in order to embrace the spiritual self fully and commit to God.

This notion of the female self as something to be acquired by women alone, as something to be strived for in order only to relinquish it to God, was profoundly at variance with masculine notions of individualism and with many Protestant notions of women's principal roles as relational subjects, as wives and mothers but not as individuals. The theology of radical Pietist groups, like that of Quakerism, allowed women and men to envision an alternative model of individualism. Imagined as a corporeal entity contrasted with the female body consecrated to marriage and childbirth, this individual would live not with men but with other women, and not for men but for herself and God.

CONCLUSION

In the theologies of Quakerism and of German Pietism as expressed in Bethlehem and Ephrata, women could define and celebrate a paradoxical

82. Ann Kirschner, "From Hebron to Saron: The Religious Transformation of an Ephrata Convent," *Winterthur Portfolio* 32 (Spring 1997): 60, and passim.

kind of selfless self. The significance of negating the self for all of these groups lay in the attainment of a spiritual closeness to God. By negating the material or the worldly self, one could achieve a more intense, authentic, and desirable spirituality.[83] But the self that was being denied was very often defined in explicitly masculine terms.[84] The reverencing of material goods was a decidedly masculine vice. Women were often disciplined for their attachment to material frippery, such as fashion, but it was men who were encouraged by secular culture to hanker after the substantial things of the world: wealth and power. Both kinds of attachments evidenced pride and self-absorption, and were not conducive to the kind of submission and self-abnegation that a proper relationship to God required.

The female self that women found in their theologies was not this kind of materially motivated self. It was, instead, a self detached from the demands of the world. For women, the obligations that could distract from God's worship were those of marriage, especially a dominant husband and dependent children. Husbands could interfere with women's spiritual lives in manifold ways. They could make unreasonable demands about which religion to follow. They could simply require attention, to themselves or their households, that might otherwise be appropriated to God's work. The care of children, who inevitably followed marriage, was regarded as particularly burdensome for women.

This reading of the connections among gender, religion, and a feminine self suggests that eighteenth-century Quakerism owed just as much to its origins in a radical vision of gender as did its seventeenth-century counterpart. While aspects of the Quaker experience show that Quakers' ideas about gender were becoming assimilated to the Anglo-American norm, others remind us that women still had access to the very radical formulations of Fox and Fell. Phyllis Mack has described seventeenth-century Quaker women's spirituality as self-abnegation or alienation. As Quakerism passed through the initial emphasis on intense bodily experience and moved toward a more organized, disciplined expression of

83. In an important essay considering the relationship of individualism to culture, family, and gender, Natalie Davis wrote that women in sixteenth-century France located a kind of "self" in the act of "giving themselves away." While women were often "given"— in marriage, for example—they could employ strategies of gift giving, estate disposal, and even marriage brokering in which they took charge of distributing their own "selves." Davis, "Boundaries and the Sense of Self in Sixteenth-Century France," in Thomas C. Heller, Morton Sosna, and David Wellerby et al., eds., *Reconstructing Individualism: Autonomy, Individuality, and the Self in Western Thought* (Stanford, Calif., 1986), 53–63.

84. On the masculine denied and the feminine embraced, see Kirschner's study of the transformation of the single men's building, Hebron, into Saron, and the values explicitly reverenced and celebrated. Kirschner, "From Hebron to Saron," esp. 61.

spirituality and collective worship, women's self-expression was limited by traditional conventions of gender. Thus a woman's ministerial calling was not an assertive, self-confident feminist achievement. Rather, Quaker women found the challenge to follow their religious calling intensely lonely, even crippling.[85] Into the eighteenth century, however, Quakerism had undergone a variety of changes. Some led to conservatism and social conformity, but others supported the radical, equalitarian tenets of the faith. The intensity of the Women's Meetings networks, and their exchange of epistles, created a transatlantic community.[86] Local communities in places like Philadelphia fostered cells of female spirituality modelled on the radical Quaker past.

The developmental trajectory of the female self did not result in a feminine self-actualizing individual in the masculine, materialist model. The self that eighteenth-century women expressed was not analogous to later notions of individual autonomy. Twentieth-century feminists are often caught between arguing for women's expanded rights and status based on an essential common humanity—man and women are fundamentally the same, thus equal—and basing their claims on qualities unique to women—men and women are different, but still equal. These often contradictory arguments would find little common ground with the ideas expressed by eighteenth-century women, who were concerned with perfecting their relationships with God rather than with men. The search by many women for spiritual identity led them to re-examine the fundamental precepts of the early modern system of gender, in particular the notion that women were largely relational creatures. These women asserted, not their civil rights, but their spiritual need for individual identity. Only in and through themselves, not through their service to husbands or children, could they find a satisfactory religious experience.

The female individual exemplified by radical religious groups and by women within the Pennsylvania mainstream of Quakerism could be translated into alternative household structures. As we will see in the next chapter, unmarried women fitted into and created a number of household forms, some of which were exclusively female communities.

85. Mack, *Visionary Women*, 381.
86. Kunze, "vessells fitt for the masters us[e].

[3]

Mary Sandwith's Spouse:
Family and Household

In the hot summer months of 1771, Elizabeth Drinker and various members of her family made their annual pilgrimage away from the city to the cooler climate of the countryside. From their summer home in Frankford or from the baths at Bristol, the Drinkers still visited with friends in Philadelphia and Burlington, or welcomed visitors from farther away.[1] Often while Elizabeth spent the entire summer in the country, her husband, Henry, spent a good deal of time attending to business in the city. Some of their five children also moved back and forth between the two residences. Henry and the Drinker children moved between two women as well. While Elizabeth stayed in the country, her spinster sister, Mary Sandwith, managed the household in Philadelphia, providing comfort and assistance to Henry and affection and attention to the children. By all accounts, the children were devoted to their aunt. In that summer of 1771 young Billy Drinker insisted that his aunt stay with him in the city, threatening, as she reported to Elizabeth Drinker, to "nail my frock" if she tried to leave.[2] Henry was similarly pleased with the arrangement. While spending weeks at a time away from his lawful wife, Elizabeth, he appreciated the domestic comforts and services that his sister-in-law provided. He was so content, he confided to Elizabeth, that he felt especially "clever . . . to have two wives."[3]

Mary Sandwith lived with Henry Drinker throughout the fifty years of her sister's marriage.[4] She never married herself, but instead became an

1. For the Drinkers in Bristol, see Elaine Crane, ed., *The Diary of Elizabeth Drinker* (Boston, 1991), vol. 1, 159–66.
2. Mary Sandwith to Elizabeth Drinker, Philadelphia, July 19, 1771, Drinker-Sandwith papers, vol. 2, p. 80, HSP. See also Crane, ed., *The Diary of Elizabeth Drinker*, xxiv.
3. Elizabeth Drinker to Mary Sandwith, Bristol, July 13, 1771. Drinker-Sandwith papers, vol. 2, p. 80, HSP.
4. Perhaps longer; Henry Drinker died in 1809, Elizabeth Drinker in 1807. Mary Sandwith lived until 1815.

essential part of her sister and brother-in-law's household. She shouldered much of the burden of domestic management that would otherwise have fallen to Elizabeth as the mistress of the family. This dynamic
was initiated almost from the start of the Drinkers' married life, when
Mary helped supervise their collective move to a house on Water Street
immediately following the 1761 wedding. She performed the same service
when the family moved again in 1771, this time to a fashionable home on
the corner of Front Street and Drinker's Alley. She oversaw many aspects
of household management, including the hiring and supervision of servants.[5] Even family friends recognized that Mary was the acknowledged
"housekeeper" of the Drinker home.[6] She also spent a lot of time caring
for her nieces and nephews. In the absence of one or both of their parents
and often even when both were at home, she fed, bathed, and dressed the
children. In 1776, while Henry and Elizabeth Drinker were attempting to
secure Henry's release from patriot captors, they encouraged their children to "look upon your Aunt . . . as one of your Earthly parents":

> . . . She has from your very Infancy upwards, both by Night and by Day,
> been as an Affectionate tender parent to you, studying & devising to serve
> & oblige you & to make things in this world easy, amusing & pleasant—
> and when you consider, as indeed you ought to a[ll] with grateful Hearts,
> that she is under no obligation to disregard her own ease, to give up her
> time & even to injure her Health for your sakes, how watchful should each
> of you be to make due returns for so much Love, tenderness & continued
> care & anxiety, in which she is continually exercised on your account.[7]

The responsibility Mary Sandwith bore for her sister's children was enhanced by Elizabeth's regular illnesses, but the affection she felt for them
was genuine and freely given. She joked with Elizabeth that it was
difficult to write frankly about the children's behavior with "Sally at my
arm, [']Aunty say I am good[']."[8]

Mary Sandwith's life and experiences raise a host of questions about
the composition of colonial urban households and about the dependence
or independence that single women sought and exercised. Although she
lived within a household headed by her brother-in-law, rather than her
own husband, Mary Sandwith in many ways was the woman of the

5. Elizabeth Drinker to Mary Sandwith, July 13, 1771, Drinker-Sandwith papers, vol. 2,
p. 80, HSP; Crane, ed., *Diary of Elizabeth Drinker*, 91.
6. Diary of Ann Warder, January 15, 1787, entry, AM 178, HSP.
7. Henry and Elizabeth Drinker to Mary Sandwith and Drinker children, Waterford,
November 24, 1776, Drinker-Sandwith papers, vol. 2, p. 96, HSP.
8. Mary Sandwith to Elizabeth Drinker, Philadelphia, August 2, 1770, Drinker-
Sandwith papers, vol. 2, p. 82, HSP.

house. She consequently was both confined and legitimated by her position as a household dependent. As the Drinker family's "housekeeper,"
she was not a domestic worker, in the way that the term might be applied
in later centuries, but a woman with authority to make household decisions. While attending to many of the duties of wife and mother, Mary
Sandwith also exercised the capacities and authority of a single woman.
She had independent means, including financial investments with Henry
Drinker and rental property of her own. She was no passive investor;
Mary Sandwith collected rent from her tenants in person.[9] She also traveled with Henry Drinker to inspect their joint investment in a New Jersey
copper mine.[10]

The household arrangement in which Mary Sandwith lived was a familiar one among her peers, for the city's economy and culture supported
a wide range of household forms. Although households centered around
a nuclear family were the most common, female-headed households
were a normal occurrence. Among this group, widows with children
predominated, but long-time widows with grown children also populated Philadelphia's neighborhoods. Many other household types were
found in the urban environment, including female-only households. In
these, women's partnerships with other women, often sisters but in some
cases friends, formed the basis of the household unit.

Unmarried women assumed a variety of positions in urban households. Incorporation into the household of another family was the most
common arrangement for single women. Women like Mary Sandwith
regularly joined the households of parents, siblings, or cousins, often
to fulfill domestic roles vacated by a wife's death. As servants and slaves,
unmarried women also played a vital role in the urban household. Domestic service was a key feature of many unmarried women's lives, particularly for younger women before they married but also for older
women who never married or who were widowed.

The Anglo-American cultural ideal of the household was organized
around hierarchical gender roles, but in Philadelphia, where such a wide
variety of household forms existed, it is clear that household roles were
more flexible. Particularly in households with children, kin, including
siblings, cousins, and aunts and uncles, as well as friends or neighbors,
substituted for mothers, fathers, wives, and husbands. Sometimes the
substitutes were identified with a particularly gendered position, as in
the case of Mary Sandwith, Henry Drinker's additional "wife." Other

9. Crane, ed., *Diary of Elizabeth Drinker,* 86. Examples of Sandwith's investments can be
found in the Drinker-Sandwith papers, vol. 1, pp. 28, 30, 33, and 36, HSP.
10. Drinker-Sandwith papers, vol. 1, p. 28, HSP.

times the household positions that unmarried women assumed were not so clearly aligned with traditional gender roles. The existence and experiences of the many women who lived within households, but not as wives of male household heads, point up the contrast between the cultural ideal of the gendered household and the reality of urban life. This chapter looks first at ideas about gender and the early modern household, and then at the differences between rural and urban households in southeastern Pennsylvania. Next, it examines the unmarried women who were a key feature of the urban household: widowed heads of household, servants and slaves, kin such as sisters, aunts, and cousins, and household partners.

GENDER AND HOUSEHOLD HIERARCHY

The household was the most important social unit in colonial America.[11] Derived from the English model of household organization and the relationship of household to government as well as the economic mode of household production, the household was a familial and affective unit, but also an economic and political entity. Significant social power and authority was conferred on the head of the household, and household dependents were expected to defer to him. Law and custom, as well as religious institutions, helped shore up the privileges and position of the patriarchal head of household by disciplining insubordinate dependents and sometimes even lax masters. That the public enforcement of domestic order might be viewed as an infringement on a man's right to run his household as he saw fit was of little consequence. The hierarchical system required that those with authority exercise it and those in a subordinate position accept it.[12]

11. Historians have long recognized the importance of the household in the political economy of early modern Europe, but have only recently begun to tackle the implications of this patriarchal form of social organization in colonial America. See especially Julie Hardwick, *The Practice of Patriarchy: Gender and the Politics of Household Autonomy in Early Modern France* (University Park, Pa., 1998); and Lyndal Roper, *The Holy Household: Women and Morals in Reformation Augsburg* (New York, 1989). Historians of early America addressing this issue include Mary Beth Norton, *Founding Mothers and Fathers: Gendered Power and the Forming of American Society* (New York, 1996), and Carole Shammas, "Anglo-American Household Government in Comparative Perspective," *WMQ* 52 (January 1995): 104–144.

12. This paragraph owes much to Shammas, "Anglo-American Household Government in Comparative Perspective." My views differ significantly from those of Daniel Scott Smith, who argues that it was not the position of household head, but the dyadic relationships of husband-wife, parent-child, and master-servant that conveyed authority. Smith, "The Meanings of Family and Household: Change and Continuity in the Mirror of the American Census," *Population and Development Review* 18 (1992): 421–56.

Gender was the core of household hierarchy. Religious texts, most importantly the Bible, and the writings of theologians such as Martin Luther taught Anglo-Americans that a proper household was governed by a patriarch and inhabited by deferential dependents. The most important subordinate was the wife. A wife demonstrated appropriate support for her husband by her deference to his authority and set the tone for the entire household. This aspect of domestic relations was neatly captured in an "Epitaph on a Man & his Wife," copied into a notebook by the Quaker minister Rebecca Jones:.

> They were so one, that nobody could say
> The which did Rule, or whither did Obey—
> *He rul'd*, because *she wou'd Obey*, and *She*
> In so *obeying, Rul'd* as much as *he*.[13]

Although Jones was a spinster whose own household looked very different from the one this passage depicts, she understood perfectly the dynamic of dependence within a marital household. Men's authority was utterly—and awkwardly—dependent on their wives' recognition of it.

The traditional assumption that women occupied a subordinate place in society and within the household was based in part on the legal and customary equation of women with wives. Marriage signified a specific, dependent legal status for women and implied a relationship to husbands and households that was equally subsuming. The common law of coverture required that wives subordinate their separate interests to their husbands' ownership or, in a few cases, management of their property. Coverture, William Blackstone noted, articulated the principle of "legal unity": the notion that men's and women's legal and economic interests were combined as one upon marriage. Thus the interests of their household were singular, and, in the same way, a woman's interests and life became equated with those of her household. On the occasion of her marriage, a rejected suitor declared to Clementina Cruikshank that "Small is the Province of a Wife, And narrow is her Sphere of Life." She should, he proposed, "guide her House with prudent care" and with such skill that her husband would "Bless the day, he gave his Liberty away."[14] This vision of a wife's duties as entirely domestic was not applicable to the large number of Philadelphia wives who worked outside their homes for wages, but the assumption that women became house-

---

13. Rebecca Jones' commonplace book, Box 12, Allinson Collection, QC.
14. Verses addressed to Clementina Cruikshank, December 8, 1768, Plumstead Papers, HSP.

hold dependents upon marriage resonated across a broad spectrum of economic and social groups.

Separate but mutually reinforcing forms of subordination to spouse and to household were challenged by the frequency with which women in urban settings slipped the bonds of both. In eighteenth-century Philadelphia the gender of households was based on Anglo-American religious and civil assumptions, but these ideas were adapted to an urban, Quaker-dominated culture. Most women lived within households headed by men at some point in their lives, mostly because marriage was the norm, but pockets of singleness existed, especially within the Quaker community, and the mortality rate ensured that many women spent significant portions of their lives as widows.[15] Women moved in and out of both the legal confines of coverture and the position of household dependents.

Eighteenth-century Philadelphia displayed many of the patriarchal features of early modern European society, but it also embraced some cultural values that made it look quite different. Like the rest of the Anglo-American world, colonial Pennsylvania regulated female sexuality through laws against fornication and bastardy; women were more likely to be tried for fornication than were men, and extracting support for a bastard child from his or her putative father was difficult work.[16] Aspects of Philadelphia's urban and Quaker cultures, however, mitigated some harsher aspects of patriarchy. Patriarchal household authority among Quakers was held in check by the regular investigations of the Quaker meeting, which worked through a committee system to ensure that Quakers practiced the kind of egalitarian domestic partnerships first encouraged by Margaret Fell and George Fox. And the urban setting itself fostered a variety of household forms.

Unmarried Women in Rural and Urban Households

The urban household was not simply a family residence during the early modern period. It was often a place of production, and its compo-

15. Alexander Keyssar, "Widowhood in Eighteenth Century Massachusetts: A Problem in the History of the Family," *Perspectives in American History* 8 (1974): 83–119; Robert V. Wells, "Quaker Marriage Patterns in a Colonial Perspective," *WMQ* 29 (July 1972): 415–442.
16. Philadelphia's extant court records are fragmentary, but for an example, see the records of the Mayor's Court for 1767–1771, HSP. On New England bastardy cases, see Cornelia H. Dayton, *Women Before the Bar: Gender, Law and Society in Connecticut, 1639–1789* (Chapel Hill, 1995), 157–230.

sition was more varied than we might imagine. Unpaid but economically essential domestic work, such as child care, food preparation, and sewing, took place primarily within the home.[17] Artisanal and retail work sites as well as merchants' offices and small taverns, or dram shops, were located within homes, often on the first floor of a multistory dwelling. This mixing of residential and commercial space was a natural outcome of the economic and affective functions of the household. Households regularly included other kin as well as apprentices, servants, and slaves. Urban households were headed by women as well as men, and could be composed of men, women, or a combination of the two without a married couple at the helm. Sometimes a fortuitous coming together of the economically needy, sometimes the product of kinship obligations, and sometimes the result of intense emotional bonds, the formation of urban households combined both economic and affective needs.[18]

By the mid-eighteenth century the city's households presented a striking contrast to households in the rural townships of Philadelphia County.[19] Only a very few women headed rural households, and even then they did so for only short periods. A 1756 census for Perkiomen Township, including the village of Skippack, shows the typical rural pattern of male-headed households. In this community, where over half the householders identified themselves as farmers, only three of the eighty-five households were headed by women.[20] This pattern was not unusual. In rural Philadelphia County townships, women comprised only 2.0 to 2.3 percent of the taxable population (those most likely to head households) during the late colonial period. By contrast, women made up between 4.5 and 5.7 percent of the taxable population in the city during those same years.[21]

17. Sharon Salinger, "Spaces, Inside and Outside, in Eighteenth-Century Philadelphia," *Journal of Interdisciplinary History* 26 (Summer 1995): 29–30. On the economic necessity and value of domestic labor, see Jeanne Boydston, *Home and Work: Housework, Wages, and the Ideology of Labor in the Early Republic* (New York, 1990).

18. For an analysis of the indivisibility of the two, see Hans Medick and David Sabean, *Interest and Emotion: Essays on the Study of Family and Kinship* (New York, 1984).

19. In a broader regional comparison of female householding based primarily on the 1790 U.S. census, Daniel Scott Smith found that urban white women were twice as likely to head their own household as rural white women. Smith, "Female Householding in Late Eighteenth-Century America and the Problem of Poverty," *Journal of Social History* 27 (Fall 1994): 93.

20. 1756 census of Perkiomen and Skippack, Pennsylvania Counties Collection, HSP. Totals for these areas, as well as a discussion of women in other parts of Philadelphia County, can be found in Karin Wulf, "A Marginal Independence: Unmarried Women in Colonial Philadelphia," (Ph.D. diss., Johns Hopkins University, 1993), 108–146.

21. These data were compiled from the extant provincial tax lists for Philadelphia County for 1767, 1772, and 1774, found in the following locations. The 1767 assessment is

Tax records also indicate that unmarried women who either headed their own household or owned taxable property (primarily land, dwellings, or livestock) in the county tended to concentrate in areas closest to the city or at crossroads, where they might operate a small inn or shop.[22] For example, Rebecca McVaugh and Elizabeth West of Oxford Township, which lay directly north of the city beyond the Northern Liberties, operated taverns. Both women owned some real estate and livestock and operated their taverns for over fourteen years. A bit closer to the city, rental property was a more lucrative investment, as the experience of Tabitha Myers illustrates. Myers lived in Southwark, and was taxed every year from 1767 to 1774. She began keeping an inn and tavern in the late 1760s, and she secured rental income from several sources. By 1774 her sole taxable property was rental income, and her assessment had increased from £15 to £24. By that time she had finished with tavernkeeping.[23]

Just outside the city, virtually all women lived within male-headed households.[24] The rural pattern derived in part from the inheritance practices of rural men, which diverged from those of urban testators. Men in the rural county tended to leave their wives a portion of the house and "supplies" from the farm's produce. Often an inheriting child, or even a tenant, was designated by the will to make particular provisions for the

in Special Collections, Van Pelt Library, University of Pennsylvania, and the 1772 assessment is at the Historical Society of Pennsylvania. Duplicates of the 1769 and 1774 assessments are at the Philadelphia City Archives. A microfilm of those two volumes is at the HSP. In compiling data on the proportion of women among the taxable population, I never included estates. The difficulty of separating estates of the deceased from custodial estates was one issue. Also, I did not count women who were taxed for their deceased husband's or his "orphans'" estates. My findings correspond to the work of other historians of southeastern Pennsylvania, most of whom have focused on Chester County, immediately south of Philadelphia County, where there were few women householders or taxpayers. These include Joan Jensen, *Loosening the Bonds: Mid-Atlantic Farm Women, 1750–1850* (New Haven, Conn., 1986), 16; Lucy Simler, "The Landless Worker: An Index of Economic and Social Change in Chester County, Pennsylvania, 1750–1820," *PMHB* 64 (April 1990): Table 3, 196; Lucy Simler and Paul Clemens, "The 'Best Poor Man's Country' in 1783: The Population Structure of Rural Society in Late-Eighteenth Century Southeastern Pennsylvania," in *Proceedings of the American Philosophical Society* 133 (1989): 241–242.

22. In a 1734 account of the landowners and "freeholders" in Philadelphia County, with two exceptions all the townships in which women held property were in the southeastern portion of the county. Women were more than 2 percent of the taxable population in every township in the eastern half of the county except Roxborough, and four of the five townships with populations that included in excess of 5 percent women were in the eastern most part of the county. Wulf, "A Marginal Independence," 133, 331–333.

23. Tax assessments, 1767–1774; "Tavern, Marriage and Pedlars Licenses, 1762–1776," HSP.

24. Lisa Wilson shows the convergence of these patterns after 1830 in increasingly urban Chester County. Wilson, *Life After Death: Widows in Pennsylvania, 1750–1850* (Philadelphia, 1992), 105–121, see esp. 106 and 121. See also Toby L. Ditz, *Property and Kinship: Inheritance in Early Connecticut, 1750–1820* (Princeton, N.J., 1986), 119–137.

Table 3.1 Rates of Female Householding in Select City Wards, 1762–1775 (in percentages)

Ward	1762	1770	1775
Walnut	13.5%		19.4%
High Street		14.1%	21.3%
Mulberry, East		13.1%	12.4%
Chestnut			15.9%
Dock, South			12.8%
North			13.2%

widow's care and comfort. These types of legacies reflected the fact that land was the principal source of rural income and were designed to help provide a widow with an adequate maintenance after her husband's death. These types of bequests probably also kept many women from heading households, however, because women were unlikely to inherit either the entire house or the entire estate. This pattern differed significantly from Philadelphia, where between 1750 and 1770 urban men who wrote wills were four times as likely as rural men to leave their wives their entire estate. Nonetheless, unmarried women played important roles within farm households. Widows could join an adult child's household, perhaps helping with some of the housework or child-care duties. Before marriage, women could work as live-in servants or day laborers, doing spinning, dairying, or other work to aid the mistress of the household or take her place in cases of illness or death. Lucy Simler's analysis of the available labor pool in Chester County from 1750 to 1820 showed free white women in a variety of roles: landholders, minor children, cottagers, and single women. According to Simler, 22.4 percent of rural laboring women were unmarried adults.[25] This percentage remained almost constant throughout the colonial period.[26] Yet in Chester County, almost all women lived within households headed by men. This pattern differed significantly from that in urban Philadelphia.

More women headed households in the city. While only 3.5 percent of households in Perkiomen Township were headed by women in the mid-1750s, the proportion of female household heads in Philadelphia was never smaller than 12 percent. Table 3.1 shows the percentage of households headed by women in selected areas of the city between 1762 and 1775, as recorded in the Constables' Returns (a form of census taken for

25. Simler, "The Landless Worker," Tables 1 and 3.
26. The calculations for 1775 yield very similar results: 1,100 unmarried women represented 21.6 percent of the 5,094 women Simler estimates in the labor pool.

Table 3.2 Estimated Population of High Street Ward, 1770 and 1775

	1770		1775	
	Male	Female	Male	Female
Householders	116	19	126	34
Wives of householders		93		95
Inmates	39	2	29	2
Servants	4	4	16	16
Slaves	30	19	14	9
Children of householders	131	132	179	179
Total	320	269	364	335

Note: The method of estimation for determining the number of wives of male household heads follows Carole Shammas, "The Female Social Structure of Philadelphiain 1775,"PMHB 107 (1983): 71, 73. The vastly higher ratios of female to male hired servants (57 to 11 in East Mulberry Ward for 1775) suggests that a fifty-fifty ratio may underrepresent female servants.

purposes of taxation).[27] Unfortunately, the small number of extant Constables' Returns makes a complete comparison impossible.

A close look at two of these areas, High Street and East Mulberry wards, between 1770 and 1775 illustrates important aspects of the late colonial urban household. The households in High Street and East Mulberry wards reveal important life-cycle transitions that affected the percentage of female-headed households, the different characteristics of male and female householders, and differences in the composition of male- and female-headed households. East Mulberry was a much larger and more populous ward than High Street. Because it encompassed two full city blocks and probably had many smaller and alley homes, the number of households was almost four times larger. The sex ratio of the population of these two areas can be estimated from the surviving materials. Tables 3.2 and 3.3 show household heads and inmates (that is, boarders)

27. Constables' Returns, 1762–1775, PCA. The constables were interested largely in whether a household head was collecting rents from "inmates" (boarders), whether inmates themselves should be taxed, and whether householders had any servants or slaves. All of these—rents, servants, and slaves—were taxable. The constables also reported the numbers and ages of children in a household, because they could be the basis for an informal reduction of the tax rate in some cases. Individual constables were highly irregular in some aspects of their reports. For example, the constables of High Street Ward for 1770 and 1775 and the constable of East Mulberry Ward in 1770 were all very lax in reporting the presence of hired servants. Perhaps this was because so many were women; the diligent constable of East Mulberry for 1775 found sixty-eight hired servants, fifty-seven of whom were female. Nonetheless, the Constables' Returns provide a unique window into colonial urban households, and the consecutive reports available for these two wards are especially informative.

Table 3.3 Estimated Population of East Mulberry Ward, 1770 and 1775

| | 1770 | | 1775 | |
	Male	Female	Male	Female
Householders	445	67	522	74
Wives of householders		326		323
Inmates	158	2	150	18
Servants	32	33	97	98
Slaves	35	24	28	19
Children of householders	531	531	540	541
Total	1,201	983	1,337	1,073

by sex as well as an estimation of the number of wives of male household heads and the sex of children, servants, and slaves. This estimation suggests that the population of High Street Ward was 46 percent female in 1770 and 48 percent female in 1775 and that the population of East Mulberry Ward was 45 percent female in both years, not unusual proportions for that place and period.[28]

These tables show Philadelphia's population growth in the 1770s in microcosm, but they also reveal several important aspects of household composition. One is the transition in the proportion of households headed by women. In High Street Ward the ratio of wives of household heads to female household heads was approximately five to one in 1770, but approximately four to one in 1775.[29] This increase was largely due to naturally and regularly occurring life-cycle transitions, primarily the death of male household heads. Among new female household heads, seven were women whose husbands had died. These widows included Mary Hall, the wife of Benjamin Franklin's partner, David Hall. Hall was moderately well off, and subsequently so was his widow. She probably managed the domestic arrangements of the family, perhaps even boarding apprentices, although by the time of David Hall's death the Hall children were old enough to assist their father in his work.[30] Similarly, after Thomas Lawrence's death, his widow, Elizabeth Lawrence, carried on the

28. Carole Shammas found a similar proportion in Chestnut Ward, where she estimates the adult population was 49 percent female in 1775. Carole Shammas, "The Female Social Structure of Philadelphia in 1775," *PMHB* (January 1983): 71, 73.

29. By comparison, in 1775 women comprised 9.5 percent of household heads in Chestnut Ward, and 10.9 percent of household heads in the east part of Mulberry Ward. The ratio of wives to female household heads was five to one in Mulberry Ward, but only three to one in Chestnut Ward. Shammas, "Female Social Structure of Philadelphia," 71, 73.

30. In 1775, William Hall was a printer. He had two indentured servants, which suggests that his father may also have had servants at some time. 1775 Constables' Returns.

upholstery business they had built. She advertised to the public that she would continue to "feather beds, mattresses, sacking bottoms, bottoming chairs, [and] cleaning the feathers of old beds."[31]

Women who headed households were less likely to have a specified occupation than men who headed households, but many did. Thirty percent of High Street Ward female householders had discernable occupations in 1770, and 40 percent did in 1775.[32] Most of the women who had occupations in 1770 kept shop and a few kept taverns; by 1775 several hucksters and a couple of spinners had moved into High Street Ward.[33]

Although a few women who did not have listed occupations took in boarders, some female household heads were widows whose sole source of income came from inheritances. As a consequence, those women who could afford to head their own households without benefit of an occupation were generally much wealthier than the average male household head. Ann Warner, for example, owned taxable property, most of it rental property, assessed at over £440 in 1769. In both 1769 and 1774, two of the four persons whose estate was assessed at more than £200 were widows who owned a large amount of real estate. Warner was one; Mary Harrison was the other. Both women owned a large amount of real estate.

Female heads of household were likely to be older on average than male heads of household, and their children had very different lives. The number of children in such households, for example, was sharply lower. Despite other differences in the two wards, in both areas women who headed households were much more likely than men to have no children co-resident at all. In 1770 more than 50 percent of the female-headed households, yet only 20 to 27 percent of male-headed households, were childless. The data are similar for 1775. Among female-headed households in High Street Ward in 1775, 32 percent included no children, whereas only 25 percent of male-headed households included no children.[34] Of course, men who headed households were more likely to be married and thus to continue producing children, than were women who headed households. The significantly lower number of children present in female-headed households also suggests that women who headed households were older than men who headed households.

31. *PG*, May 12, 1773, as quoted in Frances Manges, "Women Shopkeepers, Tavernkeepers and Artisans in Colonial Philadelphia" (Ph.D. diss., University of Pennsylvania, 1958), 105.

32. Information about women's occupations comes from the Constables' Returns as well as tax assessments, newspaper advertisements, tavern licenses, and shop inventories. See Chapter Four.

33. I assume that "spinster" referred not to marital status, but occupation. At least one "spinster" had several children, suggesting that she was a widow.

34. Wulf, "A Marginal Independence," 36.

The experiences of children who lived in female-headed households diverged from those of children who lived in male-headed households. Children who lived with their mother tended to have fewer siblings present in their home, perhaps because widows moved quickly to have their children apprenticed.[35] In 1745, for example, Jane Jones arranged for her one-year-old daughter, Mary, to be bound out to John and Mary Warner for seventeen years. The expenses of Mary's "maintenance and education" would henceforth be provided by the Warners.[36] The Overseers of the Poor bound out the children of poorer women such as Judith Exeter, a free black woman, whose daughter was bound out in 1771 for close to fourteen years.[37] In exchange for Mary Anne Exeter's service, probably to her twenty-fifth birthday (white girls were usually indentured until they were twenty-one), Hannah Steele was to provide the girl with education enough that she could "read & write a legible hand."[38]

WIDOWS KEEPING HOUSE

Most female heads of household were widows. However, other events also prevented the formation of marital households or disrupted them. Recent scholarship on mariners' families suggests that women whose husbands went to sea often contended with a daunting set of family and community needs and expectations. Because of the seasonal nature of maritime work and the cyclical economy, sailors were at sea when it was warm and when profits were good. Women could be captains of their households for as much as half of each year. Often faced with very little economic support from their spouses on the one hand, and restrictions on their own economic activities (because they were married) on the other, they worked creatively to contribute to or entirely support their households.[39] Pennsylvania recognized the unique situation of these

35. In Mulberry Ward in 1770, for example, out of 1,062 children who lived in the ward, only 82, or 8 percent, lived in homes headed by a woman.

36. "Account of Servants Bound & Assigned Before James Hamilton Mayor 1745 & 1746," HSP.

37. Lisa Wilson has estimated, based on data that Susan Klepp collected, that roughly 70 percent of widows in the late eighteenth century had minor children, and that of these widows, only 20 percent remarried. Wilson, *Life After Death*, 171–172, 210n.

38. Guardians of the Poor Memorandum Book and Indentures Made, 1751–1797, PCA.

39. Ruth Wallis Herndon, "The Domestic Cost of Seafaring: Town Leaders and Seamen's Families in Eighteenth-Century Rhode Island"; and Lisa Norling, "Ahab's Wife: Women and the American Whaling Industry, 1820–1870," in Margaret Creighton and Lisa Norling, eds., *Iron Men, Wooden Women: Gender and Seafaring in the Atlantic World, 1700–1920* (Baltimore, 1996), respectively, 55–69, and 70–91.

women, and beginning in 1718 allowed them to operate as feme soles during the period of their husbands' absence. Women could then contract and discharge debts, undoubtedly an issue of some concern for the retailers they frequented.[40] Because of the size and importance of the shipping trades, thousands of Philadelphia women may have fallen into this situation of temporary widowhood.

Mariners' wives were not the only married women who acted as feme soles. Hundreds of reports in the newspapers, as well as court records, attest to the prevalence of informal separations between men and women who remained married. Newspaper accounts alerted potential creditors that women had abandoned their husbands or men were attempting desert their wives.[41] Sometimes the court stepped in to dissolve households altogether. Anna Maria Boyser petitioned the court for separate maintenance in 1761, claiming she needed assistance because her husband had "cruelly beat her and turned her out of doors." After investigating, the court required him to pay her a maintenance of 7 shillings and 6 pence per week.[42] Deserted wives acted very much as widows, with the important exception that they could not remarry.

Nonetheless, widowhood was responsible for creating the majority of female headed-households.[43] The composition of widows' households, like that of all households, was largely determined by economics. The number and types of inhabitants of the household were especially dependent on the kind of work that widows performed in their homes, if any, and the manner of bound or hired help they could afford. For widows, the financial provisions of their husband's will were crucial. If they could command the resources of their late husband's estate, they might

40. Marylynn Salmon, *Women and the Law of Property in Early America* (Chapel Hill, 1986), 48–49.

41. A plethora of advertisements for "runaway wives" from men seeking shelter from debts incurred by their wives can be found throughout the *Pennsylvania Gazette*. Very few divorces were granted in colonial Pennsylvania, but see Merril Smith, *Breaking the Bonds: Marital Discord in Pennsylvania, 1730–1830* (New York, 1991).

42. January Session, 1761, Docket of the Mayor's Court, 1759–1764, PCA. For two similar examples, see the petition of [illeg] Motley, "Wife of Patrick," in July of 1768 and the petition of Elizabeth Keemle in July 1769, both in the dockets of the Mayor's Court, 1766–1771, HSP.

43. Although the Constables' Returns did not always faithfully record female occupations, some constables did note women's marital status more carefully. Thus, the ward returns which provide the least detailed information about occupation are conversely most explicit about marital status. In Dock Street Ward South in 1775, for example, at least 66 of 77 female heads of household were widows. In East Mulberry Ward for the same year, widows headed at least 46 of the 75 female-headed households. The Constables' Returns under counted widows in some areas when the constable chose to record an occupation instead, but for both of the wards the constables were more concerned with—or more able to determine—marital status.

take over the family's business, and they would be expected to secure the future of any children. If a widow was economically vulnerable, she might look to family, church, or the city to help with these tasks. She might even remarry, although this became increasingly unlikely for urban women.[44]

Poverty was a defining feature of many female-headed households. Widows usually made do with very little. The popular depiction of widows as typically impoverished but occasionally very wealthy bore some relationship to reality. Widows in colonial Philadelphia generally seemed to be either financially comfortable or in real distress. Widows seemed unable to retain middling status.

In High Street and East Mulberry wards in 1775, the women who headed households fell into four broad economic categories. The wealthiest women formed a small proportion of this population. Only a handful of women—and a handful of men—in each ward owned homes as well as hundreds of pounds' worth of other taxable property. These were the elite among widows, and despite the alleged attractiveness of wealthy widows in the remarriage market, many retained their independence for decades. The next, slightly larger, category included women who owned taxable property, as well as those women who had few economic hindrances, such as dependent children. For example, High Street Ward resident Jane Osborn owned five slaves but also had nine children to support; her neighbor Ann Gibbs had no children and took in a boarder for extra income.[45] Most women had some economic resources, such as discernable occupations, and they could afford reasonable rents, but their familial economic obligations far outweighed these advantages. High Street Ward shopkeeper Rachel Rhudie, for example, paid £24 in rents, well above the average for her area of the city, which suggests that she had a good income. But she also had five children, and no assistance from servants. Shopkeeper Ann Owen paid £60 in rent, but she paid no taxes because officials counted her four children against whatever income she produced. In fact women with children, despite their occupational or other income, generally paid no taxes whatsoever. A few women who headed households lived on the very margin of poverty. Roughly one-third of the total urban population in 1775 paid less than £10 in annual house rents.[46] This group represented the most marginal,

44. Susan E. Klepp, "Philadelphia in Transition: A Demographic History of the City and its Occupational Groups, 1720–1830" (Ph.D. diss., University of Pennsylvania, 1980), 118–119.

45. 1774 Tax Assessment; 1775 Constable's Return, PCA.

46. Sharon Salinger and Charles Wetherall, "Wealth and Renting in Pre-Revolutionary Philadelphia," JAH 71 (March 1985): 836.

economically vulnerable group of householders. Only a very few women who headed households, however, fell into this group.[47] Most impoverished women were simply unable to maintain their own households.

Cities have traditionally been seen as places of opportunity for independent women, as the higher proportion of unmarried women in urban rather than rural places attests. But the resources required for women to live without a marriage partner for a significant amount of time could be hard to come by in the city. One answer for women was live-in domestic service, which provided food, shelter, and even clothing. Children could be bound out, which was likely the solution adopted by many of the very poorest among Philadelphia's widows. Another strategy for garnering scarce resources might be to build another marital household. Remarriage, however, was not without its complications. Sometimes the most compelling reason to seek remarriage, to provide for young children, was also the primary impediment. Complicated guardianship arrangements, and occasionally a husband's will discouraging or even forbidding remarriage, could outweigh the eventual economic, if not emotional, imperative to remarry.

Faced with the pervasive phenomenon of widows' poverty, many scholars have concluded that these women were indeed the most defenseless of the urban poor.[48] Certainly it is essential to remember, document, and critically analyze the gendered economy that so disadvantaged women, but the creativity and tenacity with which women on the economic margins of the city constructed and maintained their households must also be appreciated. This creative energy was often developed over a lifetime of experience. Lisa Wilson has demonstrated that poor widows in early nineteenth-century Philadelphia usually came from a background of poverty, and that more financially secure widows generally came from comfortable backgrounds. Thus, it was not the experience of widowhood alone that thrust women into new economic conditions.

47. In 1775 only four of twenty-four women householders in High Street Ward, and twelve of seventy-four women householders in East Mulberry paid £10 or less in annual rents. Thus while 30 percent of total householders paid so little—probably for very meager dwellings of a single story and just over two hundred square feet of living space—only 12 to 16 percent of female householders lived in such circumstances. On the size of dwellings, see Salinger and Wetherell, "Wealth and Renting," 836. Salinger and Wetherell also compared the 1774 tax assessment with the 1775 Constables' Returns and found that women were disproportionately represented among unassessed renters, and that unassessed renters paid much less for their dwellings than assessed renters. Salinger and Wetherell, "Wealth and Renting," 835. See also Billy G. Smith, The "Lower Sort": Philadelphia's Laboring People, 1750–1800 (Ithaca, N.Y., 1990), 158–165.
48. An example of this is Shammas, "The Female Social Structure of Philadelphia in 1775."

Widows could use the economic skills they had developed throughout their lives and had observed among others of their economic status.[49] We have already seen that households headed by women were composed quite differently from those headed by men. Widows' households, however, did not follow any set pattern; rather, they were marked by wide variation. Many widows lived with their young children, and some had other kin in their households. The flexibility and resourcefulness with which Philadelphia widows approached the construction and maintenance of their households is striking. For example, Ann Battson Wishart, who was probably well over eighty years of age when she died in 1770 and spent at least the last twenty years of her life as a widow, had acted as the steward of her family's interests and allowed both of her children to continue in the family trade. Ann Battson had married Peter Wishart in 1710.[50] By 1750, Peter had died, and Ann was supporting their family by her trade as a tallow chandler. She took on apprentices, including her son, Thomas, and her daughter, Ann.[51] Eventually Thomas took over the family business, but both his mother and his sister continued to work for him. Neither of the children married. The three Wisharts lived together until the senior Ann's death, after which Thomas and Ann Jr. continued to make a home and a business life together.[52]

Widows who headed stable households either enjoyed economic security already or, like Ann Wishart, used business or artisan skills to keep their families intact. Whether wealthy or working, these women called on family, neighbors, and even government officials to help hold their households together. A common strategy was to take in boarders; a widow's boardinghouse could function as either a society sanctuary or a workingman's lodge. The households of Ann Warner and Alice McCalla, both of which included boarders, looked very different. After Ann Coleman Warner's husband died in 1754, she helped maintain her family by taking in lodgers.[53] Warner was quite wealthy, and in fact was taxed at an extraordinarily high rate for a woman.[54] Among her boarders were Elizabeth and Mary Sandwith, who stayed with her for four years after the deaths of their parents. Entertaining frequently and including

49. Wilson, *Life After Death*, 69–71, 99, 122.
50. William Wade Hinshaw, *Encyclopedia of Quaker Genealogy*, vol. 2 (Baltimore, 1969).
51. *Abstracts of the Philadelphia Monthly Meeting Records (1730–1785)*, vol. 3, p. 184, GSP.
52. Will of Ann Wishart, Sr., W1770 #342, PDW.
53. Crane, ed., *Diary of Elizabeth Drinker*, xi, and 2224.
54. By the 1760s she was rated as owning £450 worth of property, and by the early 1770s her property's worth exceeded £500. Tax Assessments for 1769–1774, Constables' Returns, 1770 and 1775.

her lodgers along with her guests, Warner made her home into a favorite gathering spot for young Quaker women.[55] Alice McCalla's household also offered entertainment as well as bed and board. In 1770 McCalla had at least three male boarders and was running a tavern on Front Street.[56] Her economic situation was far different from Warner's, however. McCalla was rarely taxed, and her assessment was among the lowest in her neighborhood.[57]

SERVANTS AND SLAVES

Households were economic units, within which work was allotted on the basis of gender, age, and skill. Very often household labor was undertaken by servants and slaves, a substantial proportion of whom were unmarried women. Young women who were bound as servants until the age of eighteen or twenty-one, somewhat older women who were hired servants, and women of a wide range of ages who were enslaved, all formed an essential part of many urban households. Unmarried female servants and slaves posed tensions and contradictions within households, even as they often provided the domestic labor that households required. While the dominant discourse associated femininity with dependence and marriage, servants and slaves could be adult, female, and dependent yet outside the strictures of marriage.

The work and social lives of servants and slaves were determined by the requirements of their masters and mistresses. In other important ways, however, they shaped household life. Personal relationships with the head of the household, religious community, and street life could not mitigate the impact of their condition, particularly for enslaved women, but the urban setting provided abundant opportunities for interaction both within and outside of the household.

The slave population of Philadelphia was small, but the prospects for freedom and for the creation of a vibrant African-American community increased over the eighteenth century. The black population of colonial

55. For examples, see Crane, ed., *Diary of Elizabeth Drinker*, 13, 15, 25, and the diary of Hannah Callender for the same period (1759).

56. "Licenses for Marriages, Taverns and Pedlars," HSP; "List of Public Housekeepers recommended July Sessions, 1773," HSP; 1770 Constables' Return, PCA.

57. Usually assessors avoided rating women at these low levels; either they commanded significant assessments or the officials let them out of the tax system completely. For a discussion of the comparative economic conditions of women like Alice McCalla and their male counterparts (almost always rated even at low levels), see Karin Wulf, "Assessing Gender: Taxation and the Evaluation of Economic Viability in Late Colonial Philadelphia," *PMHB* 121 (July 1997): 201–35.

Philadelphia constituted between 3 and 10 percent of the city's total population during the eighteenth century.[58] Pressure among Quakers to manumit slaves, a high mortality rate for black infants, and disruptions in the slave trade decreased the number of blacks by the 1770s. By 1800, Philadelphia's black population was larger, and almost exclusively free.[59] But in the years before the Revolution, enslaved people still provided a significant amount of labor. Before the 1760s, between 20 and 30 percent of the colony's labor was undertaken by slaves, and even in 1775 only one in five Philadelphia blacks was free.[60] Adult women were roughly 30 percent of this largely slave population of blacks.[61] Philadelphians were much more likely than their rural counterparts to purchase slaves, and they were also much more likely than their rural counterparts to make slaves a central part of their domestic operations. While farmers in the surrounding hinterlands employed slave women largely in household production, city dwellers tended to use black women for exclusively domestic work.[62]

Young, unmarried white women, mostly under the age of twenty-one, also constituted a significant presence in urban households. Wealthier households made more frequent use of hired servants, whose ages varied, while more modest households tended to rely on younger indentured servants.[63] Women who headed households sought indentured servants in exchange for domestic training.[64] Contracts often included a provision that indentured girls also be taught to read and write. Catrine McGinniss, for example, was indentured to Mary McCulloch for a period of thirteen years and five months beginning in October 1767. The Guardians of the Poor specified that Catrine was to be taught to "read write and cypher" as well as housewifery and sewing. Violet Pines should expect that Mary Newport, in exchange for her service for over six years, would see that she be taught to read and to "write a legible

58. Susan E. Klepp, "Seasoning and Society: Racial Differences in Mortality in Eighteenth-Century Philadelphia," WMQ 51 (July 1994): 475–476.

59. Gary B. Nash, Forging Freedom: The Formation of Philadelphia's Black Community, 1720–1840 (Cambridge, Mass., 1988), 33–34, 137.

60. Sharon Salinger, "To Serve Well and Faithfully": Labor and Indentured Servants in Pennsylvania, 1682–1800 (New York, 1987); 178–179; Klepp, "Seasoning and Society," 495.

61. Jean Soderlund, Quakers and Slavery: A Divided Spirit (Princeton, N.J., 1979), 79.

62. While black women in rural areas were directly involved in household production, keeping gardens and preserving food, urban women were rarely expected to assist in shops or trades. Soderlund, Quakers and Slavery, 62–63, and 72–73.

63. Shammas, "The Female Social Structure of Philadelphia," 81.

64. Of sixty-six servants bound to women between 1771 and 1773, for example, 80 percent were female. These female servants were most often indentured to undertake domestic chores, and were to be taught "housewifery," or "to spin and sew." "Records of Indentures in Philadelphia, 1771–1773," GSP.

hand."[65] Ann Hardcastle was obligated to see that Sarah Smith achieve literacy and "arithmetic as far as the rule of three."[66] Although it was far more usual for boys or young men to be taught a trade by men, some women apprenticed girls or women to trades. For example, in 1773 shop-keeper and milliner Mary Brown bound Lydia Whitehead to service for five years and eight months. For the first portion of her indenture, Lydia was "employed about any kind of housework," and for the last two years she was "taught the trade of a bonnet, hat and cloakmaker."[67]

Servants were vulnerable to whatever power a master or mistress could exercise. The tension between masters or mistresses and their servants was profound, and the inability of employers to control their servants' time, skills, and even body created schisms that could lead to violence. Hannah Dawser was just a girl when her master, Stephen Hutchins, was brought before Philadelphia's Mayor's Court to answer for his abuse of her. Hutchins was familiar with the court; he was brought in at least one additional time for the crime of running a "tippling house," or gaming and drinking establishment. Hutchins first appeared before the court in January 1762 for "abusing and violently beating" Hannah, and he reappeared in April to pay a fine for the crime. Hutchins paid the fine and posted a bond to ensure his good behavior and her continued safety, but there was no mention of breaking the indenture or freeing her from his household.[68] While the threat to girls and young women from male masters was quite pronounced, men were not the only source of danger in urban households. Masters and mistresses could team up to abuse women servants, as in the case of apprentice Mary King, who was attacked by Patrick Hogan and his wife, Elizabeth. Surviving court records do not indicate the nature or outcome of the case against the Hogans, but the court did take the charge seriously enough to require a bond of surety and good behavior for each of the principals, paid by Patrick Hogan, and three witnesses were named who could be called to testify in the matter.[69]

The control of masters or mistresses could be mitigated somewhat by short lengths of service. Some girls and young women moved rapidly from employer to employer, serving only a few months or a year of a

---

65. Guardians of the Poor Memorandum Book and Indentures Made, 1751–1597, PCA, entries for October 9, 1767 and June 19, 1770.

66. "Record of Indentures," April 30, 1772.

67. *Ibid.*, July 21, 1773

68. For Hannah Dawser (or Daser) and Stephen Hutchins, see January and April sessions, 1762, in docket of the Mayor's Court, 1759–1764, PCA. For Hutchins's subsequent arraignment on charges of "tippling house," see April sessions, 1764.

69. July sessions, 1772, Docket of the Mayor's Court, 1772, HSP.

longer contract. Dorothy Sugg, for example, was indentured to Elizabeth Test in the fall of 1771 for four years. Just over a year later, however, she was indentured to Hannah Dunbar for a period of two years.[70] This pattern suggests that while indenture contracts could be for very long periods, particularly when young children were involved, those contracts were not indissoluble, attenuating employers' control.

Reports from employers about servant women's illicit pregnancies testify to the frustrations inherent in a relationship that presumed hierarchy, control, and protection, but in which employers' power was rarely absolute, either to control or to protect. Servant women's pregnancies were a constant reminder that a great deal of sex occurred outside of marriage.[71] Of course, women of the lower sort were not the only Philadelphians to engage in extramarital or premarital sex. But according to Susan Klepp, there was a significantly higher rate of illegitimacy and premarital conception among the lower-middling and lower sort in Philadelphia than among the wealthier groups.[72] Moreover, pregnancy among servants or slaves was problematic for the functioning of the household. The loss of women's labor during pregnancy and their "lying in" was always emphasized as a serious financial burden, and women who were indentured usually found that their masters or mistresses acted quickly to have their period of servitude lengthened as compensation.[73] Enslaved women's sexuality created at least one other problem for slave owners and for the surrounding community. By the eighteenth century, generations of slave owners had used African women's reproduction as a form of coerced labor production.[74] Yet among Philadelphians, especially by the mid-eighteenth century, black children and families provided constant reminders, for those who wished to acknowledge them, of the essential humanity of Africans and the utter depravity of slavery.

In the case of both slaves and servants, the eighteenth-century city was in the midst of an important transition. Beginning in earnest in the 1770s, many Quakers moved to manumit slaves, and a significant urban population of free blacks developed. Philadelphians also moved from using bound servants to hiring labor, and from having households where women lived in to do domestic work to those where women lived with

70. October 14, 1771 and December 3, 1772, "Record of Indentures," October 14, 1771, December 3, 1772.

71. Sharon Salinger, "'Send No More Women': Female Servants in Eighteenth-Century Philadelphia," *PMHB* 107 (January 1983): 40–41.

72. Klepp, "Philadelphia in Transition," 87–93.

73. Salinger, "'Send No More Women,'" 40.

74. Soderlund, "Black Women in Colonial Pennsylvania."

their own families and came to work for their employers each day. Despite these transitions, most of which occurred late in the century, servants formed an important component of the urban household, and servitude was a common experience for many unmarried women throughout the colonial period.

In colonial Philadelphia, the stereotype of spinsters that depicts them either as unsociable loners, cranky and depressed by their lack of a family of their own, or as unwanted, burdensome additions to others' households, seemed seldom realized. First, adult women who never married rarely headed their own households. A few single women shared a household with another unmarried woman; they seldom lived alone. Indeed, unmarried people of either sex rarely lived alone, except for a few widowers or widows. Single women most often lived in their parents' or siblings' households. Single daughters who remained at home gradually became caregivers for elderly parents.[75] Unmarried sisters were often free to devote themselves to the families of their married siblings. These unmarried women were not unwanted, nor were they burdensome to the households they joined. Rather they played vital roles in their families, and many found this life quite fulfilling.

We know the most about elite women in this situation, largely because they appear in family papers preserved by their descendants. Deborah and Elizabeth Norris are prime examples. These wealthy spinsters chose neither to live together, nor to stay with their widowed mother, nor even to join their married sisters. Deborah Norris left her parents' country home at Fairhill while in her early twenties. She lived in the city with her brother Isaac from 1727 until 1742, when he married and moved to Fairhill. Then she lived, still in the city, with her brother Charles for twenty-four years; only during the last five did he marry and have children. Elizabeth lived at Fairhill with both parents until the death of Isaac Norris, Sr., in 1735. She remained at Fairhill with her mother until her death, and then with her brother Isaac, and lived there briefly with him, his wife, and their two daughters. As Isaac Norris, Jr., described the arrangement in 1747, "my sister Betty lives with me in the country . . . my Brother Charles lives in town and My Sister Deborah keeps his house."[76]

75. Terri L. Premo, *Winter Friends: Women Growing Old in the New Republic, 1785–1835* (Urbana, Ill., 1980), 43–44.
76. Isaac Norris, Jr., to Prudence Moore, Fairhill, November 21 1747, Isaac Norris Letterbook, HSP. For an example of unmarried sisters and brothers in eighteenth-century

The sisters' living situations were superficially similar but were actually quite different. The security of Fairhill and her place there may have brought Elizabeth some peace of mind that, at least in early years, Deborah did not have. When Deborah was twenty-eight, and Isaac went abroad, she wrote that she "fancied" herself Isaac's widow. She was expressing not only contentment with their living arrangement and a strong attachment to her older brother, but perhaps also a touch of anxiety about her future role in their household. It was probably clear to her that unless something extraordinary happened, she might never marry. The question of whether he or she would marry must have weighed heavily on her. After rumors reached her that Isaac might bring home a bride, Deborah assured him "how welcome a wife of thine w[ould] be to all of us."[77] But married sister Mary Norris Griffitts joshed she would "venter something" that a recently widowed cousin would "get two wifes befor [Isaac would] get one."[78] After Isaac did marry, Deborah lived with Charles and then with his widow.

Isaac Norris, Jr., then age thirty-eight, married twenty-four-year-old Sarah Logan in 1739. Their marriage interrupted the household arrangement of Isaac and Deborah, but it did not end the pattern of sharing quarters with siblings. Isaac and his bride took a house in Philadelphia, but then moved out of town, "into the Country About three miles" to Fairhill, which his mother vacated.[79] "Sally" Logan Norris died in October 1744, "after having lain in near a Month," leaving Isaac with two small daughters and "a resignation to the will of God."[80] His "private Loss" devastated him, keeping him "from the . . . sitting of Assembly, and Indeed from the Town."[81] Elizabeth, not Deborah, stepped in to fill the void left by Sarah Logan Norris; Elizabeth not only managed the household but also fostered an intimacy among its many members that lasted into the next generation.

By then, Elizabeth was a very wealthy woman. After their father died, she routinely lent Isaac sums ranging from £152 to £400.[82] Although she

France, see Christine Adams, "A Choice Not to Wed? Unmarried Women in Eighteenth-Century France," *Journal of Social History* 29 (Summer 1996): 883–894.

77. Deborah Norris to Isaac Norris, Jr., August 4, 1734, Norris Family Letters, vol. 1, p. 22, HSP.

78. Mary Griffitts to Isaac Norris, Jr., March 25, 1734, Norris Family Letters, vol. 1, p. 22, HSP.

79. Isaac Norris, Jr., to William Logan, June 3, 1743, Isaac Norris Letterbook, Logan Papers, HSP.

80. Isaac Norris, Jr., to Richard Hill, October 40, 1744; Isaac Norris to [William Logan] March 5, 1745, both in Isaac Norris Letterbook, Logan Papers, HSP.

81. Isaac Norris, Jr., to Richard Partridge, November 15, 1744, Isaac Norris Letterbook, Logan Papers, HSP.

82. Bonds dated 1737, 1749, 1750, Norris Family Accounts, HSP.

never owned the homes she lived in, she did own other real estate, including land in Norriton, for which she collected rents in bushels of wheat.[83] In her will she was able to bequeath an extraordinary number of personal items, including silver "plate" as well as furniture, £600 outright to niece Mary Norris Dickinson, and a comfortable living to her primary legatees, Hannah and Mary Griffitts. When Elizabeth lived at Fairhill there were a number of servants and slaves working there. Isaac Norris, Sr., had been a slave trader, but a number of his family, including himself and Elizabeth, freed slaves either during their lifetimes or at their death by will.[84] Mary Lloyd Norris willed to Elizabeth her "negro girl Dinah," probably because she surmised that Elizabeth would be staying at Fairhill. Dinah served Elizabeth for the next twenty years, until Elizabeth manumitted her. Dinah and another freed slave, Henry, each received £15 from the estate of Elizabeth Norris.

After Sarah Logan Norris died, Elizabeth became not just the household manager at Fairhill but a caregiver for two "Innocent Babes." Isaac Norris worried that they would "ever miss" their mother's "care and prudent conduct over them . . . . always with the nicest judgmnt."[85] But Elizabeth was not the only one who cared for the girls in their father's absence. Her unmarried cousin Mary Lloyd "took the active part in the care of the family" and "knew how to prepare every delicacy for the table."[86] Two other unmarried cousins, Hannah and Sarah Griffitts, also joined the household.

Elizabeth was closer to Isaac's daughters than to Charles's children; exactly the reverse was true of Deborah. While Elizabeth, living in the country, oversaw the raising of young Mary and Sarah after the loss of their mother and then, much later, their father, Deborah was living in the city with Charles. His children were almost twenty years younger than Isaac's, so Deborah's hand in raising them came a little later in her life than did Elizabeth's work with Isaac's daughters. Charles Norris's cashbooks detail Deborah's role in provisioning the household. She managed the marketing, either procuring the food herself or sending a servant to

83. Tax assessments for 1767–1774.
84. This was not unusual. Jean Soderlund clearly demonstrates that Quaker manumissions began in the 1730s, at the height of Quaker slave ownership, and peaked in the 1770s, by which time only about 19 percent of all inventoried Quakers owned slaves, and all of them freed them at their deaths. In his will Isaac Norris, Sr., freed "Indian servant man Will (born in my house) . . . on or before 2 July 1740 on condition he serve his mistress whose property he will be." Soderlund, *Quakers and Slavery*, 163.
85. Isaac Norris Letterbook, March 5, 1744, Logan Papers, HSP.
86. Charles Stille, "Memoirs of the Historical Society of Pennsylvania," *PMHB* 13 (1889): 312.

do it for her.[87] Charles's house on Second Street had very extensive gardens, which Deborah was responsible for overseeing.[88] She implored a man to part with some scarce seeds one year with such success that she promised friends they could "depend on a portion."[89]

Although in her late fifties by the time of their birth, Deborah played an active role in the lives of Charles and Mary Parker Norris's children. Mary's father, who lived in Chester County, was quite ill; so she spent a good part of the six years between the birth of her first child in 1760 and the death of her husband in 1766 away from the family while she tended to her "Daddy."[90] Young Isaac, the first of Charles and Mary Parker Norris's children, was born in 1760. By April 1761, Deborah was playing letter games with him in "which letters [we]re printed on Square Pastboards, & thrown on a Table for him to take up, what [was] told him to." She reported that he could pick out "A for Aunty, D for Daddy, I for Isaac, M for Mammy, N for Nursey," which may have fairly represented the rank of people with which the child interacted. On one occasion in 1766 when Mary Norris took the newest baby, Charles, Jr., with her to Chester, Deborah's letter revealed just how many child-centered activities occupied her day. First, there was the children's laundry to be considered: "I was in hopes of sending Chally's frocks by this Conveyance but they are not don tho Promised tonight." Then there were gifts of food for her and the children to send from the gardens: "Love to Molly with thank for her cakes and now return the basket with Artichokes, we would have sent gooseberries but they are not quite Ripe." Deborah had taken the children to "fairhill last first Day . . . they all ، . . Desired their love to thee." Of course, Deborah reported the children's concern for their mother's absence: "They one and all are now Bawling my Duty to mamma and a Kiss to Brother Chally, tell mamma we want to see them, when will they come home." In a postscript Deborah noted that the eldest child, "Debby," "is Stand by till I write that She is a very good Girl, which indeed She is."

When Deborah Norris died in 1767, she left the bulk of her fortune to the children she had helped rear. Her romantic nature was revealed in one of the several drafts she made of her will. While most wills stated that the testators wished that their "just debts and funeral expenses" be paid

87. For example, Norris Family Accounts, vol. 6, p. 14 (receipt book for 1753–54), HSP.
88. See Charles Norris to Susannah Wright, April 16, 1761; also, Charles Norris to Isaac Norris, entries for June and July 27, 1757, Norris Misc. Letters, HSP.
89. Charles Norris to James Wright, February 15, 1753, Norris Misc. Letters, HSP.
90. See Mary Parker Norris to Charles Norris, letters dated between 1761 and 1765, Norris Family Letters, HSP.

by their estates and some consigned their bodies to God, Deborah wanted a hand in orchestrating her final earthly appearance. She asked that a small token be given to all those in attendance at her "Bridal" ceremony. Then, "just as my Coffin was Lower'd down in the Grave," she wrote, "it would be quite my wish and at this time gives me great Pleasure in hopes it will be Permited" that "four young women or rather girls" would sing:

While God vouchsafes me his support
I'll in his Strength go on
All other Righteousness Disclaim
and mention his Alone.

She hoped that by singing that particular hymn, which proclaimed an independent spiritual self, both she and "those that shall be performing" would "Reap the Blessings of a Life well Spent." In return for this indulgence, she wanted the four girls to receive a copy of Tate and Brady's Psalm Book and "a silver Spoon apiece."[91] Given the tenor of her life, it was only natural that unmarried women would have played a role in her exit.

The presence of unmarried women affected household arrangements, intense and casual emotional ties, and inheritance practices. The Norris family adapted to the abundance of unmarried women among them without much trouble; indeed, Elizabeth and Deborah Norris often eased the lives of their parents and siblings. Elizabeth and Deborah Norris's experiences demonstrate that even women who did not marry could embrace household arrangements and emotional ties that mirrored the roles of wife and mother. By acting as "housekeepers" with all the domestic management functions of a wife, they played crucial roles in the household and the larger kin network. Each embraced not only child-rearing and household management but financial management as well. Elizabeth's stewardship of Fairhill left its mark on subsequent Norris women. Elizabeth and Deborah Norris's experiences confirm the centrality of domestic responsibilities for most women, but challenge the centrality of marriage to those same functions.

HOUSEHOLD PARTNERSHIPS

Among the opportunities that urban life offered women was the chance to form households together. Although women rarely lived alone, never-

91. Deborah Norris, draft of will, Logan Papers, vol. 7, p. 20, HSP.

married sisters, a widow and her unmarried sister, or a widowed mother and her widowed or never-married daughter often formed a household together. Unmarried kin took in elderly or infirm relatives. Occasionally unmarried friends formed long-term household partnerships. Quaker ministers whose frequent absences might necessitate flexible living arrangements could benefit from such partnerships. Women joined forces to share financial burdens and resources, as well as for companionship. In all of these cases, as in any other household, both economics and affection bound people together. The responsibility of providing enough income for the household to operate as well as the labor of domestic management fell to both or all partners. Rather than dividing such work along gendered lines, all-female households allocated this work according to individual skills and inclinations.

A prominent female partnership in the late colonial era was that of the Quakers Rebecca Jones and Hannah Catherall, who taught school and kept house together for at least twenty years. Jones and Catherall's household union blended emotional and economic interests. They formed and maintained a household to recognize their emotional commitment. Friends and colleagues recognized the strength and significance of their relationship, and they were a popular pair. Jones's talent as a minister, their joint work as teachers, and their individual personalities made them welcome guests for tea, for suppers, and for visits around Philadelphia and Burlington. Traveling Friends looked to Jones and Catherall as leaders of the Quaker community; they formed special bonds with other independent women.

Rebecca Jones and Hannah Catherall came from different backgrounds. Jones was the daughter of a sailor and a teacher, and was raised in Philadelphia as an Anglican. Catherall was born into a prominent Burlington Quaker family, and served as clerk of the Philadelphia Women's Yearly Meeting from 1778 to 1794.[92] Catherall was thus a "birthright" Friend, whereas Jones's connection to the Quaker community developed over time. Jones began attending Quaker Meeting when she was as young as twelve, and she was deeply affected by the preaching of the visiting English Friends Catherine Peyton and Mary Peisley. Both Peyton and Peisley were unmarried at that time; in fact, Peyton had already met the man she would later marry but was resisting marriage until she had completed her ministerial travels. These unmarried ministers set an example that other women followed. Jones reportedly slipped a note to Peyton after one meeting, asking for spiritual guidance. From that point on she was befriended by a number of ministers, and in 1758, when she

92. Crane, ed., *Diary of Elizabeth Drinker*, 21–24.

was only nineteen, she began her own ministerial career. Jones recounted that first, tenuous step towards the ministry: "Finding that no excuse would longer do, and that faithfulness was required, I stood up in great fear and trembling, and expressed a few sentences very brokenly."[93] Within a year she was approved as a minister by the Friends Monthly Meeting.

Jones and Catherall opened their school together after Jones's mother died. From 1763 until 1783 they taught boys and girls. Reports to the Overseers of the Friends Public Schools showed a thriving school, which opened in 1763 with twenty students.[94] In an era when students' attendance was erratic and peripatetic, many of Jones's and Catherall's students stayed with them for years. Martha and Mary Stackhouse, for example, were among the school's first pupils. Martha remained with them through 1768 and Mary through 1769, even though their widowed mother was struggling financially.[95] Prominent Quakers, too, including the Drinkers, sent their children to be schooled by Jones and Catherall. Sally Drinker, who tugged at her Aunt Mary Sandwith's sleeve while the latter was writing letters, began school with Jones and Catherall in April 1765; Sally's younger brother followed almost ten years later.[96] As Jones recalled, the school allowed them "a sufficiency [on which] to live comfortably."[97] A surviving account book suggests that they kept careful track of their financial relationship, sharing responsibility for household expenses and chores.[98]

Like their working lives, their social and religious lives overlapped significantly. Friends, family, and associates treated them as a couple. Invitations to tea or supper were often extended to them both, and they developed and maintained friendships as a pair. The English Quaker Rachel Wilson and her daughter, Rachel Junior, for example, corre-

---

93. Ruth E. Chambers, "A Short Account of Rebecca Jones," *The Westonian* (1907), 24–25.

94. "Overseers of the Friends Public Schools to Rebecca Jones and Hannah Cathrall Dr from 4 mo. 5. 1763 to 4th moth 5th 1764," Teachers' Accounts, Box 1, William Penn Charter School Archives, QC.

95. Tax assessments for Martha Stackhouse of Mulberry Ward for 1767–1774, in which she was assessed at a very low level and her "severall children," and their ages were noted as mitigating factors. Mrs. Stackhouse was probably paying something toward the girls' tuition. The overseers contributed to all the children's education, but some were designated "Poor scholars" and their parents probably paid nothing.

96. Crane, ed., *Diary of Elizabeth Drinker*, 115, 198.

97. Chambers, "A Short Account," 26.

98. Handwritten almanac of Rebecca Jones, 1770, Allinson Collection, Box 12, QC. In this almanac Jones noted household events ("Parlour chimney swept"), other notable dates ("Died the Widow Breintnall"), and a few debts ("HC Dr sundries 6/3").

sponded with Jones and Catherall jointly.[99] Young Anna Rawle noted in her diary in 1781 that "H.C. and R.J. dined here as usual these days."[100] Perhaps most tellingly, Jones and Catherall and their friends and family accorded their relationship a respected status.[101] In a correspondence between Jones and Catherall's mutual friends Henry Drinker and George Dillwyn, Dillwyn noted that Catherall was about to take a vacation from school. He was relieved, he said, and wished that "she & her valuable Yoke Fellow would now & then . . . make such excursions; & *not keep the Garden enclos'd so much in the Cellar.*"[102] Dillwyn's letter reveals a number of assumptions about Jones and Catherall's relationship. His use of the term "yoke fellow" implies a relationship much like a marriage, that is, one in which the partners were teamed for work and for life. He encouraged Jones and Catherall to be out among their friends and among Friends more than their school responsibilities allowed them to be. Dillwyn's use of "yoke fellow" also demonstrates the willingness of contemporaries to see two women in a committed relationship.

Like any other partners, Jones and Catherall often acted in concert and sometimes acted alone. These two prominent Quakers, one a minister and the other a very active member of the Meeting, often found themselves serving on committees together.[103] They were separated in 1784, when Jones commenced a four-year trip to Great Britain. It is unclear how this trip affected their relationship, but during her travels Jones wrote to and of Catherall regularly.

Jones and Catherall's partnership was not unique in Philadelphia. Perhaps the most common form of all-female households was the one composed of kin, usually sisters. The Hudson family provides a good example of the kind of generational and other factors that created these households. In 1767, sisters Mary, Jane, and Susannah Hudson, and their cousin Hannah Hudson all lived together in Philadelphia's North Ward. Jane died in 1768, and Hannah probably soon after. Mary and Susannah Hudson then set up another home togther in South Ward.[104] This kind of household, composed of several unmarried women, was not uncommon. The Hart sisters shared ownership of a home in North Ward; each was as-

---

99. Rachel Wilson, Jr., and Rachel Wilson to Rebecca Jones and Hannah Catherall, Kendal, October 3, 1770, Allinson Collection, QC.

100. Diary of Anna Rawle, Pemberton Papers, vol. 21, p. 72, HSP.

101. See Rebecca Jones to Edward Catherall, July 25, 1782, which she signed from "whom thou calls thy Aunt R Jones," Allinson Collection, QC.

102. George Dillwyn to Henry Drinker, Burlington, April 19, 1781, Vaux Collection, QC.

103. Crane, ed., *Diary of Elizabeth Drinker,* January 2, 1784.

104. Hinshaw, *Encyclopedia of Quaker Genealogy;* Hinshaw, "Index to Quaker Meeting Records," FHL.

sessed for one third of its value. They shared equally in both rental income from other property and rent payments on the home in which they lived.[105] The Harts evidently also kept shop together.

Women who never married, even if they came from middling or wealthy families, often had to find a way to earn money, because inheritance was so intimately bound up in the institution of marriage. Testators most often passed real property to sons but gave daughters money or other personal property, often in the form of marriage settlements, so that single women were left out of such property arrangements. Spinsters' work and occupations were often directly related to their lack of adequate inherited resources and their need to support themselves. Rebecca Rawle and her sister Elizabeth never married but lived and worked together, operating a dry-goods shop in or near their home in Upper Delaware Ward. Elizabeth Rawle died in 1758, leaving bequests to the Society of Friends and her sister Jane England. She gave the "rest and residue" of her estate to Rebecca for her life's use, providing that it would eventually go to their nephew and nieces Rebecca Cooper and Francis and Sarah Rawle. Rebecca Rawle died the following year. Her will was similar to Elizabeth's: she left the bulk of her estate to Jane England and assorted nieces and nephew. Both women identified themselves in their will not by occupation but by marital status as "single women." Neither of the Rawle sisters' 1756 tax assessments denoted an occupation; only Rebecca and Elizabeth Rawle's estate inventories reveal that they were shopkeepers.[106] Both sisters' inventories included three categories of property: miscellaneous wearing apparel, "ready money," and bonds; household furniture; and "shop goods." The largest portion of each woman's estate was "ready money."[107] Although they were clearly among Philadelphia's wealthier citizens, the Rawleses did not have extensive household furnishings. Their possessions did, however, include a

105. The Harts were not unusual; many extended families had two or more unmarried women among their number, many of whom chose to live near one another. In the 1760s and 1770s, for example, the Armitt, Clampfer, Griffith, Hart, Hudson, Hyde, Lloyd, Morris, Paschall, and Steel households included two or more unmarried women. Among women who were taxed in those years, forty-two lived in the same ward as an independent female relative. Thirty-two lived with or near only one, and ten women lived with or near at least two relatives.

106. The 1756 tax assessment under-reported the number of women shopkeepers. Thirty-eight women on that tax list were identified as shopkeepers, but at least an additional twenty-four kept shop. The same phenomenon was true of women tavernkeepers. Patricia Cleary, "'She Merchants' of Colonial America: Women and Commerce on the Eve of the American Revolution" (Ph.D. diss., Northwestern University, 1989), 121.

107. In almost no other cases of inventoried wealth among women taxables was this the case, but note that among shopkeepers, a large amount of cash in various forms (such as pistoles, etc) was not uncommon.

large amount of silver "plate," one indication of wealth and status.[108] Their shop goods were also modest, consisting primarily of fabric and other dry goods.[109] Another example of a working partnership was that of glover Mary McCutchen and her partner, Sarah Dean, who lived in East Mulberry Ward during the late 1770s.[110]

The households of Jones and Catherall, the Hyde, Hudson, and Rawle sisters, and the partners McCutchen and Dean all attest to the importance of economics in forming all-female households. These household arrangements displayed the same interests as others, combining affective relations with economic partnership. Households composed of women reflected the combination of opportunities and restrictions on women's lives in the colonial city. Economic opportunities were more expansive than in the countryside and allowed women to live independent of marital households. Those opportunities were not so great and cultural views not so expansive, however, as to encourage individual women to strike out on their own; in a city where few people lived alone, that would have seemed peculiar in any case. The group living situations that women created reflected this combination of needs, opportunities, and pressures.

CONCLUSION

Historians have long acknowledged the tenuous connection between prescribed gender roles and the practice of daily life, noting that women's behavior has only rarely conformed to dominant ideologies of femininity. The realities of life and work have rarely afforded women the opportunity to engage only in prescriptively "feminine" activities, even had they wished to do so. But there has nonetheless been an assumption that it was within the domestic realm, as wives and mothers, that gender norms could be most easily achieved and enforced. Within urban households we can see this process at work. Yet we can also see the ways in

108. The Rawleses were each rated at £20 in 1756, which placed them in the top 40 percent of taxables. Within their own neighborhood, however, they were among the very wealthiest, as no taxable in Upper Delaware Ward was rated within the top 10 percent of the city's taxables. 1756 Tax Assessment. The Rawleses averaged under £100 worth of household goods, which places them well below the median of £267 that Thomas Doerflinger found in merchants' estates. Doerflinger, *A Vigorous Spirit of Enterprise: Merchants and Economic Development in Revolutionary Philadelphia* (Chapel Hill, 1986), 129.

109. Inventory, Estate of Elizabeth Rawle, W1758 number 96; Estate of Rebecca Rawle, W1759 number 210, PDW.

110. 1775 Constable's return for East Mulberry Ward identified Dean as McCutchen's "partner."

which gender became simultaneously detached from and more attached to sex. Often women were expected to perform feminine domestic tasks whether or not they were wives or mothers. Women such as Mary Sandwith acted as replacements or supplements for their female kin. Within other households, women and men performed tasks usually assigned to the opposite sex. In households headed by women, women performed the public and occupational roles customarily assumed by men. Widows were the most numerous among household heads. Women who shared households also acted in masculine roles, especially if they also worked together. The potential for women to assume such roles was limited. When a man resided in a household, he most often assumed the masculine roles and tasks. In the Norris family, for example, Isaac and Charles both performed as patriarchs while their sisters acted the maternal and wifely role. But even when unmarried women acted in a domestic fashion, undertaking the responsibilities of wife and mother for a man not her husband and for children not her own, she was still not a wife and not a mother. Like Mary Sandwith, she could conduct her own affairs with a degree of independence unavailable to married women.

The gendering of the household, through the domestic functions and identities assigned to unmarried women, was imperfect. It allowed women who were not ultimately subordinate, through law or custom, to act as both household dependent and as independent individual. For married women, and within the dominant model of womanhood, that combination should have been unimaginable. In urban places, however, that combination was practical, and even necessary.

As the urban and increasingly cosmopolitan culture of Philadelphia came to embrace gender in ways at once essentializing and yet distinct from the identities created in European agricultural society, the gender of household functions and the importance of their gendered performance changed. Large numbers of women in colonial Philadelphia lived in households that departed from the traditional composition in which a patriarch ruled his wife and children. In the nineteenth century, the fevered pitch of domestic discourse would clash ever more apparently with the growing population of women who chose never to marry.[111] This contradiction may have been most pronounced in places like Philadelphia.

For colonial Philadelphians, the urban household, in its many and varied forms, helped shape urban culture, even as it was shaped by the urban economy. The patriarchal philosophy and practice of household

111. Jensen, *Loosening the Bonds;* Lee Virginia Chambers-Schiller, *Liberty, a Better Husband: Single Women in America: The Generations of 1780–1840* (New Haven, Conn., 1984).

government was a distinguishing characteristic of early modern Anglo-America. The idea that men would rule over their households expressed, more than any other single concept, the basic premises that governed daily life. The importance of hierarchy, the autonomy of the individual man within the realm of his home, the reflection of the royal government's relationship to its subjects in the rule of men over their household dependents, and the preponderant importance of gender as a means and a signifier of power relationships—all of these ideas were encapsulated in the concept of the patriarchal household. Countervailing trends, including economic and demographic factors, dissenting theologies and political philosophies, sentiment, and the expansion of public culture, meant that a culture of household governance could develop quite differently in different places.[112] Quaker culture and the opportunities the urban economy afforded women contributed to a plurality of household forms in Philadelphia. That women appeared within households in so many different roles, and that households appeared so varied, augured ill for a strictly patriarchal culture. The impact of women and their households on neighborhood communities is the subject of the next chapter.

112. On comparative household government in the seventeenth-century Chesapeake and New England, see Norton, *Founding Mothers and Fathers.*

[4]

Rachel Draper's Neighborhood: Work and Community

Even in a city as large as Philadelphia, with a transient population and a seaport buzzing with daily arrivals and departures, dense webs of relationships underlay urban neighborhoods. Thus, when John Barker, the constable of Philadelphia's High Street Ward, set out to enumerate the residents of his district in 1775, he encountered familiar faces and families of long residence. Among the householders he greeted while making these rounds was the widow Rachel Draper, a tavernkeeper. Rachel Draper had lived in High Street Ward for over twenty years by the time Barker came to make his Constable's Return. Her husband, James, a tailor who had earned a modest living, had died relatively young. The September 8, 1763, *Pennsylvania Gazette* carried a notice that "ALL Persons indebted to James Draper, Taylor, deceased, by Notes or Book debts, are requested to make speedy Payment; and those that have any Accounts against said Estate, are desired to bring them in, in order that they may be adjusted by me RACHEL DRAPER, Administratrix." Rachel Draper was the sole executor of her husband's estate, a common phenomenon among Philadelphia's lower sort. The larger and more complex an estate was, the less likely it was that the widow was named as the sole executor, or even as a co-executor. After administering the settlement of her husband's estate, Rachel Draper set about making a living for herself and her two young daughters. She held onto the house, but her financial status was precarious. She was considered too poor and too burdened by the costs of supporting her young children to pay any taxes.[1]

Like many others among Philadelphia's working poor, Draper used

1. Information on the Drapers was compiled from the Philadelphia Monthly Meeting Births and Burials, 1686–1829, GSP; Hannah Benner Roach, "Taxables in the City of Philadelphia, 1756," *Pennsylvania Genealogical Magazine* 22 (1961–1962): 3–41; *PG*, September 8, 1763; Tax Assessments and Constables' Returns. On tailors' wages, see Billy G. Smith, *The "Lower Sort": Philadelphia's Laboring People, 1750–1800* (Ithaca, N.Y.: 1991), 119–

a variety of economic strategies to meet her family's needs. She was granted successive city licenses to operate a "dram shop," or small tavern, probably right in her home on Chancery Lane. She was a tavern-keeper from at least 1767 through 1773, and perhaps for much longer. To help with the annual rent of £14 on a house and lot that served as both residence and place of business, Draper took in boarders: Jacob Potts was boarding there in 1770, and Thomas Draper, no doubt a relation, was boarding there in 1775.[2]

By 1775 Rachel Draper had lived in her neighborhood for at least two decades, the last twelve years of which she had headed her household. Although clearly economically marginal, Draper was in some ways a success story. She never fell into the transiency that marked the lives of so many among Philadelphia's laboring population. She not only kept her family fed and clothed, but she also made sure that her two daughters received an education. Amy and Patience Draper attended Rebecca Jones and Hannah Catherall's school from the time they were, respectively, seven and five years old until they turned thirteen. The girls' tuition was paid directly to their teachers by the overseers of Philadelphia's Quaker public school system, but their mother contributed to their education. Many working parents apprenticed their children at a young age simply to cover the costs of their care. Rachel Draper's commitment to provide her daughters with food, clothing, and lodging as they attended school is thus all the more remarkable.[3]

Rachel Draper's circumstances as a working, unmarried woman were far from unique. She lived and worked alongside such women as upholsterer Elizabeth Lawrence, tavernkeeper Susannah Harditch, and tallow chandler Ann Wishart. Each of these women was a neighbor of Draper's and a resident of long tenure. Each had extensive ties to the community. These women, and others like them, helped to shape urban community and urban culture in the eighteenth-century city. As independent women, they could act legally and economically in ways that their married sisters, bound by coverture, could not. Although historians have

123. On widows' estate management, see Lisa Wilson, *Life After Death: Widows in Pennsylvania, 1750–1850* (Philadelphia, 1992), 50–52.

2. Will of James Draper, 1763, #34, PDW; "List of Public Housekeeper's Recommended," July 1767, Mayor's Court Docket, HSP; "A List of Public HouseKeepers recommended July Sessions 1773," HSP. 1770 and 1775 Constables' Returns for High Street Ward, PCA. Draper's rent of £14 in the 1770s placed her among the bottom half, but not the bottom third, of renters. Sharon Salinger and Charles Wetherall, "Wealth and Renting in Pre-Revolutionary Philadelphia," *Journal of American History* 71 (March 1985): 836.

3. Philadelphia Monthly Meeting Births and Burials, 1686–1829, GSP; Teachers' Accounts, William Penn Charter School Archives, Box 7, Teachers' Accounts, QC. On transiency among the working poor, see Smith, *The "Lower Sort"*, 21–26, 150–175, 199–200.

emphasized the importance of all women in creating social networks, unmarried women not only maintained existing ties of kinship and friendship but also created community ties that facilitated their independence. They exchanged credit and debt, rented property to and from their neighbors, served drinks, bought and sold goods, and engaged in friendly, practical, or even hostile conversation. Neighbors often worshipped together. Some were related by blood or marriage. Unmarried women were central actors in the creation and maintenance of the economic, religious, familial, and broadly political networks of association that defined urban life.

This chapter examines the significance of gender and work in creating the networks of association that defined urban community, focusing on the ways in which unmarried women's work enhanced their importance to the communities in which they lived. The urban economy thrived in large measure because of women's paid and unpaid labor, and work was an essential feature of most unmarried women's lives. Work was central to the identity of many middling women who had trades or occupations, as well as poorer women who labored in domestic service or for daily wages. Work often defined a woman's place in the community, and work shaped her economic and social interactions with neighbors.

NEIGHBORHOOD COMMUNITY

Community was generated by the interaction among households. Eighteenth-century Philadelphia was a "walking, talking" city, where important social knowledge was formed at close range.[4] As Stuart Blumin describes it, this "face to face society" was "highly personalized," a place "in which people . . . frequently interacted within an environment small enough so that they could recognize each other as individuals, understand something of each other's personalities and character, and in many cases know and use each other's names."[5] Although Philadelphia was the largest American city by the time of the American Revolution, it was still small by today's standards, smaller in fact than Bozeman, Montana, in the 1990s. A significant portion of the population was quite mobile, as in any other seaport city, but a stable base underlay the transient flow. In such a setting, where daily interactions were so intimate and individualized,

4. Peter Thompson, "A Social History of Philadelphia's Taverns, 1683–1800" (Ph.D. diss., University of Pennsylvania, 1989), 536.
5. Stuart Blumin, *The Emergence of the Middle Class: Social Experience in the American City, 1760–1900* (Cambridge, 1989), 26.

what roles did women play in generating and maintaining dynamic community interaction?

The heart of every community was a network of association. Studying social networks has helped historians to unravel the ways in which early modern peoples in particular communicated and granted meaning and value to a variety of relationships.[6] Networks were regularly created through familial connections of birth and marriage. This most fundamental of networks often led to other kinds of associations—of religious groups, of shared economic interests, and of politics. Networks helped early modern people cope with a world that was quickly expanding across oceans and continents through commerce and migration and yet was still bound by expensive, slow methods of communication and travel. Through whom one was known and for whom one could or would vouch were critical aspects of the networks that underlay daily relationships of co-religionists and family members, as well as the increasingly tenuous and impersonal relationships of credit and debt.[7] The intensity and diligence with which letter writers undertook their exchange of gossipy information about friends, family, neighbors, and local dignitaries underscore the importance of such news in the first information age.

While eighteenth-century urban neighborhoods contained communities of interest based on networks of association formed and maintained by men and women, including familial, religious, and economic networks, they were also communities of place. Multiple networks of association existed among neighbors, reinforcing geographical community. Neighbors relied on each other for a variety of services and kindnesses, and could be brought together in times of crisis; during the Revolution, for example, Philadelphia militias grew out of neighborhood associations.[8] Daily interaction—the walking and talking that scholars have emphasized as characterizing the early city—gave shape to a geographically based, neighborhood community.

One day in the mid-1760s, a "Country man" sauntered into Elizabeth Paschall's shop on Market Street. As he and Paschall were chatting, their

6. Charles Wetherell, "Network Analysis Comes of Age," *Journal of Interdisciplinary History* 19 (Spring 1989): 645–51.

7. On the importance of reputation, see Toby L. Ditz, "Shipwrecked, or Masculinity Imperiled: Mercantile Representations of Failure and the Gendered Self in Eighteenth-Century Philadelphia," *Journal of American History* 81 (June 1994): 51–80; and David S. Shields, *Civil Tongues and Polite Letters in British America* (Chapel Hill, 1997), 275–307. On the advance of impersonal economic relationships, see Cornelia Hughes Dayton, *Women Before the Bar: Gender, Law, and Society in Connecticut* (Chapel Hill, 1996).

8. Steven Rosswurm, *Arms, Country, and Class: The Philadelphia Militia and the "Lower Sort" During the American Revolution* (New Brunswick, N.J., 1987).

conversation worked its way around to kidney stones. The man confided that he was once "in Extreme torture & could not make water." The cure? A "Good old woman pounded some onions Raw & warmed them & applyed [them] to his Belly," which "quickly Gave him Reliefe."[9] Two aspects of this conversation bear scrutiny. First, shopkeepers held a uniquely contradictory authority. Customers' authority lay in their decision to buy or not; shopkeepers' authority lay in their position as arbiters of quality and purveyors not just of goods but of information.[10] The country man, then, offered to this urban woman his own knowledge of medicine in exchange for the information she had to offer. Second, the authority in this conversation always returned to women. Paschall, the shopkeeper, was authoritative not only because of her position as proprietor and her medical expertise, but because she could record his story. The "good old woman" who cured the kidney stones possessed knowledge and skills of such significance that they could be exchanged secondhand in an urban locale. In daily interactions, neighbors exchanged news and information of specific importance to their community as they bought and sold from one another. Who was escorted home by the constable late at night after making so much noise in the streets? What could be done about the impoverished family living in the tiny basement of an alley house? The city authorities planned to bill the owners of private water pumps for repairs, and they were not going to fix the leaky one on the corner until the money was secured![11]

Women played crucial roles in forming and maintaining these networks of exchange and association during the eighteenth century. Historians have shown how women contributed to economic, political, and kinship networks through their marriages, solidifying existing connections or creating new alliances. Margaret Hunt has demonstrated the extent of English women's participation in capital formation in this critical period, and the ways in which, both through the laws of coverture as well as their own patterns of bequest and inheritance, women actively shaped networks of economic association. Nancy Tomes's careful reconstruction of Elizabeth Drinker's visiting patterns confirms that Drinker used visiting as a way to cement social ties among her fellow Quaker

9. Elizabeth Coates Paschall Receipt Book, CPP. Paschall's shop carried some apothecary materials, so the customer would have been clued to her interests in medical issues; perhaps he went to her store for that purpose.

10. Richard Bushman, "Shopping and Advertising in Colonial America," in Cary Carson, Ronald Hoffman, and Peter J. Albert, eds., *Of Consuming Interests: The Style of Life in the Eighteenth Century* (Charlottesville, Va., 1994), 246–251.

11. Carl Bridenbaugh, *Cities in Revolt: Urban Life in America, 1743–1776* (New York, 1955), 296.

elites. Other women used such socializing to repair fractured political relationships.[12]

Unmarried women also became active in the public networks of association that became increasingly important in the eighteenth century. As unmarried household heads, they were invited to join the voluntary associations that fed the poor, resisted British taxes, and created circulating libraries.[13] Their greatest impact, however, was on local, neighborhood community. Unmarried women, particularly heads of household who lived and worked in their neighborhoods for decades, were central to the networks of both interest and place that defined the urban community. Technically, all individuals engaged in these network formations, but women, as heads of household, took responsibility for the exchanges that informed the community's own interests: about crime, about property, and about other neighbors. Because female unmarried heads of household also interacted economically—directly, on their own behalf, rather than indirectly, on behalf of a spouse, parent, or master—with their neighbors, such women could not only maintain ties of family and sociability but create new ties as well. By buying, selling, engaging, or providing services for a neighbor, the nub of a network—an exchange—was created.

Rachel Draper, widow and tavernkeeper, exemplified the women who created community through their residence and their work. Draper's neighborhood lay immediately north of the city center. For purposes of governance, the Philadelphia Common Council divided the city into wards as early as 1704. High Street and North wards were two of the three small, centrally located wards. They encompassed houses on streets and alleys in two square blocks bounded by Market Street on the south, Mulberry (Arch) Street on the north, Front Street on the east, and Third Street on the west. The Delaware River docks were a block to the east, and both the large city markets and the courthouse were located on Market Street, just to the south.[14] An Anglican church and the Baptist church

12. Kathleen M. Brown, *Good Wives, Nasty Wenches, and Anxious Patriarchs: Gender, Race and Power in Colonial Virginia* (Chapel Hill, 1996), 247–282; Margaret Hunt, *The Middling Sort: Commerce, Gender, and the Family in England, 1680–1780* (Berkeley, 1996); Nancy Tomes, "The Quaker Connection: Visiting Patterns Among Women in the Philadelphia Society of Friends, 1750–1800," in Michael Zuckerman, ed., *Friends and Neighbors: Group Life in America's First Plural Society* (Philadelphia, 1982), 174–195. In the 1750s Esther Edwards Burr used her visiting efforts to try to heal the significant breeches among New Jersey's warring political factions. Brendan McConville, *"These Daring Disturbers of the Public Peace": The Struggle for Property and Power in Early New Jersey* (Ithaca, 1999).
13. See Chapter 6.
14. By 1775 the city markets along Market Street extended from Front to Fourth streets. John F. Watson, *Watson's Annals of Philadelphia* (Philadelphia, 1850), vol. 1, pp. 63, 65, 362–63.

were located in this neighborhood on Second Street, and the Quaker Meeting House was at the southwest corner of Market and Second.

Although it was settled much later than New York or Boston, Philadelphia by mid-century was larger than either. In 1770, the population exceeded 25,000, small in comparison to London, but large by colonial standards. In 1770, the constable counted 135 households in High Street Ward; just five years later, there were 160. Twenty-five additional households squeezed into what would now be called one city block. Several inns and taverns made the area a popular gathering spot. Across Market Street lay the heart of the mercantile community, William Bradford's London Coffee House, but within the neighborhood itself were numerous other taverns. Most of these had long-time women proprietors. By 1775 Rachel Draper had been licensed to sell "spirituous drinks" in her "dram shop" on Chancery Lane, the small alley that cut between Arch Street and Coombs Alley, since at least 1767. Elizabeth Coarse served drinks at the southwest corner of Mulberry and Front for at least as long as Draper, and Susanna Harditch had kept a tavern on Front Street since at least 1755. William Whitebread, another long-time resident who served variously as tax assessor and tax collector of High Street Ward, operated the King's Arms Inn across Second Street from the Christ Church parsonage.[15]

Proximity to the market made this area an attractive residence for a variety of artisans, retailers, and professionals. Three occupational groups predominated. Merchants accounted for the largest single category, but High Street Ward actually had a smaller percentage of merchants than other central wards, and the merchants in High Street Ward were not among the very wealthy. Merchant George Robotham, for example, was rated at a much lower tax than his neighbor, tallow chandler Ephraim Bonham. Shopkeepers were the next largest occupational category. The clothing, hat, and shoe trades, including cordwainers and tailors, comprised a larger group than merchants.

Within High Street and North wards, neighborly connections were common, routine, and vital. Often neighborly obligations coincided with family obligations, for family ties both within and between households were common. In North Ward, for example, three pairs of spinster sisters

15. In 1756, 1769, and 1774 High Street Ward had more taxed and licensed tavernkeepers than other central wards. Thompson, "A Social History of Philadelphia's Taverns," 392, 399; Mayor's Court Docket for July Sessions, 1767, HSP; "List of Tavernkeepers City of Philad. who do not sell wine 1755," Richard Peters' Cash Book, HSP; J. Thomas Scharf and Thompson Westcott, *History of Philadelphia, 1609–1884*, 3 vols. (Philadelphia, 1884), vol. 2, p. 980.

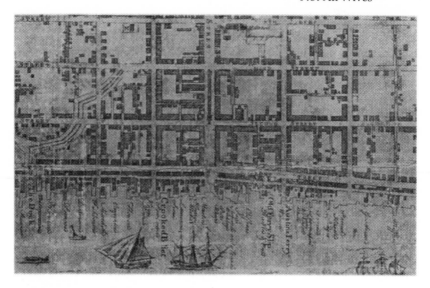

3. This detail of Philadelphia in 1762 shows High Street and North wards, bounded by Market Street on the south, Mulberry (or Arch) Street to the north, Front Street on the east, and Third Street to the west. Courtesy of The Library Company of Philadelphia.

kept shop during the late 1770s. The Hudson, Hart, and Roberts sisters all benefited from family connections. Elizabeth and Ruth Roberts, for example, inherited money and real estate from their aunt Jane Nicholas, also a shopkeeper and North Ward resident. Widow Mary Tongue lived close to her niece, Elizabeth Shewell, who was also widowed.[16]

Neighbors looked to one another to perform fundamental services. Witnessing and executing wills were among the most vital. When writing his will, cordwainer Samuel Cheesman had his neighbors serve as witnesses and executors. Shopkeeper Mary Tongue asked her neighbors Joseph Riddall and Benjamin Gibbs to witness her will. Estate appraisal was another task that neighbors often performed. When Mary Jacobs died, her neighbors John Drinker and Stephen Collins inventoried the estate. Mary Bevan was tended in her last illness by neighbor Miriam Potts, and when Bevan died, two other neighbors appraised her estate, including the debts owed to Potts.[17] Neighbors and resident kin were natural

16. Will of Jane Nicholas, Book P #349, 1773; Will of Mary Tongue, Book P #509, 1774, PDW; Will of Peter Sonman "Practitioner of Physick," #235, 1776, PDW. In 1774 two long-resident families merged when Margaret Attmore married John Head. AM10155, vol. 2, p. 18, HSP.

candidates for services pertaining to estate settlement. Their proximity was an obvious advantage, particularly when wills had to be written, signed, and witnessed quickly, but they might also know details about the contents of estates to which even kin might not be party. Women's participation in these relationships, as testators, executors, and witnesses, confirmed their importance to the fair and orderly transfer of property, clearly one of the community's priorities.

Networks of obligation and reciprocal service, such as those fostered by family ties or requested in times of crisis and death, were not the only kinds of networks that urban neighbors created. Residents also banded together for a variety of causes. In 1761, for example, neighbors Walter Goodman, Ephraim Bonham, Thomas Campbell, and John Young served as managers of the lottery designed to finish the building of St. Paul's Church on Second Street. Neighbors occasionally engaged in heated legal action, as in 1760, when resident Edmund Milne, a silversmith, brought a lawsuit claiming libel against William Whitebread, Jr. The case was no doubt complicated by Whitebread's extensive ties within the community. His father served High Street Ward in a variety of elected and appointed capacities. The foreman of the inquest was yet another High Street Ward resident and local magistrate, Evan Morgan.[18]

The association of men managing the church building lottery and the legal entanglements of Milne and the Whitebreads appear to be largely male preserves. Certainly men were the vast majority of those who appeared in court and handled public finance. But when women were unmarried, particularly when they headed households, they were expected to participate in these activities. Rachel Draper's neighbor Mary Harrison was one of four people to lend money to the Philadelphia Common Council for poor relief in 1767.[19] Other women acted in their own interests and in the interest of public order by prosecuting criminals. Mary Bevan appeared in court to complain of trespassing, and Rachel Rhudie prosecuted Ann Quigly for theft.[20] Court appearances and public charity

17. Will of Samuel Cheesman, #413, 1770; Will of Mary Tongue. For other examples see the wills of Peter Sonmans; Susannah Harditch (#175, 1779), James Rickey (#140, 1776), and William Honeyman, (# illeg. 1774); estate inventories of Ruth Adams, Mary Attmore, Judith Benezet, Mary Bevan, Susannah Harditch, Mary Jacobs, and Jane Nicholas, PDW, which were performed by one or more residents of High Street or North wards.

18. Accounts of the St. Paul's lottery can be found in the PG, January 29, and March 12, 1761. The Milne-Whitebread case material is located in the Balch-Shippen Papers, vol. 2, p. 84, HSP. For another example of neighbors' legal wrangling, see Cuthbert Landreth v. William Cox, 1744, Margaret Morris Lawrence Collection, HSP.

19. The others were Sarah Mifflin, Joseph Richardson, and John Maes. MCC, 720.

20. Records of the Philadelphia Mayor's Court, 1766–1771, HSP. Women's petitioning activities also fell into this category. See Tabitha Myers's inclusion among those who

contributed to community health. These activities knit men and women into a community of shared values—in these cases, the protection of private property and care for the neediest city-dwellers.

Perhaps the most important connections created by urban neighbors were those based on socioeconomic status. Historians have long looked to cities as the seedbed of a class consciousness, particularly among the nascent working and middle classes. Although the distribution of wealth was less unequal during the colonial period than later in American history, families were still distinguished by property and occupation. In city neighborhoods, socioeconomic standing played a role in forming networks of association and cementing ties of friendship. A unique document allows us to examine how this worked.

Beginning in the mid-1750s, North Ward shopkeeper Elizabeth Paschall, who had conversed with the "Country man," kept a record of medical information she collected and dispensed. In this journal, Paschall recorded interactions with a variety of individuals who either contributed to or were the beneficiaries of her medical knowledge, from the man who suffered from kidney stones to the botanist John Bartram. Paschall lived in a house she inherited from her father on the north side of High or Market Street in North Ward, immediately west of High Street Ward. She was a woman of means, owning not only the house in North Ward but also a "country seat," called Cedar Grove, in what is now part of Philadelphia's Fairmount Park. Paschall was widowed in 1742, and remained unmarried until she died in 1768.[21]

As a lay medical practitioner, Paschall exchanged information with a wide variety of people, including relatives, neighbors, and servants.[22] Her mother, siblings, and cousins, as well as her children, appear time and again as the sources and recipients of her medical knowledge. Her servants were more often her patients, but several provided Paschall with information about their experiences and those of their relatives.

Neighbors held a unique position between those with whom one chose to associate, such as friends, and those one could hardly avoid, such as relations. Paschall could not control who lived next door, down the street, or in the alley behind her, but she chose her "neighbors." The ways in which Paschall identified her relationships with the people in her

petitioned for a regulation of the nightly watch in the Northern Liberties. Scharf and Westcott, *History of Philadelphia*, vol. 1, p. 261.

21. Information on Elizabeth Paschall is drawn from William Wade Hinshaw, *Encyclopedia of Quaker Genealogy* (Ann Arbor, Mich., 1936–1950); and Fiske Kimball, "Cedar Grove," *Pennsylvania Museum Bulletin* 118 (1928): 5–24.

22. Karin Wulf, "A Marginal Independence: Unmarried Women in Colonial Philadelphia," (Ph.D. diss., Johns Hopkins University, 1993), 41–45.

neighborhood suggests that women like her understood their position within their communities in terms of socioeconomic identity and position. Neither household members nor relations by blood or marriage, neighbors anchored and defined the physical and conceptual space this urban woman inhabited. Elizabeth Paschall's categorization of "neighbors" is significant for several reasons. Chief among them is that her neighborhood was clearly defined. With only one exception, the people she specifically identified as neighbors came from North Ward or High Street Ward, and probably from the southern sections of each, nearest to Market Street.[23] For example, David and Mary Deshler, both of whom Paschall identified as "neighbors," lived at the southern corner of Church Alley and Third Street. Paschall's friend the midwife Mary Sindry was a long-term resident of North Ward.[24] Thomas and Elizabeth Lawrence, the upholsterers, lived on the other side of Second Street, in High Street Ward. A good portion of her other friends also lived in that area or in Mulberry Ward, where Paschall's sister-in-law and sometime business partner Mary Coates lived. For example, Paschall's friends Eliza Wartnaby and her husband, William, a blacksmith, lived in Mulberry Ward, as did John Knight, a baker, and his wife.[25]

Although many of Paschall's neighbors were "middling sorts," tradesmen and artisans rather than merchants, they were also for the most part on solid financial ground.[26] This fact indicates that "neighbors" were not just the people who lived close by but those who shared common interests and socioeconomic status. Paschall's interactions with her servants suggest an intimate relationship, but they also recognized distance and station. Phebe Robinson told Paschall about her father's dreadful bout with "Costiveness" (constipation), which was so painful "that he Could not help Continually Crying out." Phebe found it "Dreadfull to hear his Cryes." Finally, "an antient woman" advised him to drink a warm mixture of "hoggs Lard & . . . Mallasses." Paschall valued Phebe Robinson's story so much that she recorded the information in her "receipt book." Yet, she identified the source as "our Phebe." Similarly, Polly Webb was "our Polly Webb" and Nancy Donaldson Park was "our Nancy Donaldson that maryed Joseph Park."[27] By identifying her servants in this way,

23. Mathias Bush was rated in 1756 in Walnut Ward. Possibly he moved either before or after Paschall described him as a neighbor.
24. Sindry (also Lindry) was rated as a taxable in North Ward from 1756 through 1774.
25. All appear on the 1756 tax list.
26. This is based on information from the 1756 tax list, which muted differences among taxables' wealth among the lowest groups. Paschall's "neighbors" were rated above these questionable lower categories.
27. Paschall Receipt Book, 20, 41, 43, 21, CPP.

Paschall also emphasized her own position in relation to them. Similarly, her identification of "friends" and particularly of "neighbors" implied a unity of interests and experiences. Paschall found neighbors in those who shared both a community of place and a community of interest.

Paschall and her neighbors were also property owners whose voices could legitimately be joined with other householders. In 1743, for example, the property-owning members of the southern North Ward enabled the construction of Church Alley. Paschall, her brother-in-law John Reynell, and ten other men and women signed a release backing Joseph Fox's sale of a lot 66 feet by fifteen feet, which would become the alley.[28] From the earliest days of her widowhood, Elizabeth Paschall took on the duties of property ownership and the concomitant "neighborly" connections it implied. That the property she owned had been willed to her by her father rather than her husband underscored her independent position in the community and her independent capacity, indeed obligation, to be "neighborly."

How would someone like Rachel Draper, who was not of the same economic group as the wealthy Paschall, have entered into such a neighborhood? Who would have constituted her neighbors? Two factors worked to make women like Draper "neighbors" even to those who possessed far greater wealth. First, communities of interest overlapped with communities of place. Draper was a Quaker. Within her own neighborhood, she found common ground with a number of other Quakers, and her daughters attended the Quaker school located just around the corner. Second, daily exchanges fostered by close quarters created opportunities for new communities of interest among neighbors. Economic exchange was particularly important in this respect. The identity that work offered, as well as the exchanges it entailed, could make neighbors of those who lived nearby.

WOMEN'S WORK AND THE URBAN ECONOMY

Women's work was vital to Philadelphia's economy, but the extent and range of this work has been particularly hard to uncover. Scholars who study the occupational structure of early American cities have had to rely on sources that mask the work of women and other economically marginal groups, including laboring men, servants, and slaves. As Richard Oestreicher has noted, the Philadelphia of 1800 according to many of

28. "Release of lot . . . ," Charles Morton Smith MSS, vol. 4, no. 33, HSP.

these sources was "a very strange place indeed," for it appears that merchants, shopkeepers, and other such white-collar workers comprised 42 percent of the labor force. Of course, the city's eighteenth-century labor force looked nothing like this. Rather, Philadelphia was "a much more plebeian place with a minority of the prosperous and propertied surrounded by armies of servants and dressmakers, carters and dock hands, shoemakers' apprentices and journeymen bakers."[29] In short, the city was dependent on goods and services provided by laboring men and women. But the remaining inventories of merchants' goods, the records of indenture, and even tax records that nominally recorded occupations paid little attention to recording women's work in any systematic way. Thus sources have in some measure "hidden" women's work.

In addition, eighteenth-century culture was ambivalent about the meaning of women's work in general and about the economic contributions of domestic work in particular. *Present for an Apprentice: or, a Sure Guide to Gain both Esteem and Estate* circulated widely in the Anglo-American world. In Philadelphia, Benjamin Franklin printed the fourth edition of this book of advice for young, working men embarking on life's journey in 1749. The author cautioned that young men of the laboring sort should consider marriage an expense, rather than a financial gain, as "the portions, received with wives, pay so large an interest, by the increase of family expenses, that in the end the husband can hardly be said to be a gainer."[30] Of the economic benefit of women's labor, there was no mention.[31]

Although some source materials reflect the eighteenth-century elision of the significance of women's economic contributions, it is clear that women's work was both ubiquitous and necessary. A common assumption is that widows, who were the majority of unmarried women, were reliant on their inheritances.[32] A husband's estate formed the bulk of a widow's wealth, and thus her own economic condition was utterly dependent on the state of his estate at his death and then on the provisions

29. Richard Oestreicher, "The Counted and the Uncounted: The Occupational Structure of Early American Cities," *Journal of Social History* 28 (Winter 1994): 355–356.

30. [Sir John Barnard], *Sir John Barnard Present for an Apprentice: or, a Sure Guide to Gain both Esteem and Estate . . .* (Philadelphia, 1749), 65.

31. On the value of domestic work, see Jeanne Boydston, *Home and Work: Housework, Wages, and the Ideology of Labor in the Early Republic* (New York, 1990); and Claudia Goldin, "The Economic Status of Women in the Early Republic: Quantitative Evidence," *Journal of Interdisciplinary History* 16 (Winter 1986): 375–404.

32. Lisa Wilson, "A 'Man of Business': The Widow of Means in Southeastern Pennsylvania, 1750–1850," *WMQ* 44 (January 1987): 40–64. See also the exchange between Wilson and Deborah Gough in "Communications," *WMQ* 44 (October 1987): 829–839.

of his will. There are two problems with this assumption. The first is that it portrays widows as peculiarly financially dependent. In fact, economic interdependence, not independence, was the rule in this period. Men as well as women relied on inheritance and on transfers of wealth rather than strictly on accumulation through income. If anything, women aided men in this respect; the laws of coverture guaranteed men access to any property their wives possessed at marriage and gave them rights to their wives' earnings during the marriage. Men from George Washington to the famously "self-made" Benjamin Franklin prospered through this legally mandated transfer of wealth. The second problem with assuming that inheritance was widows' sole source of income is that it casts women as only passive recipients of wealth, rather than generators of wealth. A widow's inheritance, after all, was the product of her own as well as her husband's capital and labor. In addition, many widows who inherited subsequently increased their holdings through investment or through income-producing occupations.[33]

The urban economy gave women more options for producing income or supplementing their capital than did strictly agricultural regions. Although widowhood often meant a difficult economic predicament, some female entrepreneurs flowered financially after they were widowed. Their experiences suggest that, as for men, familial, friendship, and economic connections helped them establish small businesses. Born in 1707, Hannah Breintnall was a little like Deborah Franklin. Mrs. Franklin often kept shop and accounts for her husband, but while Benjamin Franklin lived a long life during which Deborah was the distinctly subordinate partner in his ventures, Hannah Breintnall's husband died, leaving her to make her own way financially. She took up the most common occupations for female entrepreneurs: keeping a shop and tavern. During the early 1750s, Hannah Breintnall was the proprietor of the Hen and Chickens Tavern on Chestnut Street, and by the mid-1750s, she was making a fairly good living. Then she decided to change her occupation and opened an optician's shop, where she sold spectacles "of the finest Crystal . . . set in Temple, Steel, Leather or other Frames" and other optical aids, such as magnifying glasses and telescopes. This business, along with significant rental income, strengthened Breintnall's financial condition considerably. In 1767, her wealth was assessed at £30, which placed her among the top 10 percent of taxables assessed that year. After she died in 1770, Breintnall's estate was assessed at £161. Among her possessions were items of shop inventory, including "93 spectacles of sundry

33. Wilson, "A 'Man of Business,'" 57–59.

sorts & sundry cases," "20 silk watch strings," "99 thimbles," "4 shoe-makers hammers," and "a servant girl's time for 3 years."[34]

Hannah Breintnall was not unusual. She married, bore children, became widowed, managed businesses and finances, and provided for her family. The typical picture of the colonial entrepreneur and provider assumes his masculine gender.[35] But many women like Hannah Breintnall, some more and some less successfully, acted independently to support themselves and their families. Widows could rarely afford to be passive guardians of their portion of a husband's estate, and many did not remarry. It was clear to many widows that they would have to take on the financial responsibility of their own and their family's care.

Women who never married—even those from middling or wealthy families—often had to generate more wealth than they inherited because fathers most often passed real property to sons but gave cash or other personalty, often in the form of marriage settlements, to daughters.[36] Spinsters' work was usually directly related to their lack of inherited resources and their need to support themselves. Rebecca Rawle was the widow of Francis Rawle and inherited much of his considerable property and businesses.[37] At the same time, Francis Rawle's aunts, Rebecca and Elizabeth, were operating a small dry goods shop and eking out a living. These two spinsters, despite their family's privileged socioeconomic standing, worked largely because, while they probably inherited a bit, that bit required supplementing.

Constables' Returns for 1775 do not specify the occupations of most women heads of household. But, most women whose occupations were recorded by the constables came from the middling and lower sort.[38] The records also suggest that female heads of household rarely did do-

34. The tax assessor for Philadelphia's Chestnut Ward in 1756 assessed her taxable wealth at £16, which placed her squarely in the middle ranks of the city's taxables. Advertisement quoted in Frances May Manges, "Women Shopkeepers, Tavernkeepers, and Artisans in Colonial Philadelphia," (Ph.D. diss., University of Pennsylvania, 1958), 53–54, 76; will and estate inventory of Hannah Breintnall, W-1770 #409, PDW; Book O, 541, HSP.

35. Thomas Doerflinger, *A Vigorous Spirit of Enterprise: Merchants and Economic Development in Revolutionary Philadelphia* (Chapel Hill, 1986).

36. On inheritance practices in early America, including sex differentials, see Carole Shammas, Marylynn Salmon, and Michael Dahlin, *Inheritance in America from Colonial Times to the Present* (New Brunswick, N.J., 1987), chaps. 1–3.

37. Rawle's tax assessment for 1767 was £280, surpassed that year by only one other widow, Mary Masters. On Rebeca Rawle's assumption of her husband's ferry license, see MCC, 687.

38. Tax records from the 1750s through the 1770s confirm these patterns. In 1756, 31 percent of women among the lowest 30 percent of taxables had discernable occupations, as did 5 percent of those among the top 10 percent. In 1772, despite different taxation methods, these figures had changed very little. At that time 29 percent of women among

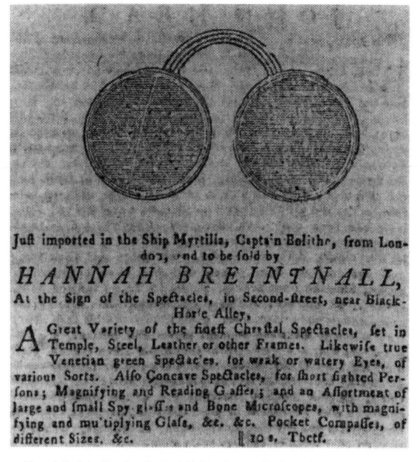

Just imported in the Ship Myrtilla, Captain Bolithr, from London, and to be sold by

HANNAH BREINTNALL,

At the Sign of the Spectacles, in Second-street, near Black-Horse Alley,

A Great Variety of the finest Chrystal Spectacles, set in Temple, Steel, Leather or other Frames. Likewise true Venetian green Spectacles, for weak or watery Eyes, of various Sorts. Also Concave Spectacles, for short sighted Persons; Magnifying and Reading Glasses; and an Assortment of large and small Spy-glasses and Bone Microscopes, with magnifying and multiplying Glass, &c. &c. Pocket Compasses, of different Sizes. &c. ‖ 10 s. Thctf.

4. Hannah Breintnall's advertisement for her shop goods, *Pennsylvania Gazette*, December 28, 1758. Courtesy of The Library Company of Philadelphia.

mestic work for pay outside their own home. The largest group of women whose occupation was noted was retailers, including a bookseller, seven dramshop or tavern operators, nine hucksters, and forty-four shopkeepers. Women who found employment in a smattering of craft occupations included a baker, a distiller, a glover, three mantuamakers, one sievemaker, a soapboiler, three spinners, one tailor, one tinker, and an upholsterer. Among women in service jobs, there were three boardinghouse

the lowest group, and 5 percent of those in the highest group, had occupations. Wulf, "A Marginal Independence," 95.

keepers, an innkeeper, one laborer, one midwife, six schoolmistresses, and two washerwomen. Tax records confirm that the largest number of women were employed in retail work, but that women also worked in service and craft occupations.[39]

Women's occupational opportunities were more restricted than men's for several reasons. Women were less likely to get specialized training in a craft or skill than were men. Female servants, for example, usually were trained only in "housewifery." Strictly limited access to capital prevented most women from creating businesses on their own, with the exception of some retail establishments headed by wealthier women. Widows of tradesmen were sometimes able to continue in their husbands' work, but other women had a hard time entering trades. Perhaps most importantly, the close association of domestic labor with women made it difficult for them to do other kinds of work, simply because whatever the size or economic status of their household, they were responsible for child care and housework. This labor, which was so critical to the functioning of the household economy, left women little time and energy to apply to another occupation. Thus, women who needed income—that is, the majority of married women as well as the vast majority of unmarried women—looked to work that could be fitted around other obligations and used their domestic skills.

Women's work in the eighteenth-century city can be divided into two broad categories: gender-specific work, primarily domestic labor, and nongender-specific work that both men and women performed. Shopkeeping and other mercantile activity, trades, and unskilled labor were all primarily male preserves in which some women could find employment. A degree of gender segregation appeared, however, even within such occupations as retailing or artisanal work.

Among gender-segregated occupations, domestic service was the most significant and visible source of employment for women. Cleaning houses; growing, butchering, preserving, and cooking food; making, repairing, and laundering clothes; caring for children—all of these were tasks that kept women moving in and out of the house and at close quarters with their neighbors. For poorer families, it was deemed both more appropriate and more economical for women to perform such tasks

39. Of the 425 women who were taxed between 1756 and 1774, 29 percent had nondomestic occupations that can be discerned from the assessments, constables' returns, licenses, newspapers, or other sources. Sixty percent of those women (75) were shopkeepers, and a number of these women had second jobs: six as tavernkeepers, two as milliners, and one as a brazier. Twenty-six percent of the taxed women were tavernkeepers, and 22 percent were employed in other occupations, including baking, bonnet making, chandling, innkeeping, teaching school, sieve making, and wine making. Wulf, "A Marginal Independence," 88–89.

themselves at home. The work required long hours and a strong back. Water for laundry and cooking had to be fetched from a pump. Although urban women did not have to go very far to get water, they still had to haul many gallons a day.[40] Caring for apprentices, servants and slaves, or boarders was also part of women's domestic labor in families of tradesmen or artisans. Even for merchants or others whose work brought income to the family without requiring extensive household labor, the value and extent of domestic labor was enormous.[41]

Female servants performed a large portion of this work. In colonial American cities, as in Europe, domestic service was an increasingly important part of the changing urban economy and reflected the growth of middling classes. In the American South, where domestic work was performed largely by enslaved women, white servants were rare. In the North, however, particularly in mid-Atlantic cities, a variant of the European pattern prevailed. Domestic household servants were not simply the preserve of the rich and titled but became a critical part of the household economy of the middling classes.[42] Whereas in a merchant's home servants would perform purely household tasks, in the home of an artisan a "maid of all work" would lend a hand in the workshop, then contribute to the household tasks of cooking, cleaning, and sewing.[43] In Chestnut Ward, one of the smaller, central, and wealthier areas of Philadelphia, 38 percent of households hired servants, most of them adult women. In East Mulberry Ward, populated by more modest households, servants were still important; 15 to 20 percent of households there employed female domestic servants.[44]

40. Philadelphia's plentiful water pumps are described in Carl Bridenbaugh, *Cities in Revolt: Urban Life in America, 1743–1776* (New York, 1955), 106, 296. On the acquisition of water and household work, see Bridget Hill, *Women, Work and Sexual Politics in Eighteenth-Century England* (New York, 1989), 107–111.

41. On the types and difficulty of housework for women in eighteenth-century England, most of which would apply to colonial Americans, see Hill, *Women, Work and Sexual Politics*, 103–124.

42. In eighteenth-century French cities, middle-class families hired an increasing percentage of the servant population. Cissie Fairchilds, *Domestic Enemies: Servants and Their Masters in Old Regime France* (Baltimore, 1984), 14; Sarah C. Maza, *Servants and Masters in Eighteenth-Century France: The Uses of Loyalty* (Princeton, N.J., 1985), 266–277. For Philadelphia, see Carole Shammas, "The Female Social Structure of Philadelphia in 1775," *PMHB* 107 (January 1983): 80–81.

43. D. A. Kent, "Ubiquitous But Invisible: Female Domestic Servants in Mid-Eighteenth Century London," *History Workshop* 28 (Autumn 1989): 119–120.

44. 1775 Constable's Return, PCA. See also Carole Shammas's reconstruction of the female population of Chestnut and East Mulberry wards in "Female Social Structure," 69–83. In East Mulberry in 1775, 9.4 percent of households employed hired servants, 85 percent of whom were female; 17.3 percent of households employed bound servants, about 50 percent of whom were female. Roughly 16 percent of households then employed female servants.

Servants could be either indentured or hired for a day, a week, or a year. Female indentured servants came primarily from three groups. The first were adult women who signed indentures before departing Europe or upon arrival in America in order to pay for their passage. Captains of ships from England, Ireland, and Germany would advertise their wares in the newspaper, listing servants alongside Irish beef, Scotch herring, and other goods. In the spring of 1773, for example, Captain William McCulloch invited those customers who were interested in servants to come view them individually on board his ship. Adults such as Rachel Walker, who was then indentured to Philadelphia merchant Walter Shea Walker, generally signed indenture contracts for four to seven years.[45] The second type of indentured women were poor girls bound out by the city or by their parents. Indentures could provide some training as well as bed and board. The majority of girls bound out by the Guardians of the Poor from the 1750s were quite young, ranging from just a few years old (it was not uncommon to see girls bound out at age four or five) to their early teens.[46] Almost half of the girls contracted to masters and mistresses in Philadelphia were entitled to an education, although usually just enough so they could "read and write," under the terms of their contract. A third category of indentures was made privately, apprenticing girls and boys to specific trades. It is not possible to estimate the size and character of this population, although more boys than girls were trained for trades. Families also sent children to relatives' households in exchange for their care and training in a marketable skill.

Over the eighteenth century an increasing percentage of indentured servants were women, and waged servants became more common. While women were a growing proportion of all indentured servants (constituting roughly 30 percent of all indentures signed in the early 1770s, up from 15 percent in the 1740s), indentured servitude was in decline. The changing nature of the city's economy made the flexibility of hired workers more appealing to employers.[47]

The kinds of domestic work that servants did depended on the type of

45. Sharon Salinger, "'Send No More Women': Female Servants in Eighteenth-Century Philadelphia," *PMHB* (January 1983): 29; Salinger, *"To serve well and faithfully": Labor and Indentured Servants in Pennsylvania, 1682–1800* (New York, 1987); see also the Records of Indentures, 1771–1773, HSP.

46. Between 1751 and 1757, for example, the Guardians of the Poor bound out girls (to masters and mistresses in the city only) for periods ranging from six years and nine months to twenty-four years and nine months. The range was generally related to age, with indentures generally expiring at age twenty-one, although for African-American girls, the age was higher (probably twenty-five). Guardians of the Poor Memorandum Book and Indentures Made, 1751–1797, PCA.

47. Salinger, "'Send No More Women,'" 31–32, fn. 7; Salinger, *"To serve well and faithfully."*

household in which they worked. Female servants in elite households often worked alongside their mistresses, who undertook burdensome domestic labor themselves. Hannah Callender, for example, regularly hired women to do washing and nursing, but did a great deal of sewing, ironing, and gardening herself.[48] According to the diary of her sister Elizabeth Drinker, Mary Sandwith ironed, a tedious chore. Hired servants could be expected to perform any range of tasks and to be flexible about accepting different assignments. Housework, then as now, encompassed a diverse set of tasks, and servants' contributions to the household naturally depended on the means, needs, and occupations of their employer. In many cases servants were not a luxury but an economic necessity. Tavernkeeper Peter Paris, for example, employed two women; doubtless their tasks included cleaning and provisioning the tavern. Skinner Jacob Shriener was not a wealthy man, but he employed a hired woman. He and his wife had six children ranging from one to sixteen years old. The servant would have had to assist Mrs. Shreiner in the formidable task of caring for and outfitting a family of nine on a meager budget. Shopping, cooking, child care, and a modicum of cleaning were among the chores that kept her day very long and full.[49]

Some kinds of domestic work were quite specialized, and servants were not pressed into performing them. Rather, women were hired specially to perform such jobs. One was whitewashing, or the regular painting of interior walls.[50] A perennial task, white-washing was left to women hired for the occasion. Hannah Griffitts asked a cousin for a reference when the woman she usually employed for this work was unavailable. Griffitts then sought further reassurance. "[Can I] have any Dependence on the negro woman thou mentioned to me, as a good white washer[?]," she wrote. "I never (before) knew such a difficulty to get one." When Griffitts was finally able to contract for this work, she reported that "the old woman has plastered & Whitewash'd the little Hut," her Norris Alley home.[51]

Work that was seen as feminine was often linked to domestic skills, specifically to providing care and personal services for others. Chief

48. Susan E. Klepp and Karin Wulf, "Cultural Crosscurrents: Quaker Marriage and Constrained Sensibility in the Eighteenth-Century Delaware Valley" (paper presented to the Philadelphia Center for Early American Studies, May 16, 1997).

49. For the Paris and Shreiner households, see the Constable's Return for East Mulberry Ward, 1775, PCA.

50. Whitewashing was seen to have some hygienic value. Hill, *Women, Work and Sexual Politics*, 118.

51. Hannah Griffitts to Margaret Morris, n.d; and [2nd] Hannah Griffitts to Margaret Morris, n.d., Howland Collection, Box 3, folder 2, QC.

among these were nursing, midwifery, and mortuary work. Nursing seems to have been a specialized skill, but it also commingled with midwifery and laying out the dead. In an era when doctors were just beginning to acquire formal training, medicine was often administered by lay persons. Nurses were not simply women who happened to care for the sick, however. They were addressed as "Nurse," and some specialized in infant care, others in infectious diseases.[52] The Pennsylvania Hospital for the Sick Poor used doctors who contributed their time, but paid a regular staff consisting of an apothecary as well as a "Steward, Matron, Nurses, Servants, & c."[53] Matron Esther Weed died in 1767 after serving the hospital for seven years "in so conscientious and careful a Manner, as to give great Satisfaction to the Managers, Physicians, and all others concerned for the Prosperity and Usefulness of the Institution."[54] The Overseers of the Poor and the Almshouse Managers regularly hired and paid for nursing care for expectant and postpartum mothers. In April 1758, the overseers paid Mary Pane "ye midwife for her deliv[ering] 2 wom[en]." In the same month they paid Catharine Denny and Hannah Cott for nursing children, and Precilla Cowley for nursing and "laying out" (preparing for a funeral) the body of Elizabeth Hixon.[55]

Midwives such as Mary Pane were always in demand. The earliest newspaper obituaries include this affectionate notice of January 1730: "Yesterday was interred here the Body of Mary Bradway, formerly a noted Midwife . . . . aged just One Hundred Years and a Day. Her Constitution well wore to the last, and she could see to read without Spectacles a few months since."[56] Despite increasing use of schooled physicians, midwives seem to have found regular, constant employment. The College of Philadelphia and the Pennsylvania Hospital began to train and employ doctors in the mid-1750s, and more Philadelphia physicians travelled to elite European medical schools for their education. The pioneering obstetrical practice of Dr. William Shippen and the expansion of his practice to include elite patients such as Elizabeth Drinker suggests that the process of usurping midwives' autonomy was underway. Yet

52. Hannah Callender Sansom discussed her smallpox nurse, as well as her children's infant nurses and wet nurses. See entries for January 1758 and November 1769 in the diary of Hannah Callender, APS.

53. See the accounts of the Pennsylvania Hospital, *PG*, February 23, 1769 and February 21, 1771.

54. Ibid., January 8, 1767.

55. In April 1758, the Overseers of the Poor paid women four times for nursing. "City of Philad:a for Disbursements for the Poor" for 1758, Christopher Marshall's Diary "B,", HSP. Manges addresses mortuary work in "Women Shopkeepers, Tavernkeepers and Artisans," 111–112.

56. *PG*, January 6, 1730.

midwives seem to have maintained large rosters of patients and to enjoy high esteem.

Even women who, later in the century, chose to have doctors rather than midwives deliver their babies hired nurses for their newborns. Breastfeeding was a matter of choice for elite women; Elizabeth Drinker nursed her own children until her doctor insisted that she quit, whereas her friend and school-fellow Hannah Callender Sansom sent her children out to a wet nurse. After nursing her son Henry for almost eight months, Drinker reported that she turned him over to "S. Oats, whose Breast he willingly suck'd."[57] Wet-nursing supplied poorer households with some extra income, perhaps at a critical moment when a woman was prevented from income-earning activities by virtue of recent childbirth. Mrs. Greenman advertised her availability in 1766, noting that she had "a good Breast of milk, not above a month old." She claimed good references, and was willing to travel to the child's home or to take the child into her own.[58]

Women's responsibility for the attending the dead was both social custom and economic opportunity. Women regularly stayed with women friends who were either sick or in labor, and with friends' children who were sick. Once a person had died, however, professional services were engaged. Some women, like Precilla Cowley, both nursed the ill and prepared the dead body for burial, while other women provided specialized mortuary and funerary services. It is likely that Cowley, who was paid by the Overseers of the Poor, provided comprehensive services because her clients could not afford better. When Quaker Judith Benezet died in 1757, her estate detailed the variety of payments made to women who participated in the final arrangements. The estate paid "sundry expenses for cleaning the house, putting the goods in order for the Vendue [estate auction], & subsistence for ye Maid & Housekeeper 'till all was sold & finish'd." Ann Read was paid for whitewashing the house, Mary Belle for maid service, and Elizabeth Hawksworth for her work as both housekeeper and nurse. In addition, Sarah White made "a shrowd" for the corpse, and Mrs. Hyde provided muslin for the "winding sheet, ribbons & c."[59] Other common services included laying out the dead and attending to the body, both before and during the funeral.[60] Lydia Darragh ad-

57. Elaine Forman Crane, ed., *The Diary of Elizabeth Drinker* (Boston, 1991), vol. 1, p. 163.

58. *PG*, February 27, 1766.

59. Estate inventory of Judith Benezet and Estate Account by Anthony and Daniel Benezet, W1765, #217, PDW.

60. For example, see expenses paid to "Several Women attending the Death" of Ann Stinson, Account of the Estate of Ann Stinson, A1757, #72, PDW; payment of £2 to Ann

vertised in the *Pennsylvania Gazette* that "she intends to make Grave-Cloathes, and lay out the Dead . . . as she is informed a Person in this business is much wanted in this City."[61]

Women found other employment that required domestic skills in a nondomestic setting. Laundry and cleaning public areas, for example, were jobs usually filled by women. In 1723, for example, the Philadelphia Common Council paid Mary Whiteaker two shillings "for sweeping ye Court House & Stalls twice a week."[62] Demand for these jobs increased as the city grew.

Like other laborers, women could expect low wages for such work. Billy Smith has calculated and compared the income and minimum budgetary requirements (for food, shelter, and clothing) for laboring families. He found that even with the extra income provided by women's wages, most laboring families existed on the edge of poverty.[63] The low wages paid to working women contributed to this situation. Although the evidence permits only generalizations, it is clear both that women and men had differential employment opportunities, with more skilled work available primarily to men, and that women were paid from one-quarter to one-half of the wages that men could command for similar work.[64] In urban areas, the greater demand for more specialized skills and trades benefited males more than females, especially because domestic service was women's primary employment. But it appears that when specialized work was called for, wage differentials shrank so that women earned perhaps one-half to two-thirds of the wages that men commanded. Smith offers the example of a married couple employed by the Pennsylvania Hospital during the late 1780s. John Baldwin whitewashed walls and fences for just over five shillings a day. Elizabeth Bald-

---

Perdue from the estate of Lynford Lardner for "laying him out makeing a shroud and tending the berring." Receipt from Ann Perdue, Lardner Family Papers, Box 2, FF 13.

61. *PG*, February 6, 1766, as quoted in Manges, "Women Shopkeepers, Tavernkeepers and Artisans," 112; see also the payment of November 4, 1748, to Grace Dwitte for "laying out & assisting at burial of Samuel Coates," Receipt Book of Samuel and Mary Coates, 1740–1756, Gratz Collection Case 17, Box 3, HSP. For Mary Symonds's funeral in 1773, Darragh also provided funeral clothing of "black Buckles & Buttons." Account of James Reynolds, Executor [for Mary Symonds], W1773, #297, PDW.

62. *MCC*, 232.

63. Smith, *The "Lower Sort,"* 92–125.

64. Gloria Main, "Gender, Work, and Wages in Colonial New England," *WMQ* 51 (January 1994): 49–50; Paul G. E. Clemens and Lucy Simler, "Rural Labor and the Farm Household in Chester County, Pennsylvania, 1750–1820," in Stephen Innes, ed., *Work and Labor in Early America* (Chapel Hill, 1988), 118–119, 142. See also Carole Shammas, "The World Women Knew: Women Workers in the North of England During the Late Seventeenth Century," in Richard S. Dunn and Mary Maples Dunn, eds., *The World of William Penn* (Philadelphia, 1986), 110–113.

win did laundry, cooking, some light housekeeping, and nursing for about half that amount per day.[65]

Unmarried women faced economic pressures particular to their situation. They needed to work, but remunerative employment was scarce. A handful of cases of bawdy house brought before the Philadelphia Mayor's Court in the 1760s and 1770s attest to the unsurprising existence of prostitution in the seaport, but prostitution must have been a last resort. Reported instances of prostitution among poor women increased sharply only after the Revolution.[66]

Domestic service did have some economic advantages, in particular the security of room and board.[67] Unmarried female domestic servants who lived with their employers were provided with food and sometimes with clothing. A regular annual salary of £10 might have compared favorably, at least in economic terms, with the situation of a mistress of a laboring household.[68]

Retailing goods or food and drink provided the next largest group of occupations for women after domestic service. Women accounted for perhaps as many as half of all retailers in the eighteenth-century city, although women's retailing was generally conducted on a smaller scale than men's and was less likely to be combined with wholesaling.[69] Retailing was appealing in part because, as Patricia Cleary has pointed out, it required only a modest investment (depending on the extent of the establishment) and was one that "a woman with few skills could enter."[70]

Over the eighteenth century, retailing became an increasingly viable economic option for women. Retailing increased in importance as imported consumer goods washed over the colonies, a process that intensi-

65. Smith, The "Lower Sort," 92, 112.
66. For example, the case of Susannah Collins in the October 1770 and January 1771 sessions of the Mayor's Court records, 1766–1771, HSP. For prostitution in the late 1780s and after, see Smith, The "Lower Sort," 22–23, 35, 168.
67. Kent, "Ubiquitous But Invisible," 115–117.
68. For annual wages paid to female domestic servants, see Elaine Crane, "The World of Elizabeth Drinker," PMHB (January 1983): 28. Drinker paid servants in the 1760s and 1770s between £61/2 and £12 annually. Other accounts suggest an average of £10. Phineas Bond paid Alice Russell this annual rate in 1769. Phineas Bond Receipt Book, HSP. Lynford Lardner paid Sarah Antrobus £12 annually in the mid-1750s. Lynford Lardner Journal D, Lardner Family Papers, HSP. These wages may be compared with the budget shortfall for laboring families, even at full employment; see Smith, The "Lower Sort," 92–125. Sharon Salinger points out that the average length of employment for servants in the Drinker household was three and a half months, but this may say even more about the appealing flexibility of domestic employment. Salinger, "Send No More Women," 34–35.
69. Patricia Cleary, "'She Will be in the Shop': Women's Sphere of Trade in Eighteenth-Century Philadelphia and New York," PMHB 119 (July 1995): 184–185.
70. Ibid., 195.

fied at mid-century.[71] Benjamin Franklin commented on the replacement of his plain earthenware bowl and pewter spoon with china dishes and silver cutlery; his famous remark is emblematic of the transition that was occurring within middling households. Not only were these goods available in newly enlarged quantity and variety, but they were in demand by a new clientele.[72] As Franklin noted, his wife wanted the plate in their household to be as nice as their neighbors', and thus the Franklins' collection of such goods grew as their "wealth increased, augmented gradually to several hundred pounds in value."[73] Goods conferred or designated status in a new way, and the proliferation of goods allowed middling families access to the kinds of status items previously available only to the very rich.[74] This increase in the availability and variety of consumer goods prompted the elaboration of retail establishments, and of the activity of shopping itself. Shops developed advertising and display strategies designed to appeal to consumers. Retailers and consumers calculated quality, affordability, and fashion. The act of shopping, and of making these calculated choices, placed consumers in a newly elevated role.[75]

Women were well positioned to take advantage of both the retailing and the consumption of goods.[76] Provisioning the household (or "marketing") was long thought to be a feminine responsibility, but the new dynamics of class and status competition were specifically gendered.

71. For a general account of this economic transition, see John J. McCusker and Russell R. Menard, *The Economy of British America, 1607–1789* (Chapel Hill, 1985); on the impact of the influx of such goods, see T. H. Breen, "An Empire of Goods: the Anglicization of Colonial America," *Journal of British Studies* 25 (1986): 467–99.

72. Lois Green Carr and Lorena Walsh, "Changing Lifestyles and Consumer Behavior in the Chesapeake," in Cary Carson, Ronad Hoffman, and Peter Albert, eds., *Of Consuming Interests: The Style of Life in the Eighteenth Century* , (Charlottesville, Va., 1994), 59–166.

73. Benjamin Franklin, *The Autobiography and Other Writings*, ed. Jesse L. Lemisch (New York, 1961), 92.

74. Cary Carson, "The Consumer Revolution in Colonial America: Why Demand?" in Carson, Hoffman, and Albert, eds., *Of Consuming Interests*, 528.

75. Richard L. Bushman, "Shopping and Advertising in Colonial America," in Carson, Hoffman, and Albert, eds., *Of Consuming Interests*, 233–251, esp. 246–251.

76. Accounts against the estate of Lynford Lardner, a cousin of the Penns who held a number of provincial positions, give some idea of how extensively wealthy Philadelphians relied on women retailers for good and services. Lardner died in 1774, and accounts for the several years before his death show that he and his wife, Katherine Lawrence Lardner, were regular customers of at least three female establishments, including most prominently the Steels. In 1773 and 1774 the Lardners' account with Rebecca Steel amounted to almost £40; their purchases from Mary Steel in October of 1774 alone totaled over £46. Accounts of the Lardner estate with Rebecca Steel and Mary Steel, Mary Eddy, and Anne Sparks, Lardner Family Papers, Box 2, FF 13. Other accounts of the Lardners, especially with Rebecca Steel, can be found in Box 2, FF 8, Accounts and Memo Books, 1754–1756 and 1763–1764, Box 2, HSP.

The demonstration of gentility that the acquisition of even cheaper versions of luxury goods afforded the middling sort required very specific enactments of masculine and feminine qualities. Thus, tea drinking, an eighteenth-century phenomenon that scholars often point to as the quintessential ritual of consumption because of the accoutrements it required, was undertaken by both men and women and yet was a highly feminized ritual; women controlled the tea table.[77] So, too, shopping was becoming feminized. Both men and women shopped, but the increasing attention of retail advertisements to their female clientele and to items of female apparel testifies both to women's importance as consumers and to the importance of feminine attire to class aspirations.[78] As retailers, women could tap the very market they helped comprise. Female shopkeepers among the middling or elite whose customers came from the same networks of association could help determine fashions.

Philadelphia retailing experienced these eighteenth-century trends with peculiar force, in large measure because of the size of the city and its long tradition of extensive merchant activity. Retailing depended on wholesale availability of goods. The city was an entrepot, where goods from the countryside surrounding Philadelphia were exchanged for finished goods arriving from abroad. In a single day, merchants might trade in wheat from the country and fine cloth from France. By the end of the colonial period there were three sizable markets in the city, the largest being the central market on High (later called Market) Street. Market stalls were the largest single repository of small-scale rural production, while the merchants' wharfs received imports.[79] City auctions, or vendues, were held regularly to dispose of goods ranging from estate items to goods damaged in trans-shipment.[80] Retailers both large and small looked to this range of suppliers for their wares.

Retailing varied widely. At the lower end of the scale, hucksters purchased cast-off, second-quality, damaged, or otherwise less desirable merchandise, which they then hawked through the streets. Peddlers who moved from the city out into the countryside with imported or finished goods were regulated and licensed, and were almost exclusively male. Hucksters who carried goods through the city were usually female. Hucksters could acquire goods for their baskets from a variety of sources.

77. On the significance of tea drinking, see David S. Shields, *Civil Tongues and Polite Letters in British America* (Chapel Hill, 1997).
78. Bushman, "Shopping and Advertising."
79. On the expansion of public and private wharves, see Scharf and Westcott, *History of Philadelphia*, vol. 3, pp. 2151–2158; on the growth of shipping between 1750 and 1775, see Doerflinger, *A Vigorous Spirit of Enterprise*, 173–178.
80. On vendues see Doerflinger, *A Vigorous Spirit of Enterprise*, 171.

Fresh food was brought into the city from the hinterlands on market days, when the city's famously extensive markets could be overwhelmed with meat, cheese, butter, and produce, along with homespun cloth and other hand-made goods. Any goods left by the end of the day, unsold or of inferior quality, were sold to hucksters, who might make a tiny profit by reselling them. Walking outward from the city center, hucksters might find customers among those who could not get to the market—for example, housewives confined at home who had no servants to make their purchases, and laboring families for whom a trip to the market or first-quality fresh goods were a rare luxury.

One step up from hucksters were those women who operated tiny shops within a corner of a room, sometimes buying only small lots of goods to sell at a time. Two women retailers who operated shops in Philadelphia during the 1750s illustrate the range of goods that shopkeepers might carry and the range of success they might enjoy. Neither approached the success of the wealthiest shopkeepers, male or female. Ann Stinson died in 1757 after a modestly successful career. Her estate was valued at just under £80, half of which comprised inventoried goods that appeared "In the Shop." The small size of her retail inventory and the small variety of goods she carried suggest she catered to a working population. She had a silver watch in stock, but she carried mostly rough goods, including thirty pairs of "oznabrigs [sic] & cheque Trowsers," twenty-five woolen jackets, and some "coarse stockings." For housewares she carried some pewter dishes and some "potts & pans."[81]

Compare Stinson's shop goods with those of Ruth Webb, who died just two years later. In partnership with Mary Taggart, Webb had created a much more specialized and successful retail establishment. Webb and Taggart carried a large variety of imported spices such as cloves, various liquors including rum, and a variety of fine fabrics. Webb, who was single, had emigrated from Ireland during the mid-1730s. After working as a servant, she began a partnership with Taggart, another Irish immigrant. By 1756, the two were jointly assessed for taxes and were listed as residing in Mulberry Ward. Webb's will named Taggart and shopkeeper Mary Coates as executors of her estate. After specific legacies to two relatives and four other female friends (including £50 to Coates), Webb willed the remainder of her estate—probably over £400—to Taggart; of course Taggart also received her half of their joint shop goods. While Ann Stinson apparently conducted a very modest business, serving people who could afford only work clothes, Webb and her partner served a

81. Stinson was taxed for £12 in 1756; Inventory of Ann Stinson's Estate, A1757, #72, PDW.

[145]

wealthier clientele. Webb and Taggart, selling more luxurious imports, also made a better living.[82]

Webb and Taggart benefited from an essential component of any entrepreneur's success: their connections. Webb's personal, religious, and economic associations with the natal and marital families of Mary Coates helped her establishment. As a former servant in the home of Coates's step-father, the wealthy Quaker merchant Samuel Coates, Webb may have worked in his business. When she started her shop with Taggart, the two Quakers counted on assistance and patronage from their friends and co-religionists. Coates's merchant husband, Samuel, purchased small items from Webb; Coates herself bought goods at auction in partnership with Webb and Taggart.[83] For women, drawing on networks of association was good business; indeed, it may have been the only way to do business.[84]

A handful of elite women shopkeepers operating during the third quarter of the eighteenth century, including Mary Coates, Magdalena Devine, Elizabeth Paschall, and Mary and Rebecca Steel, were very prosperous and carried extensive inventory. For these women, as for many successful male entrepreneurs, economic, social, kinship, and religious circles all overlapped; shopkeeping mixed easily with their other social obligations. They shopped in each others' stores, bought wholesale goods together, and circulated within the same group of friends. Coates, Paschall, and Rebecca Steel bought goods together at vendue for sale in their respective shops. They purchased goods from each other when these items were not available from their own inventories, or when one happened on a better wholesale price. In 1749, for example, both Paschall and Steel purchased tea from Coates.[85] While Rebecca Steel's shop was on Elizabeth Drinker's regular shopping circuit, Drinker also visited the Bristol baths in the company of merchant Magdalena "Dilly" Devine.[86]

---

82. Ruth Webb was received by the Philadelphia Quaker Meeting on January 29, 1737 (10th month 29, 1736), from Lurgan, Ireland. Albert Cook Meyers, *The Immigration of the Irish Quakers into Pennsylvania, 1682–1750* (Swarthmore, Pa., 1902), 295. Will of Ruth Webb, L175, 1759. Patricia Cleary notes that Webb was a servant in the home of Mary Coates's stepfather, Samuel Preston. Cleary, "She Will Be in the Shop," 194. Taggart also came from Lurgan Meeting, in 1750 with her husband, John. Hinshaw, *Encyclopedia of Quaker Genealogy*; Roach, "Taxables in Philadelphia." It is possible that Webb and Taggart were sisters; a list of Quakers living in Philadelphia between 1757 and 1760 lists Taggart in Mulberry Ward as living with a sister.

83. Receipt book of Samuel Coates, 1740–1756, Gratz Collection, HSP; Cleary, "She Will Be in the Shop," 194.

84. Doerflinger, *A Vigorous Spirit of Enterprise*, 45–69.

85. Mary Coates Receipt Book, 1748–1759, Coates-Reynell Collection, HSP.

86. Crane, ed., *Diary of Elizabeth Drinker*, on Rebecca Steel 7–8, 18, 25, 31, 48, 70, 76, 417; on Devine at the baths, 162–165.

These women retailers also shared more than friendship; Coates and Paschall were sisters-in-law, and the Steels—Rebecca and Mary—were mother and daughter.[87]

Retailing was an increasingly viable option for women in the colonial city, as consumer demand increased and could support specialization as well as a wide range of retailing venues. Related employments, such as millinery, which combined both craft work and retailing and which also depended on both availability of fine imports and consumer demand for fashionable items, expanded as well.

Opportunities in tavernkeeping also increased as the city grew. A few gathering spots, such as the London Coffee House on Market Street, catered to a new clientele of merchants who wanted not just to exchange business talk but to engage in the whole realm of discussions that were beginning to constitute public discourse. The only women welcomed there were servers. Most taverns, however, remained gathering spots for neighbors or work-fellows, providing modest provisions and drink at a low price. For many women like Rachel Draper, tavernkeeping was a reasonably good prospect. Peter Thompson found that women tavern-keepers had smaller establishments than those kept by men, but that the percentage of women in the field remained significant throughout the colonial period.[88] In 1773, for example, of the 170 Philadelphia publicans recommended by the Mayor's Court for tavern licenses, forty-three, or one quarter, were women.[89] In some areas of the city there were as many or more female as male publicans. Tavernkeeping could also be combined with shopkeeping in a single establishment, which may have made it especially appealing to women.[90]

A few women worked in the specialized trades supported by the urban economy, especially after mid-century. Most probably had husbands or

87. Mary Langdale married Samuel Coates, the brother of Elizabeth Coates Paschall. I speculate that Rebecca Steel was the mother of Mary Steel for the following reasons: Rebecca Steel named Mary Bartram as an executor of her will, in a codicil dated 1783 (Estate papers of Rebecca Steel, W1784, #380, PDW). Mary Steel married Isaac Bartram in the North District Quaker Meeting, in 1779. Bartram was son of the botanist and disowned Quaker, John Bartram. Bartram was also fifty-four years old at the time (it was his second marriage), and thus it is conceivable that he married a child of Rebecca Steel's marriage of the late 1730s. The two had no children, and Mary Steel Bartram died in 1818. This would also explain why, although other evidence suggests a significant business operation, Mary Steel was never taxed or appeared on a Constable's Return; until her marriage, she was living in her mother's house.

88. Thompson, "A Social History of Philadelphia Taverns."

89. "List of Public Housekeepers, recommended July Sessions, 1773," HSP.

90. Ruth Webb, discussed above, also held tavern licenses for at least the three years prior to her death. See the list of Philadelphia tavernkeepers for 1755–1757 in Richard Peters's cash book, AM 2988, HSP.

fathers who had worked in these trades and perhaps already established workshops that they could assume. Among those who made their living supplying the many seaport industries, Sarah Jewell continued the rope-walk her husband had founded, making ropes and rigging so necessary for shipbuilding, while Hannah Beales continued her father's fishnet-making business.[91] No guilds kept women in Philadelphia from pursuing trades, as they did in early modern Europe, but the complications of acquiring apprentices and gaining master status were enough to discourage most women. Informal pressure from loose organizations of artisans may also have had a hand in discouraging women's participation in such trades.

Marriage, Work, and Community

Almost all urban women worked either within or outside the home, and most probably worked for pay. Economic connections that women made while working could be a critical outgrowth of other relationships, particularly among family members, but the formation of economic networks was also a fundamental opportunity provided by neighborhood. Unmarried women were in a unique position to take advantage of such opportunities, and they did so largely out of economic necessity. The better-developed a woman's personal networks of association were, the better her chances were of surviving economically in the city. Women, like men, accessed credit and debt networks by exercising familial and economic resources, including personal relationships. Because women had much less access to trans-Atlantic credit, however, wholesale merchant work was an unlikely pursuit, whereas local credit networks such as those employed by small retailers were much more readily available. Women such as the shopkeepers Mary Coates, Elizabeth Paschall, and Rebecca Steel, who purchased wholesale goods together, used their familial and neighborhood connections to further their economic goals.

By forming economic connections and networks, work also became an important source of personal and community identity. Although not all workers identified with their work, many did, especially those whose work enmeshed them in networks of obligation and association. Contributing to the association of work and identity was the way that work became bound up with the community's needs and one's place in the community.

91. Manges, "Women Shopkeepers, Tavernkeepers, and Artisans," 97–115; on Sarah Jewell see 102.

The Wishart family of High Street Ward, headed by Ann Wishart, Sr., provides a good example of the ways in which work identity, family ties, and economic networks became intertwined with community position. After the death of her husband, Wishart supported herself and her children through her trade as a tallow chandler. Scattered evidence attests to their success. For example, Ann owned an enslaved man who helped with the chandling business. In addition to a workshop, the Wisharts also operated a retail shop, attached to their home at the corner of Front Street and Pewter Platter Alley, where they sold their wares.[92] The family lived close together, and Ann's daughters echoed their mother's strong attachment to entrepreneurial work. One daughter, Jemima Edwards, was a widowed shopkeeper who lived just a few blocks away from her mother and two unmarried siblings.[93] Thomas and Ann, Jr., were apprenticed as chandlers and continued to live with their mother in High Street Ward until her death in 1770. They stayed together, jointly administered their mother's estate, and practiced her trade. In the 1770s Thomas was elected tax assessor of High Street Ward, a recognition of the family's position in the community. Two other clues point to the importance of Ann Wishart's identification with her craft. First, she apprenticed not only her own two children to the trade, but at least one other young person at the request of the Quaker Meeting.[94] The Meeting's recognition of Wishart's trade suggests the significance of her work to her position within the community. Second, when Wishart penned her will, she identified herself as "Ann Wishart Sen. of the city of Philadelphia in the Province of Pennsylvania a tallow chandler."[95] This sort of declaration was unusual for women, and points to the centrality of Wishart's occupation to her identity within the community.[96]

92. The Wisharts had long-standing accounts to provide candles for the Norris family. Norris Family MSS, Family Accounts, vol. 1, pp. 106–123; vol. 2, pp. 2, 3, 18, 30, 39, 55, 66. For the Wisharts' shop, see the references in Ann Wishart Senior's will to the "largest Front Shop," and to the "Implements for carrying on the Chandling Business."

93. Jemima Edwards was a legatee in her mother's will. Edwards's estate inventory of 1768 shows a fairly successful retail operation, with bonds and credits in the thousands of pounds. Estate papers of Jemima Edwards, W1768, #171, PDW. Edwards was rated for taxation in Lower Delaware Ward in both 1756 and 1767.

94. In 1750 the Quaker meeting "allow[ed] Anne Wishart five pounds for taking Samuel Farmer, Apprentice, to learn the trade of a Tallow Chandler." *Abstract of the Philadelphia Monthly Meeting Records (1730–1785)*, vol. 3, p. 184, GSP.

95. Will of Ann Wishart, W1770, #342, PDW. Like many other Philadelphians, she reached out to neighbors to witness her will; Thomas Wharton lived two blocks away, and Caleb Jones lived just a few houses north of the Wisharts on Front Street. "A Directory of Friends in Philadelphia, 1757–1760," *PMHB* 16 (1892): 222, 229.

96. Among Wishart's High Street Ward neighbors, for example, Joseph Potts did not identify his work, whereas six other men, from merchant to cordwainer, did. Wills of Joseph Potts, 1771, # 371; John Bleakley, 1769, #272; Samuel Cheesman, 1770, #413; William

For unmarried women like the widowed Ann Wishart, longtime residence and an occupational identity were often linked. Philadelphia's tax officials tended to identify women by their marital status instead of their occupation. However, women who headed households over a long period were more often identified by occupation.[97] A small group of twenty-three women were taxed every year between 1756 and 1774. Another fifteen were taxed for eleven or more years, and sixty-six women were taxed for five to seven years. Two features of the most persistent group of twenty-three women taxables are significant. The first is that these included neither the wealthiest nor the poorest among female taxables; most were among the middling group. Furthermore, the tax assessors identified more than half of the most persistent female taxables by occupation.[98] The implications are twofold: an occupation made long-term independence viable, and persistent community position seemed to be the key to acquiring an occupational identity that was recognized, at least by the tax officials.

Residential longevity was a key factor in developing networks. Women seemed to be somewhat better at this than men. In the only area of the city where neighborhood reconstruction is possible, a much higher percentage of women than men were long-term residents. In High Street Ward only 35 percent of men listed on the 1770 Constable's Return reappeared on the 1775 return, whereas 57 percent of women did.[99] These women could become neighborhood anchors, fixtures within their communities and essential components of the dynamic of urban interaction that defined daily life for eighteenth-century Philadelphians. Whereas married women operated within the urban matrix of relationships and networks in many ways defined by their spouse, for some unmarried women, particularly widows and spinsters who became neighborhood anchors, their own occupational identity became just as important. Their connection to the community ultimately came not from their connections

---

Honeyman, 1774, # illeg.; Thomas Lawrence, 1775, #86; James Rickey, 1775, #140. The convention in wills was for women to identify their marital status. This may have been related to their age at the time they wrote their wills, as women seemed to write them quite late. Wishart, on the other hand, wrote hers in 1759 (eleven years before her death), when she was probably still very actively chandling.

97. For a summary of residential patterns among taxable women see Wulf, "A Marginal Independence," 78–80. More than 80 percent of women taxed for more than five years stayed in the same city ward.

98. Occupations were noted for eleven of the twenty-three most persistent taxables; of those who were taxed for between eleven and eighteen years, over half had discernable occupations. Among women who appeared on the tax rolls for six to eight years, less than a fifth were identified with an occupation.

99. Karin Wulf, "Assessing Gender: Taxation and the Evaluation of Economic Viability in Late Colonial Philadelphia," *PMHB* 121 (July 1997): n. 62; 1770 and 1775 CR, PCA.

through a husband or father, but through their own economic contributions to the community. By building individual relationships and networks, they came to have a community position of their own.

CONCLUSION

The pre-Revolutionary city was defined by the interdependencies of its residents. Whether or how urban dwellers defined their own place within this system in class terms, they relied on interlocking networks of association to structure their economic, familial, religious, and political experiences. These networks were composed of men and women whose needs, interests, and wants overlapped in complementary ways. In economic terms, these relationships included wholesale and retail purchasing, rental arrangements, and credit and debt exchanges. In familial and religious terms, these networks created communities of affinity and belief. In political terms, networks of association came to play a larger and larger role in the formation of new identities and actions.[100]

Marital status as well as gender created a context for women's experiences and for women's place in an urban community. Although the economic and political connections of men came to define urban political consciousness in the late eighteenth century, unmarried women entered into these networks in ways that were different from both men and married women. They acted on behalf of themselves as individual contractors of relationships, and on behalf of their families. The most pronounced associative relationships were contracted by working female heads of household. Women such as Rachel Draper were enmeshed in the multiple networks of association, particularly economic ones, that constituted urban community in the eighteenth century.

Unmarried women were vulnerable to poverty. The city provided more occupational opportunities than the countryside, but women still faced difficult restrictions on their work, and many widows bore the costs of caring for children. Without networks of association and support that could help them economically, women often turned to welfare. Sometimes all that their friends could do was place them in the hands of officials.

100. Richard Ryerson and Steven Rosswurm, for example, have traced the formation of radical committees and militias to networks of association that were neighborhood-based. Ryerson, *The Revolution Is Now Begun: The Radical Committees of Philadelphia, 1765–1776* (Philadelphia, 1978); Rosswurm, *Arms, Country and Class.*

[5]

Ann Dunlap's "Great Want":
Poverty and Public Policy

Living in mean housing along Philadelphia's Tun Alley, widowed and pregnant Ann Dunlap suffered severely through the harsh winter of 1761–1762. She was not alone. With the end of the Seven Years War on the American continent in 1760, the prosperity of wartime requisitioning had given way to an economic slump. The combination of economic ills and the cruelly cold weather placed the poorer population of Philadelphia in acute distress. Standard mechanisms for poor relief were incapable of handling either the volume or the character of need in this critical period. The skyrocketing prices of essentials required to stave off starvation and freezing, particularly firewood, made needy a whole new population.

Dunlap's neighbors, Margaret Trotter and a woman known to us only as Isaac William's wife, appealed on her behalf to one of the ad hoc, privately organized charitable groups formed to ameliorate the emergency conditions of that winter. The two women described Dunlap as "Lying in & in great want." The Committee to Alleviate the Miseries of the Poor, a private relief organization of "Gentlemen" with "benevolent intention," borrowed key practices from public relief officials, such as determining need and merit through a system of recommendation. Once the committee acknowledged an individual's neediness, it issued a numbered ticket for wood, blankets, or stockings (the principal provisions). This system was designed "to prevent Impositions of ill designing persons who may feign a pretence of Indigence" so that "a just & equal distribution may be made among those who are real objects of charity."[1] Through the offices of the Committee to Alleviate the Miseries of the Poor, Trotter and Williams were able to deliver to Dunlap two blankets and a pair of stockings. It was not much, but those items might save Dunlap and her baby

---

1. Accounts and Minutes of Committee to Alleviate the Miseries of the Poor, Box 1 and Oversize #26, Wharton Willing Papers, HSP.

from the cold and keep them from needing more extensive ministrations, such as a visit from the Overseers of the Poor or a sojourn in the city almshouse.

Ann Dunlap's experiences during that terrible winter illustrate fundamental features of urban poverty and poor relief in early America, some familiar to most historians of the period. The regularity of urban poverty and its origins in both personal events, such as a death in the family, and large-scale events, such as price increases, are well understood. A number of scholars have also explored the changing nature of poor relief during the eighteenth century. Relief commonly was provided in two forms: out-relief, in which officials supplied the poor with small sums of money, either intermittently or regularly in the form of pensions, or with specific, necessary goods and services; and institutionalization, in which the poor were confined to an institution and often made to work for their keep. Extensive out-relief was replaced by an almost exclusive reliance on institutionalization in the later eighteenth century.[2]

Historians have observed, but rarely fully explored, the female character of poverty and poor relief in early America.[3] The experiences of Elizabeth Boon demonstrate the range and regularity of women's reliance on relief. In 1751, Boon was an inmate of the almshouse, reported reasonably fit, with two children, "one Joseph Boon at Cohasik, & Daughter at Hanover in the Jerseys."[4] These children may well have been quite young and bound out as a prerequisite of Boon's acceptance into the almshouse. It is unclear how long she remained in the almshouse after 1751, but in 1758 the Overseers of the Poor paid William Keith fifteen shillings for her

2. The most influential work on poverty and poor relief includes John K. Alexander, *Render Them Submissive: Responses to Poverty in Philadelphia, 1760–1800* (Amherst, Mass., 1980); Gary B. Nash, "Poverty and Poor Relief in Pre-Revolutionary Philadelphia," *WMQ* 33 (January 1976): 3–30; Nash, *The Urban Crucible: Social Change, Political Consciousness and the Origins of the American Revolution* (Cambridge, Mass., 1979); and Billy G. Smith, *The "Lower Sort": Philadelphia's Laboring People, 1750–1800* (Ithaca, N.Y., 1990).

3. A large literature has addressed the role of the expansive, interventionist state in perpetuating inequalities between men and women in the nineteenth and twentieth centuries. As Linda Gordon has written, the fundamental achievement of this literature lies in teaching that "welfare as an academic topic or a social issue cannot be understood without particular attention to the situation of women and the gender system of the society." Linda Gordon, "The New Feminist Scholarship on the Welfare State," in Linda Gordon, ed., *Women, the State, and Welfare* (Madison, Wisc., 1990), 30. Few historians of poverty and poor relief in early America have remarked on the significance of women and gender. A recent exception is Elaine Forman Crane, *Ebb Tide in New England: Women, Seaports and Social Change, 1630–1800* (Boston, 1998). See also Robert E. Cary, *Paupers and Poor Relief in New York City and Its Rural Environs, 1700–1830* (Philadelphia, 1988); and Lisa Wilson, *Life After Death: Widows in Pennsylvania, 1750–1850* (Philadelphia, 1992), 59–100.

4. "A List of the Names of the Poor in the Alms House," Box 7A, SMC.

rent.[5] In 1770, she was collecting a widow's pension, which ranged from £5 to £7 per year from a private group, the Society for the Relief of Poor and Distressed Masters of Ship, Their Widows and Children. After six years of this support, a committee was ordered to inquire "very particularly" into her "Circumstances," lest she be spending her meager funds inappropriately, for example, by renting a high-priced house like another woman whom the committee forced to move to cheaper lodgings.[6] Boon's familiarity with both public and private charity exemplifies the ways in which women drew on poor-relief resources at different stages of their lives and the recurrent character of their poverty.

Ann Dunlap's and Elizabeth Boon's experiences also highlight the predominance of unmarried women among the poor and within the poor-relief system and of ideas about gender in shaping both poverty and poor relief. Throughout the colonial period, women comprised a substantial majority of recipients of both out-relief and institutional relief. There are two basic reasons for women's predominance among poor-relief recipients in Philadelphia. First, cultural imperatives and social practices disadvantaged women economically, making them especially vulnerable to poverty. The women who received relief were largely poor as a result of life-cycle and systemic developments, including pregnancies or other medical conditions, that kept them from working, child care responsibilities that hindered their work opportunities, and the low wages women could command. Most of them, like Dunlap and Boon, were unmarried.

Cultural ideals of gender played a critical role in women's poverty and their access to poor relief. Over the colonial period, poor-relief officials were increasingly inclined to connect femininity with dependence and thus with an appropriate posture for relief; they associated masculinity with independence. Officials created a poor-relief system that could accommodate and reinforce these ideas about gender. When they identified women who were not adequately dependent or men who were not adequately independent, officials acted to discipline such transgressions by withholding relief. Thus notions of gender were central both to the production of the population of the poor and to poor-relief operations.

This chapter examines the ways in which public policies dealt with the conditions of poverty experienced by so many unmarried women. A close look, first at the place and treatment of men and women within the system of public poor relief in colonial Philadelphia, and then at the gen-

5. "City of Philad:a for Disbursements for the Poor," 1758–59, recorded at the back of Christopher Marshall's Diary "B,", HSP.
6. Records of the Society for Relief of Poor and Distressed Masters of Ships, Their Widows and Children, 1765–1781, HSP.

dered rhetoric of poverty and dependency, demonstrates the continuing, significant role of gender in the midst of major changes in the conception and enactment of poor relief.

POOR WOMEN AND POOR RELIEF

Until 1766, public poor-relief administration in early Philadelphia consisted of both out-relief and successive institutions built to house the poor. After 1766, a new program of institutionalization restricted poor-relief monies to the "Bettering House," a joint almshouse and work-house, and, in principle, ended out-relief. On the whole, out-relief was the most flexible, appropriate, and desirable form of assistance for women, largely because it could be combined with low-waged or part-time work, and allowed a woman to keep her children. Institutionalization was a last resort, in cases of debilitating illness or advanced age, and was likely to result in the binding out of children.

Pennsylvania's first poor-relief act, passed in 1706, provided for a tax of one penny per pound of assessed wealth for the expenses of the Overseers of the Poor.[7] The public poor-relief process was set in motion when individual Philadelphians notified the mayor that a person without resources was in need. These referrals might come in the form of a complaint, as when Jane Collins informed Mayor Robert Strettel in October 1751 that "a poor man who lodges at her house is very doestitute of every thing necessary to support life and must perish if not speedily relieved." With winter coming, Collins could probably ill afford to keep the man herself. After the mayor received notice of need, he directed the overseers to "inquire into the Circumstances" of the potential aid recipient. The overseers' findings determined whether the individual was suited to the almshouse, deserving of a pension or other out-relief, or required removal to another locale. Like the town clerks of New England, the overseers sometimes sent impoverished folk beyond the town's boundaries or made application to other polities for their care. Usually, however, overseers paid for out-relief, which consisted of small sums of money or specific essential items such as winter firewood, an occasional loan for rent, maintenance for pregnant indigents during their "lying in," apprenticeships for poor children, and burial costs. Poor-relief authorities tried to address the needs of poor Philadelphians, from cradle to grave, through the intermittent and need-specific aid provided by out-relief.

During the early eighteenth century, Philadelphians built three sepa-

7. Peter Parker, "Rich and Poor in Philadelphia, 1709," *PMHB* 99 (1975): 3–19.

rate institutions to house those for whom out-relief, small pensions, or intermittent aid were insufficient. Never intended to replace out-relief, the almshouse built by Quakers in 1717, the city's public workhouse built as a punitive facility in 1719, and the city almshouse built in 1732 all sought to handle the poor who could not care for themselves at all, even with financial assistance.[8] These institutions worked hand in hand with the city's Overseers of the Poor. Out-relief and institutionalization could serve the same constituents consecutively. The needy poor sometimes moved from out-relief pensions to the almshouse as their conditions worsened, or, more rarely, vice versa as they improved. Usually, however, the two forms of relief were designed to serve different situations, which more often than not meant serving different constituents.

Although the early poor-relief records are fragmentary, it is clear that throughout the eighteenth century, the majority of the dependent poor were women. Women outnumbered men among recipients of out-relief, and they appeared in equal or larger numbers in the almshouses. In 1739, for example, twenty-two of the thirty-one pensioners supported by the overseers were women. Thirteen of the eighteen times that the overseers made additional payments in cash or provided wood or articles of clothing, both to pensioners and to non-pensioners, those benefits went to women. Overseers also paid for lodging outside of the almshouse for two poor persons, both of whom were women. Funeral services, including purchasing "winding sheets" to wrap the corpse, grave digging, burial fees, and even liquor to serve the mourners, went three times out of four for the burial of poor women.[9]

By mid-century, Philadelphia's population had changed, but the demography of poverty and poor relief remained much the same. Philadelphia's population had grown to over thirteen thousand in 1750, and the city had experienced its first waves of non-English European immigration. The reports of the Overseers of the Poor for 1751–1752, including a list of pensioners and a sheaf of poor-relief applications, as well as a descriptive list of almshouse inmates for that year, reveal that men and women were in different circumstances and had different requirements for assistance.[10] Women outnumbered men among pensioners, almshouse inmates, and applicants for aid. Most of these men were severely sick or disabled, while most of the women simply lacked financial and fa-

---

8. For more on the building of the almshouses, see Nash, "Poverty and Poor Relief"; Stephen Edward Wiberly, Jr., "Four Cities: Public Poor Relief in Urban America, 1700–1775" (Ph.D. diss., Yale University, 1975).

9. 1739 "Poors Day Book," Gratz Collection, Case 17, Box 4, HSP.

10. The unique confluence of the overseers' reports, the almshouse warden's reports, and petitions to the mayor represents a snapshot of the entire public poor-relief system.

Table 5.1 Men and Women Petitioners for Relief,
1751–1752

Reason	Men	Women
Illness	11	8
Abandonment	0	5
Poverty	3	11
With children	0	7
Total	14	31

milial resources. Very likely as a consequence of these different experiences and sources of poverty, men and women were treated very differently by poor-relief authorities.

Only one-quarter of the women who applied for aid were sick, disabled, or prevented by physical incapacity from working, while three-quarters of the men were (see Table 5.1). A few of the women were legally married, some to jailed debtors and others to men who had abandoned them, but most were not; all lacked the financial advantage of a husband's wages.[11] Among the thirty-one women who petitioned for aid, twenty-six unmarried women labored under familiar conditions of female poverty: they had bastard children, they were sick, or they were old. "Seduced by the promise of Marriage," Elizabeth Humber had found herself "with child by Daniel Spencer." Backed by the testimony of "several credible citizens," she took Spencer to the Mayor's Court in expectation of an order that he provide a maintenance for their child, but apparently he refused to appear. So, when she "hourly expect[ed] to fall into Labour," she became dependent on the overseers. Humber had "behaved well in two different Services," but servitude was no preparation for the expense of bearing and raising a child.[12] Few female occupations, in fact, paid enough to enable women to support children, and the care children required interfered with women's employment. "By reason of her two children," for example, Mary Doyle was "rendered unable to get her living and maintain them." Doyle was a nurse by profession and was "of Unblamable Behavior," but, "having been a Long time out of Employ," she asked the overseers to bind out her five-and-a-half-year-old son. They agreed to do so, but only on the condition that she take a younger

11. Comfort Boyd and Susanna Condon, for example, were both married to jailed debtors. The husbands of Ann Pillets Singer, Mary Driver, and Mary Howell had simply abandoned them. Mayor Strettel to Overseers, November 25, 1751 (concerning Ann Pillets Singer), March 29, 1751 (regarding Howell); August 6, 1751 (regarding Driver), Box 7A, SMC.
12. Mayor to Overseers, December 12, 1751, Box 7A, SMC.

Table 5.2 Men and Women Pensioners, 1709, 1739, and 1751

Year	Men	Women	Total
1709	4	10	14
1739	9	23	32
1751	9	33	42

Note: Peter J. Parker, "Rich and Poor in Philadelphia 1709," *PMHB* 88 (1975): 3-19; "Poors Day Book," Gratz Collection Case 17 Box 4, HSP; "List of Pensioners," Box 7A, SMC.

son with her to New York. Only two weeks after Doyle requested help, her older son was bound to Peter Wistar for fifteen and a half years.[13] Someone like Doyle seemed to require only temporary help. The overseers hoped that helping such women once or twice would prevent them from falling into long-term or permanent poverty. In this case, by taking responsibility for indenturing her child, the overseers helped Doyle restructure her household so she could be self-supporting.

As among petitioners for aid, women predominated among those who received out-relief in 1751–1752 (see Table 5.2). Thirty-three women and nine men collected regular pensions in 1751, in addition to three women who lodged or nursed children for whom the overseers were responsible.[14]

Although many more women than men applied for poor relief and received out-relief, almost equal numbers of men and women resided in the city almshouse. In the same year that women comprised three-quarters of the applications to the Overseers of the Poor for temporary relief and four-fifths of the pensioners paid regularly by the overseers, there were twenty-six female and twenty-four male almshouse residents.[15] At first glance, this parity might suggest some equivalency in poverty between men and women in this aspect of the poor-relief system, but male and female almshouse inmates generally had different reasons for needing help. More men than women came to required institutional care because of illness or disability (see Table 5.3).

Half of the men resident in the almshouse were severely disabled: among them five were "lame," three blind, and two "paralitick." Only half as many women were disabled, and only a few of them were as severely affected as the men. Two women were called "paralitick."

13. Mary Doyle's application for relief, March 15, 1751; Mayor to Overseers, March 16, 1751; Memo of Overseers re. Doyle's eldest son, March 31, 1751: all under William Attwood, SMC.
14. These included Mary Coulton and Ann Neville, each for "a Child she has in keeping." Overseers of the Poor, HSP.
15. List of Almshouse Inmates, 1751, Box 7A, SMC.

Table 5.3 Condition of Men and Women Almshouse
Inmates, 1751

Condition	Men	Women	Total
Illness	1	5	6
Disability	12	6	18
Aged	4	5	9
Fit	7	3	10
Pregnant		2	2
Disorderly		2	2
Unspecified		3	3
Total	24	26	50

Jane Murphy suffered from a "crampd hand & Foot" and Mary Middleton and Honor Gemee had "disordered" eyes. Mary Marrot's daughter was described as "Crazy." Only one man entered the almshouse sick, but five women did.[16] Most of the men assigned to the almshouse were in the most dire circumstances. The characteristics of the almshouse inmates indicate that women more often found themselves in poverty, not because of calamitous loss of limbs or senses, but through a series of misfortunes that meant the difference between a "Maintenance" and institutional help. For instance, women entered the almshouse if they had no where else to bear their children.[17]

The Overseers of the Poor and other relief authorities treated men and women very differently, awarding out-relief to guardians caring for disabled women, or even to the women themselves, and discharging sick men from the almshouse. The Overseers of the Poor often tried to keep disabled or sick women out of an institution. For example, "Crazy" Mary Charton lived in Elizabeth Heany's house at the corner of Chestnut and Second Street, receiving two shillings, six pence a week from the Overseers of the Poor. Some such pensioners were considered incapable of handling their own funds. The overseers paid "Crasy" Bridgit Sullivan's unusually large pension of seven shillings, six pence to Catherine Smith. They also noted that Sullivan's rent was £12 a year, so perhaps Smith was her landlord. Mary Mills was bedridden, and "an Old Woman" received a pension of five shillings on her behalf. Other notes jotted by the overseers indicate that aged or ill female pensioners often maintained their own lodgings (usually in someone else's house) rather than go to the almshouse.

16. This may be related to the opening of the Pennsylvania Hospital for the Sick Poor in 1751. See the discussion below of the Hospital for the Sick Poor.
17. In 1751 two women gave birth at the almshouse.

In addition to the seemingly different standards of health required of men and women for admission to the almshouse, different standards were applied when it came time to release inmates. The almshouse warden who made a survey of inmates in 1751 described twelve men and women as "hearty" or fit, but recommended that only one of the women be discharged. Elizabeth Boon, for example, seemed "fit to do something for her own Maintenance," but the warden did not suggest that she leave the almshouse to do it (although she was discharged some time later). On the other hand, almost every man the warden described as "fit" was slated for release. Tellingly, the warden identified most by occupation. He judged sixty-year-old James Sidbotham, a barber, able to "do for himself" and butcher Jonathan Richards, though "very ragged," "well enough to go out." He assessed Hugh Ross, an "old Taylor," and Gabriel Green, another "old Barber," as in shape to "go out during the summer." Thomas Tanten, "an old infirm lame Butcher," had been in the almshouse since 1748, but the warden thought he nonetheless "yet might phaps do something" for his own keep. The warden simply called Thomas Savory "no proper person for the Alms House." Clearly men who seemed able to support themselves gained the enmity of the warden's pen and an escort out of the institution, while plenty of able-bodied women remained in care.[18]

This evidence shows that at mid-century the practice of poor relief was still largely shaped by the needs of those it served most frequently and in the largest numbers: poor women without spouses. Out-relief served mostly women, because it granted women intermittent aid suitable to their experiences of intermittent poverty. Consignment to the almshouse was reserved for men with serious physical impairment and for women who needed temporary lodging.

After mid-century, in part because of economic crisis, poor-relief practices in Philadelphia underwent significant changes. Between 1765 and 1775, urban poverty reached new heights and new extremes. The depression that followed the Seven Years War brought rising costs for food, clothing, and housing that were exacerbated by attempts to pay off war debt through taxation. Of course, high prices for basic necessities pressed hardest on the city's poor. In addition, high rates of immigration worsened unemployment, further straining the city's poor-relief resources. In response to these pressures, in 1765 the overseers raised the poor tax by two-thirds.[19]

The increase in poverty did not, however, fundamentally change the

18. "A List of the Names of the Poor in the Alms House," Box 7A, SMC.
19. Nash, *The Urban Crucible*, 255–56, 260, 322; Nash, "Poverty and Poor Relief," 14.

character of the poor population. Poor women, mostly without husbands and many with children, still comprised the bulk of the needy poor and still consumed the majority of the Overseers of the Poor's time and money. The most extreme effects of poverty were usually felt in the winter, but even in the overseers' accounts for late August, 1768, it is clear that for women poverty was seasonless. At their weekly meeting, always held at seven o'clock in the evening at the courthouse, the overseers confronted·the problems of eight needy people. Seven of them were women, and four of them were women with children. Fanny O'Brien was familiar to the overseers because they had been dealing with her situation all month. She had a very sick child, was pregnant again, and her husband was "absent." The overseers gave her money three times in August alone. Finally in September, realizing that additional small sums could not support the various needs of O'Brien and her children, the overseers sent them to the almshouse.[20]

With these kinds of situations increasing, additional funds were insufficient to maintain the system of cooperation between the Overseers of the Poor and the Almshouse Managers, and out-relief was all but eliminated. Previously, the overseers had evaluated all applicants and decided which form their relief, if any, would take. After 1766, funding for this process became controversial, and money raised by the poor tax and other means (the overseers had collected fines, for example, for public swearing) was increasingly restricted to paying for institutionalization of the poor.[21]

The change in allocation of public monies was mandated by a shift in

20. August 4, August 11, August 25, September 8, 1768, Minutes of the Overseers of the Poor, 1768–1774, PCA.
21. Traditionally, the overseers had a claim to fines laid by the Mayor's Court for swearing in public, entertaining strangers, chimney fires, and certain violations of city watch regulations. In addition to this fine money, legacies left by philanthropic Philadelphians or property seized or bartered by poor residents in exchange for care accounted for the bulk of the overseers' treasury, and they were quite creative and aggressive in the acquisition of funds from these sources. For example, in 1767 Isabella Edwards signed over her dower right in a house and lot on Front Street. The house was rented to Thomas Williams for £30 a year, and the overseers got one-third of that rental money in consideration of their promise to care for Edwards. Minutes of the Overseers of the Poor, July 14, 1768, PCA. Edwards's daughter Rachel owned the other two-thirds of the house. Rachel brought the matter of a small mortgage still on the house to the attention of the overseers in hopes they would recognize their responsibility for paying a proportionate part of it. They did, and assigned a collector to collar the rent money, paying two-thirds of it to Rachel after deducting her part of the mortgage. The overseers also collected ground rents from a number of individuals as part of bequests or exchanges. In 1768 a June meeting of the overseers reported collecting ground rents on nine properties, including Isabella Edwards's. Minutes of the Overseers of the Poor, June 9, 1768, PCA. In a similar case, Elizabeth Howard (or Havord), died while in the care of the overseers in 1758. Howard's property was then administered by then-Mayor William Plumstead, and soon after the

policy deeming institutionalization the exclusive method for dealing with the impoverished. Perhaps encouraged by the English workhouse movement, and certainly inspired by Benjamin Franklin, a group of philanthropists, most of them wealthy Quaker merchants, proposed building a new "Bettering House" in place of the old almshouse.[22] The Bettering House would be composed of two parts—an "almshouse" for those incapable of working, and a "workhouse"—and would be built as a joint venture between private contributors and the government. Part of the allure of the new institution was the promise that it would be self-sustaining, or at least less dependent on taxes, through inmates' work at such tasks as weaving and picking oakum.[23] In exchange for providing substantial funds to construct the Bettering House, the new managers would receive rights to tax money raised for poor relief, as well as fines and legacies. In essence, the money that had previously funded the activities of the Overseers of the Poor would now be controlled by the managers of the Bettering House, and out-relief would be phased out.[24]

The Overseers of the Poor disagreed with this plan. Part of the controversy about the most efficient way to aid the poor was related to the different constituencies served by the almshouse and out-relief. While the majority of out-relief recipients were and always had been women, almshouse inmates were as likely to be male as female. The overseers cited all the reasons that poor women since the 1730s had preferred out-relief in the form of small sums of money or vital goods (such as firewood) and services (such as midwifery) over almshouse admissions. They snorted at the suggestion that all of Philadelphia's poor were suited to institutional living. First, some could not be put to the kind of work available in the almshouse because of "age, Infirmity, or sickness" but "found means at present to support themselves upon a small pension." Second, moving to the almshouse meant forfeiting a home, neighbors, and perhaps possessions, which would be "cruel" to those who needed only short-term help. The overseers did not explicitly mention pregnant women, but as frequent users of short-term relief they were probably foremost on the overseers' minds. Third, the physical accommodations

---

overseers were collecting rent on her house from Sarah Steward. Minutes of the Overseers of the Poor, 1758, Christopher Marshall's Diary B, HSP.

22. Nash lists the religious affiliations and occupations of the founders in "Poverty and Poor Relief," p. 15 fn. 38.

23. As Nash points out, Philadelphia poor taxes were extraordinarily regressive, raising the least from the wealthiest and the most from those who could least afford them. Ibid., 19–20.

24. Ibid., 19. See also the description of the 1766 law "for the Better Employment, Relief and Support of the Poor, . . . " establishing the new system, in Alexander, *Render Them Submissive*, 88–90.

of the almshouse were inadequate. "In the case of man and wife especially," they reported, the lack of "apartments" suitable for joint lodging was "a great discouragement to many." No overseer, and by implication no Almshouse Manager, could "in discretion" advocate that married couples, no matter what their financial position, live "in a separate state." Lastly, the overseers warned that the poor simply did not like the almshouse. The "wicked & profligate" among them "would rob & steal rather than go in or wd be begging." The Almshouse Managers were dissatisfied with this report of conditions among the poor and demanded that the overseers visit each of their pensioners and encourage them to go to the almshouse. The overseers agreed on the condition that the managers accompany them, but the managers demurred.[25]

The problem was not resolved to the overseers' satisfaction, primarily because the Almshouse Managers now had access to tax money, while the Overseers of the Poor did not. Despite their misgivings, the overseers resolved on June 23, 1769, not to pay pensions or provide short-term aid but only to recommend "proper objects" to the almshouse. Poor women who had depended on the overseers to provide aid during times of crisis were now given an unpleasant choice: the almshouse or nothing. The overseers then referred some needy poor to the almshouse and the new workhouse and, only through July 1769, added some to the list of pensioners. They composed lists of "Real Objects of Charity . . . . recommended to the Mayor as such . . . . obtained orders for Relief at the House of Employment," and "Necessitous Persons to whom small sums were Advanced for their immediate Relief." Tellingly, from March through July 1768, they now referred twice as many women as men to the House of Employment and gave "small sums" of out-relief to almost three times as many women as men.[26]

Once the Overseers of the Poor quit providing significant out-relief, the new Bettering House was ostensibly the only form of public assistance to the poor.[27] Women still comprised the majority of relief recipients, and now of the institutionalized poor. Between 1768 and 1775, while admis-

25. June 12, 1769, Minutes of the Overseers of the Poor, 1768–1774, PCA.
26. June 23, 1769, and March–July 1768, Minutes of the Overseers of the Poor, 1768–1774, PCA.
27. Intermittent records suggest that the overseers may have continued to provide ever smaller sums of out-relief, and that in fact the Bettering House managers may have come around to doing the same. See the "Accounts of Contributors to the Relief and Employment of the Poor" for May 1773–May 1774, in which small sums or weekly allowances were paid for those "whose Circumstances rendered it less expensive than to be admitted into the House." *PG*, May 18, 1774. See also Alexander, *Render Them Submissive*, 96–98. These sums were small, and the payment of these sums was contested, as the source of revenue for the overseers kept shrinking.

sions to the Bettering House climbed sharply, women consistently comprised 60 percent of inmates. Women were also now more often confined to the almshouse side of the Bettering House and men to the workhouse, suggesting that ideas about who was fit and unfit to work were still structured along gendered lines. Between 1768 and 1775, three out of five women were in the almshouse, while three out of five men were in the workhouse. This division between the almshouse and the workhouse may also reflect women's conditions, such as pregnancy and postpartum, during which they would not be of use in the workhouse.[28]

Philadelphians criticized the Bettering House for its failure to lessen the tax burden and to decrease the number of poor. Not only was poverty not being reduced, as Franklin counseled, by "driving [people] out of it," but new inmates were regularly added to the Bettering House.[29] In addition, residents of the Bettering House were deeply unhappy. The proud announcement in July 1770 that fourteen inmates had been discharged, "several of whom behaved during their residence very orderly and have obtained places of service," was followed by less auspicious developments. The managers began reporting runaways in December of that same year; when their monthly reports specified the sex of runaways, they noted that twice as many women as men had "absconded without leave of the steward." [30] Certainly conditions in the Bettering House were bleak. The punitive aspects of the Bettering House were dramatically different from the "small sums" and pensions that had kept poor Philadelphians, and particularly women, somewhat independent. Women besieged visiting British doctor Robert Honyman, begging him "to try to get them out." [31] He expressed surprise at their desire to escape: he may not have known how many were committed against their will. Between 1769 and 1775, more than twice as many women as men were committed to the Bettering House as "vagrants" or "disorderly strolers." In 1770, the first full year of operation, sixty-one women and only twenty-four men were committed to the workhouse for the mandatory term of one month.[32]

28. Almshouse Managers Minutes, 1768–1775, PCA. Births in the Bettering House were lower than one might expect given the number of pregnant women who had been aided by out-relief programs. Between nineteen and twenty-seven children were born in the Bettering House each year between 1770 and 1775.

29. Nash, "Poverty and Poor Relief," 18, 26–27.

30. The managers of the Bettering House did not consistently report runaways or the sex of runaways, but when they did, women outnumbered men by two to one. For example, the managers reported that ten women and five men ran away from the Bettering House in December 1770. Almshouse Managers Minutes, PCA

31. Quoted in Nash, "Poverty and Poor Relief," 27.

32. Almshouse Managers Minutes, January–June 1771, PCA. On the revision of laws on commitment to the workhouse, see Nash, "Poverty and Poor Relief," 25–26.

Gender, Dependence, and Poor-Relief Policy

Historians often have represented the turn toward institutionalization of the poor as a class-based response to the increasing evidence of systemic poverty, particularly among able-bodied men.[33] The increasing stratification of wealth in the late colonial period, some argue, was representative of the effects of an emerging economic system. Men were unable to get work or to support themselves and their families on the low wages prevailing in the seaport. Wealthy beneficiaries of this economic system looked to punish the poor, describing poverty as the result of a lack of industriousness or moral character. Institutionalization perfectly fitted elites' reasoning, because it could force industry upon the slothful. It also removed the poor from the sight, and perhaps the conscience, of the rich by confining them to a specific geographical and cultural location. This reading of the development of poor-relief policies during the colonial and early national periods fits some aspects of that complicated story. Most important, the prevailing analysis of poverty and poor relief has underscored the critical connection between transitions in welfare policies and the tensions inherent in the nascent identification of class interests in eighteenth-century Philadelphia.

That account of poverty and poor relief in early America, however, misses the consistent centrality of women and gender. Historians often explain women's role in poor relief as simply indicative of adherence to traditional ideas about poverty and relief. Thus, the "traditionally poor" (widows and the elderly), are contrasted with the "new poor" (able-bodied men). This interpretation fails in two respects. First, it treats as unproblematic women's "traditional" poverty and their place in the poor-relief systems. While historians who examine men's changing relationship to poverty and poor relief in the late eighteenth century emphasize that poverty among men was a structural feature of the emerging capitalist economic system, they often fail to stress that poverty among women was endemic to the economic system that had long been the basis of Anglo-American society. Similarly, historians have not adequately contended with the overwhelming evidence that women—especially unmarried women—were the predominant recipients of poor relief throughout the colonial period. The change toward institutional forms of relief had a far greater impact on poor women than poor men.

33. The most influential study is Alexander's *Render Them Submissive*, which emphasized elite desire for social control and concluded that "class division was a vital force in the revolutionary era." (174). Other key texts include Nash, "Poverty and Poor Relief," and Steven Rosswurm, *Arms Country and Class: The Philadelphia Militia and the "Lower Sort" during the American Revolution* (New Brunswick, N.J., 1987), 24–29.

Authorities rescinded out-relief, the form of poor relief that had most often benefited women and that was most applicable for the kind of intermittent poverty that women experienced.

Second, the prevailing analysis has missed the essential role of gender in the rhetoric about poverty, and in shaping the changes in poor-relief policies and practices during the late colonial period. A key factor in the triumph of the Bettering House was the increasing attention paid to male poverty, characterized by a shift in the rhetoric linking ideas of gender and dependency. Those two ideas had become deeply entwined. The cultural connection of femininity and dependence had long been the cornerstone of relief policy and practice, because women's supposed mental and physical frailties, as well as their legal and economic limitations, made them ideal candidates for benevolent care. This pairing was sometimes challenged by relief practices that encouraged women's independence through out-relief, but the rhetoric describing female poverty regularly stressed women's naturally weak and dependent state. Masculine dependence was usually problematic, as demonstrated by the unwillingness of relief officials to aid any but the most disabled men. In the mid- to later-eighteenth century, an increasingly shrill discourse decried male dependence as indolence, and as the source of severe poverty.

Linkages of gender and dependence were critical to officials' evaluations of candidates for poor relief. Officials wanted to know whether an individual should receive assistance from the city or the charity to which he or she had applied, or whether that person should be treated elsewhere (either in another locale or by another group). More importantly, they wanted to know whether a needy individual was deserving of assistance. This assessment required careful attention to the person's background, behavior, and condition of poverty. Usually justices of the peace, representatives of the mayor, or the mayor himself would direct the overseers to investigate candidates for relief and to determine the form that relief, if warranted, should take. In 1751, for example, the Mayor Robert Strettel alerted the overseers to the problems of Martha Adams, who was "represented ... incapable to maintain her Self & Child being very Poor." Strettel instructed the overseers to "inquire into her Circumstances and do for her as you shall find right."[34] Men in charge of private charities, from the Committee to Alleviate the Miseries of the Poor, which aided Ann Dunlap in 1762, to religious and occupational organizations, such as the Society for the Relief of Poor and Distressed Masters of Ship, Their

34. Robert Strettel to the Overseers of the Poor, December 12, 1751, Box 7A, SMC Box 7A, HSP. Strettel usually instructed the overseers to provide such relief "as you shall judge right." Many of his directions, as well as those of William Plumstead, can be found in the Dreer (Mayors of Philadelphia), Society, and Balch-Shippen Collections, at the HSP.

Widows and Children, shouldered similar evaluative responsibilities. They, too, sought to identify "proper objects" of charity, and to distinguish them from unsuitable or undeserving persons.

The basis of official evaluations was conformity to gendered standards of behavior and self-presentation. Officials appraised men with an eye to either serious disability, which prevented work, or age sufficient to retard labor. In other words, men's access to poor relief was always measured by their relationship to productive labor. James Armstrong, for example, was presented to the Overseers of the Poor in 1750 as "an ancient Inhabitant past his labour." Thus he was a resident of the city for sufficiently long to warrant assistance, and he was incapacitated by age. The overseer investigating Armstrong found that he had been "a Ditcher and Sawer of Wood," and gave him "1S for ye present."[35] Armstrong's previous history of work was evidence that he deserved some relief in his old age. However, as we have seen in the case of male almshouse inmates, officials' judgments about men's access to relief could be much harsher than that meted out to Armstrong. The almshouse warden judged even men with serious disabilities able enough to earn something toward their living and thus ineligible for further aid. Interest in keeping poor men working intensified over the eighteenth century. The founding of the Pennsylvania Hospital in 1751 was a turning point, for one of the institution's primary goals was "saving and restoring useful and laborious Members to a Community."[36] Once the Bettering House was founded, it became the obligation not only of the criminal poor, previously installed in the city workhouse, but of all poor persons to contribute to the work of the institution.

With poor women these evaluations were more complex. Officials were interested in women's labor, and in helping women to remain reasonably self-sufficient. But ideas about femininity that stressed women's domestic nature, as well as the social realities shaped by those ideas, mediated evaluations of women and work. Policy-makers and poor-relief officials were well aware of the special nature of unmarried women's poverty, and its foundation in pregnancy, the costs of caring for children, and the shortage of work that paid women enough. Their commitment to gendered ideals of women's roles as household dependents, however, meant that they evaluated unmarried women's adherence to those ideals. Despite the fact that most women who needed poor relief were unmarried, and were not the dependent of an individual man, officials still

35. Wm. Lawrence to the Overseers of the Poor, March 19, 1750, with a note by Sam. Hasell, Society Collection, HSP.
36. PG, June 6, 1751.

looked for indications of dependence or traits associated with dependence, such as subordination and submissiveness. Thus, officials were unwilling to see many men in the position of social dependence, but they were committed to seeing women in that role.[37]

Women who came to the attention of officials with circumstances that fitted these preconceived notions of women's dependence were generally treated somewhat better than those whose situations suggested more independence. These women's cases were also presented to the overseers or to the mayor in different ways. Mary Marrot's appeal to the city for better almshouse conditions, for example, was conveyed in a satirical tone. In 1751 the Overseers of the Poor were told that Marrot and her daughter were "thankful" to be "so well provided for, with all the necessities of Life, and in so plentiful a manner, yet, as they were both brought up in a delicate way," they found that meals at the Almshouse were "generally too gross for their Stomachs." If the overseers should find that Marott's case was "fairly represented," then she should be provided with "tea, Coffee, Chocolate or any thing else that you verily believe will be more agreeable to their palates."[38] Marrot's original request is not longer extant, and perhaps she only mentioned to the almshouse warden or to a visitor that the food was inadequate in quality or quantity. In any case Marrot became the butt of a joke.[39] The city always expected that recipients of their charity would express their appreciation appropriately; in fact, inmates at the Pennsylvania Hospital for the Sick Poor were required to sign a note of thanks upon their discharge.[40] Marrot thus defied several sets of expectations, the most important of which was that women on poor relief display dependent, submissive qualities. Marrot's requests, as well as her invocation of a more genteel background, attempted to invert the relationship of benefactor to recipient. She expressed an expectation of deserving better than what was offered, placing the poor-relief authorities in the position of having displeased her. This was unacceptable.

37. Although the evidence is fragmentary, it is clear that evaluations could also be constructed along racial lines. Among the few women who were deemed fit to be released from the almshouse and likely to work, for example, was Hannah More, a woman who had born a "mulatto child" and was thus seen as "a likely woman and hearty." List of Almshouse Inmates, 1751, Box 7A, SMC.

38. William Plumstead and Edward Shippen to the Overseers of the Poor, March 29, 1751, Box 7A, SMC.

39. The warden noted that Marrot and her "crazy" daughter shared a room at the almshouse, and that Marrot was an "old French woman." Francophobia may also have contributed to the derisive tone of the memo.

40. See number XII, "all Patients, when cured, sign Certificates of their particular Cases, and of the Benefit they have received in this Hospital, to be either published, or otherwise disposed of," in the "Rules . . . of the Pennsylvania Hospital," printed in the *PG*, March 24, 1752.

Contrast Mary Marrot's reception with that of Mary Gough, a petitioner for aid in 1771. Former Overseers of the Poor Samuel Rhoads, Levi Hollingsworth, and Samuel Fisher asked the current overseers to look into Gough's situation, as she had a "large Family & no means of Support." Rhoads, Hollingsworth, and Fisher explained that Gough was "recommended to us [from the] Overseers of the Poor as an honest Industrious, sober woman" who had "depended on the Bounty of a few of her Neighbors (except the small relief she at times obtain'd from us)." Because of her character and conditions, they thought that Gough was "still worthy" of help. Gough was presented in an entirely different posture from that of Mary Marrot. Gough was a mother with young children. She had the support and recommendation of the former Overseers of the Poor and of the neighbors, who found her compelling enough to warrant their charity. She came to the attention of the overseers not through a direct petition, but through the offices of others in the community. This representation of Gough's situation matched officials' need to find women dependent and domestic.[41]

The fallacy of this discourse of evaluation, however, was its detachment from the actual practices of poor relief. Despite officials' denunciations of the unworthy poor and, despite their attempt to enforce explicitly gendered notions of deservedness, the rates and roots of urban poverty often kept them from acting upon these ideals, particularly where women were concerned. As we have seen, officials were ready and willing to turn men out of the almshouse if they could be expected to care for themselves at all. In some cases, these expectations were clearly unreasonable, but the deep connection between men and productive labor, as well, no doubt, as the availability of work—even if it was dismally unremunerative—encouraged Philadelphia poor-relief officials to turn men back to the streets. Very few women received such harsh treatment. Mary Gaskall, for example, was an accused thief and assailant, but she still commanded the attentions and relief of the Overseers of the Poor. Over several years between 1768 and 1771 she was twice tried at the Mayor's Court, but received help from the overseers when she became sick. In January 1768, Gaskall was accused of stealing from George Knorr.[42] Brought

41. See also the case of Ann Matthews, denied assistance in 1751. Matthews had no children, and she also came to the city authorities directly, without an intermediary. Her petition was denied after the overseers reported that they did not "find the above person proper object." Box 7A, SMC.
42. January 1768 session in the Docket of the Mayor's Court of Philadelphia, 1766–1771, January 1768 session, AM 30353, HSP. Gaskall's alleged victim, Knorr, was indicted for assaulting Jacob Maag in 1772. "Philadelphia Court Records," SMC.

before the mayor and his court, she pleaded not guilty but was indicted. A jury found her not guilty (although she had to pay court costs). Three years later, Elizabeth Boyer claimed that Gaskall assaulted her.[43] There is no record of the outcome of that appearance, but the overseers did note that in July 1768, only six months after Knorr accused her of stealing, she was so ill and so poor that she was a candidate for the House of Employment. The managers recognized that she was too ill to be moved and so paid Elizabeth McClure fifteen shillings for Gaskall's upkeep.[44] Gaskall was certainly not the only person whose need, rather than her character, was evaluated. The magnitude of urban poverty, especially among women, usually exceeded the desire and ability of authorities to distinguish between worthy and unworthy women. Their sex alone, and, more importantly, the authorities' association of femininity with dependence, warranted aid for women. Therefore, rather than conclude that Mary Gaskall's brushes with the law and the contentious relations with her neighbors, which resulted in theft and assault, made her unworthy of relief, officials provided aid to meet her needs.

Poor-relief officials relied on the idea that women were innately dependent. This notion undergirded Anglo-American patriarchy as inscribed in law and custom. But poor-relief authorities also understood women's "dependence" to be economic in origin. Women's material deprivation made them socially dependent. Thus poor-relief authorities were often working back and forth between the ideology and the material reality of women's dependence. They daily dealt with the socially rather than naturally produced effects of women's condition. Authorities were well aware of the difficulty that women faced in raising children alone. Far from hidden, the challenges for poor women of carrying, bearing, and caring for children was occasionally a very public spectacle. On an August morning in 1734, for example, a poor woman made her way to the Quaker Meeting House at the corner of Philadelphia's Market and Second streets. The *Pennsylvania Gazette* reported that she "was found in Labour in the Great Meeting House Yard." After she had been "deliver'd there of a Boy," the Overseers of the Poor ordered her "convey'd away in a chair . . . to a more convenient Place."[45]

Newspaper notices of abandoned children also reminded Philadelphians of the difficulties that poor mothers faced. In September of 1751, for example, a "child of about two months old, supposed to be a Molattoe,"

43. Docket of the Mayor's Court of Philadelphia, 1766–1771, January 1771 session, SMC.
44. Minutes of the Overseers of the Poor, 1768–1774, PCA, entry for July 28, 1768.
45. *PG*, August 1, 1734.

was found in an alley near the house of the prominent Quaker Edward Shippen.[46] The Overseers of the Poor asked city residents for their help in identifying the mother so that she could be charged before the magistrates. Another notice in 1756 pointed out the lengths to which a woman might go to relieve herself of the economic burden of children. While traveling out of the city, Elizabeth Colbert had agreed to give her daughter, Mary, to "some person near Brandiwine meeting house, on the road leading from Philadelphia to Lancaster." The stranger on the road had offered to take Mary on as a servant until she came of age, but wanted a two-month trial period before an indenture contract was signed. If after two months time both parties were pleased, Mary would be returned to Philadelphia "in order to get her bound." Colbert leaped at the chance to place her daughter. She was so eager that she failed to acquire either the name or the residence of the obliging stranger. After more than two months without a word about Mary or about her indenture, Colbert described herself as "very uneasy" and thus "obliged to enquiry in this publick manner."[47] In 1768 the overseers took little William Miller to the alms-house after neighbors reported that his mother beat him. When the same neighbors reported that she also left a much younger child home all day "without any victuals and quite Naked," the overseers stormed the house in Biddle's Alley and took the second child to the almshouse.[48] The public birth in 1734, Colbert's notice of her missing daughter in 1756, and the removal of two children from the custody of the working mother in 1768 all testified to the pressures that poor women with children confronted.

Alice Harper's story was particularly distressing. On June 18, 1768, Mrs. Ann Flint applied to the Overseers of the Poor for aid. Seven weeks earlier, Alice Harper had left her infant boy, Matthia Graf, in Mrs. Flint's care. Harper promised to pay Flint nine shillings a week for the short time—"four days or a week at farthest"—that she planned to be "in the Country." After duly nursing the child for six weeks more than arranged, Flint began to worry "that the said Harper intended to leave the Child upon her Hands." Flint wanted the overseers to send the child to the almshouse and to reimburse her for her time and expenses and suggested that the overseers sell at auction any goods Harper had left in her rented

46. Ibid., *PG*, September 26, 1751. On Edward Shippen, see Jean Soderlund, *Quakers and Slavery: A Divided Spirit* (Princeton, N.J., 1985), 37, 197; Frederick B. Tolles, *Meeting House and Counting House: The Quaker Merchants of Colonial Philadelphia, 1682-1763* (Chapel Hill, 1948). For examples of other notices of abandoned children, see *PG*, for February 18, 1755, November 8, 1764, January 15, 1767, April 23, 1767, May 12, 1768, January 13, 1773, and June 28, 1775.
47. *PG*, March 4, 1756.
48. Minutes of the Overseers of the Poor, Sept. 8, 1768, PCA.

rooms at George Plum's house. The overseers sent a committee to inventory Harper's belongings, probably in hopes of securing funds to offset the costs of Matthia's care. "On Searching a Cloaths Press they found an old Bundle, but as it did not appear fit for their inspection, Mrs. Plum took it down in the Yard, and on examining it found therein the bones of a child tyed up in a White Cloth, or Hankerchief." This discovery was reported to the coroner, who ordered an inquest held that evening. The coroner was of the opinion that the dead child had been "tied up in a quilt or petticoat . . . untill the flesh was entirely consumed." The jury declared the manner of death unknown. The next month the overseers reported £11 as the "nett proceeds of Alice Harpers Goods, sold at Publick Vendue."[49] Women like Elizabeth Colbert and Alice Harper, who left their children in others' care, illustrate the desperation of some poor mothers. Whether they indentured their children or tried to support them through a patchwork of economic strategies, poor mothers' responsibility for children was the most substantial factor in the economics of their household. The length of indentures made by the Guardians of the Poor suggests the very young age at which children were apprenticed; the poorer they were, the younger they left home for apprenticeship.[50]

These women's stories provided unsettling public testimony about the difficulties that poor women regularly faced. With children to care for, and without husbands or partners, these women were stark reminders of the social costs of the legal, cultural, and economic compact of coverture. That compact suggested that women exchanged their independence for the material care provided them by a benevolent patriarch. Poor women, the vast majority of whom came before poor-relief officials either unmarried or separated, confronted that ideal with the reality of material deprivation. Sometimes that deprivation was the result of misfortunes such as illness or disability, but women often became poor by doing the very things defined as inherently feminine, such as having and caring for children. The cultural construction of gender in this period, which emphasized the essential dependence of women, was in large measure responsible for producing female poverty.

The reality of female poverty made it very difficult for poor-relief officials to enforce their ideas about gender and dependence, at least as far

49. This incident was recorded in the Minutes of the Overseers of the Poor, June 11, 1768, and July 28, 1768, PCA.

50. Of two "mulatto" girls bound by the Guardians of the Poor in the 1750s, for example, Hester (no last name given) was bound for just over twenty-one years, while Abigail Rice was bound for just over twenty-four years. Their racial identity guaranteed that Hester and Abigail would be bound for longer terms than was usual for white children. Guardians of the Poor Memorandum Book and Indentures Made, 1751–1797, PCA.

as women were concerned. Pulled both by a desire to see women as behaving in an appropriately feminine way and by their own obligation to provide for the materially deprived, the authorities often had to serve the latter at the expense of the former. Thus women such as the accused criminal Mary Gaskall were treated relatively benignly by the system, while men with even considerable infirmity were deemed unsuitable candidates for relief.

The stories of impoverished married women also undermined the conventional linkage of gender and dependency. The cases of Mary Cooper and Comfort Boyd illustrate the inverse dependencies that developed with poverty. Struggling to maintain her disabled husband, Mary Cooper broke her leg in 1751. Although they "hath paid rents and Taxes during the above time and never had any Complaint," their combined conditions led them to petition Mayor Robert Strettel for relief. The Coopers had lived in Philadelphia for "thirty years and upwards During which time they . . . Behaved Themselves honestly and justly." Their mutual disabilities left them without the means to "purchase Even a loaf of Bread." Strettel was moved by the Coopers' plea and perhaps their "honest" poverty and ordered the city's Overseers of the Poor to inquire into the situation. If the overseers should find their situation to have been fairly described, Strettel thought they would "do well to relieve them."[51] In this case, Mary Cooper's husband was probably a financial liability. For most women, however, a husband's absence meant the difference between the margin of poverty and destitution. Comfort Boyd's husband languished in jail for debt after a summer bout with "favour and ago" (fever and ague), while his wife pleaded with the city authorities for aid. Repeating the phrase "your poor petitioner" eight times in a one-page petition, Boyde stressed the illnesses of her three children and the likelihood that without some assistance in either providing for her family or releasing her husband, she would "become a town Charge."[52] What else was she to do? With a missing husband and three small and sick children, she could hardly leave home to work. On the other hand, many women saw no other choice.

Unlike most other women seeking poor relief, Cooper and Boyd were both married and reasonably healthy, but they too experienced the trauma of losing a husband's financial support. For many women, that loss was irreplaceable. Without the employment opportunities available

---

51. Petition of Robert and Mary Cooper, January 24, 1752, Box 7A, SMC.
52. Petition of Comfort Boyd, January 15, 1752, Box 7A, SMC. Overseers for Philadelphia and Moyamensing had some difficulty in determining whose responsibility Boyd was, but it appears that her petition for poor relief was favorably received.

to men and very often with children to care for and, in Cooper's case, a disabled husband as well, women had to rely on the intermittent assistance provided by the Overseers of the Poor through small pensions, goods, and services. The institutional solution was not always practical. Nor did it adequately address the short-term needs of poor women. After 1769, women like Cooper, Boyd, and countless others were condemned to the House of Employment or the streets. As the admissions records of the almshouse and the workhouse show, many chose the latter and were then unwillingly committed to the former.

Philadelphians acknowledged the problem of female poverty and its complex relationship to the ideology of innate female dependence through two other public policies: warnings out and taxation. Warning out dependent paupers who had no legal claim to residence saved money, and removing poor women was an important savings, for not only were poor women numerous, but poor women were also much more likely than men to have dependent children or to be expecting children. As a consequence, authorities moved much more frequently to warn women out of the city.[53] Another example of attempts to remove poor women comes from the court system, in which women who were unable to pay their fines were much more often than men ordered to leave the colony.[54] The threat that pregnant women could pose to the city's pocketbook was clear. For example, over the months between April 1758 and March 1759, thirteen poor and pregnant women received poor relief. A few needed

53. In Philadelphia, women were far more likely than men to be sent or removed from town; men were more likely to be assisted. A rough count shows that of the ten men and twenty-four women who were given funds to leave Philadelphia, or whose passage was paid, only two men were directed to leave the city (sent or turned out), while seven women were (sent or removed). Several other women were passengers in conveyances of people who collected their fares from the overseers, or possibly were accompanied by deputies or sheriffs. Accounts of the Overseers of the Poor, 1758–1759, in the back of Christopher Marshall's Diary "B," HSP. On women and warnings out in New England, see Ruth Wallis Herndon, "Women of 'No Particular Home': Town Leaders and Female Transients in Rhode Island, 1750–1800,'', in Larry D. Eldridge, ed., *Women and Freedom in Early America* (New York, 1996), 269–289.

54. The Mayor's Court, a court which adjudicated minor criminal cases including felony stealing, almost always assigned fines as a part of punishment. Very often convicted criminals would languish in the workhouse, unable to raise the money to pay their fines and gain their release. Poor convicts submitted countless petitions to the mayor and his Common Council, hoping for a remission of their fines. The council often remitted poor women's fines on the condition that they secure a bond for their debt and leave the colony. Men, too were ordered to leave, but not in the same numbers. In considering petitions from men, the council noted that "whilst they remain in Confinement they can have no means of raising the money." MCC, for October 3, 1752, 561. The council never took a similar view of a female convict's ability to pay fines through money raised by her labor.

only food or cash; most needed medical attention. Philadelphia's overseers paid for nursing care for all but one pregnant woman who came to their attention. Nursing during the postpartum "lying in" was in greater demand than even midwifery.[55] Mary Mackinary gave birth in late April 1758; throughout the next month she received firewood and cash as well as nursing care. Similarly, the following February the overseers awarded Mary Dawson a weekly pension of five shillings for the four weeks following the birth of her child. Such women represented a great expense. Not only did they require money and services, but also their children gained legal residence if they were born in Philadelphia and thus would be eligible for poor relief. The overseers tried to "convey mary neal out of town" by giving her three shillings, but unfortunately for them, she must have been in an advanced state of pregnancy. The account notes the three shillings given to Neal on December 23; just six days later Granny Pauling submitted her bill for nursing Peg Neal during her lying in, and three months later, Neal still needed occasional sums from the overseers.[56]

It might be tempting to credit warning-out practices as expressions of emerging class tensions and increasing poverty rather than of the continuity and centrality of gender to public policies for dealing with the poor, but city officials treated propertied as well as poor women as objects of benevolence. Tax assessors routinely excused women from taxation completely, even when they possessed demonstrable taxable wealth.[57] Assessors also habitually under-assessed the wealth of women who paid taxes. Through warnings-out, taxation practices, and poor relief, policy makers and enforcers walked a precariously fine line between acknowledging the role of dependence in creating female poverty and emphasizing the need to help women because of their "natural" dependence. These policies and practices were essential to maintaining a fractional reality in the fiction of women's essential dependence.

The inability of officials to enforce their ideas about gender and de-

55. Laurel Thatcher Ulrich, *A Midwife's Tale: The Life of Martha Ballard Based on Her Diary, 1785–1812* (New York, 1991), esp. 188–193, describes the "lying-in" period and the role of lying-in nurses as distinct from midwives. It appears that several women paid by the overseers did both kinds of tasks. Mary Pane "delivered" Elizabeth Gibbons (July 29, 1758) as well as two unnamed women and was paid for "laying" several others. But Granny Pauling performed no midwife services, restricting her care to the "lying in." See Overseers Accounts 1758–1759, entries throughout, for Pauling and Pane. See also Judith Walker Leavitt, *Brought to Bed: A History of Childbirth in America* (New York, 1986).

56. Overseers Accounts, 1758–59, HSP.

57. Women who were excused possessed taxable wealth comparable to or greater than men taxed at low levels. Karin Wulf, "Assessing Gender: Taxation and the Evaluation of Economic Viability in Late Colonial Philadelphia," *PMHB* 121 (July 1997): 201–235.

pendence as far as women were concerned may have made them even more committed to enforcing them for men, especially as the rates of poverty climbed after mid-century. Even though the probable sex ratio of the poor, and certainly the sex ratio of the relieved poor, changed very little, authorities began to focus on male poverty. (Historians have followed suit.) Whereas the discourse of evaluation in the earlier period contrasted the "worthy" poor or "proper objects of charity" with the unworthy and the improper, by the 1760s a new language was developing to describe the problems of poverty. Increasingly, authorities and philanthropists contrasted a shocking inclination to "live in Sloth and Idleness" with "industrious" poverty, claiming to find more of the former and less of the latter as the eighteenth century advanced. The "industrious" and the "idle" replaced the worthy and the unworthy as the principal categories of the poor.[58] These new categories, however, largely described different types of poor men, whereas the previous categories had contrasted women ("proper objects") with men (not proper objects).

The construction of institutions to house the poor reflected this sentiment. The Bettering House, with its division between the almshouse and the workhouse, would force the idle into industry. The managers of the Bettering House asserted that the poor would learn the habits of order and regularity that would suit them for work and thus for their eventual climb out of poverty. Good manners, punctuality, diligence, and, of course, the work itself were designed "as well to inure them to Labour, as to contribute to their support."[59] As one Philadelphia writer commented, "A man may be suspected of being deficient in industry, temperance, or honesty . . . who is not possessed after a certain number of years, of a moderate share of property."[60]

The insistent discourse concerning masculine indolence reflected a heightened attention to the presence of able-bodied men among Philadelphia's poor and needy.[61] Certainly the precarious economic condition

58. See Alexander, *Render Them Submissive*, 49–53, and 86–102, for a good description, albeit a very different interpretation than that presented here, of the developing categories of the "idle" and the "industrious" poor.

59. Quoted ibid., 95.

60. "Elector," *Pennsylvania Journal*, October 3, 1781, as quoted in Alexander, *Render Them Submissive*, 51.

61. Public notices of charitable intentions, activities, and philosophies flooded into the newspapers after 1760. Among the many examples, notices of "charity sermons" preached, see the PG, March 10, 1763, December 27, 1764, and March 26, 1772; a "public" evening for the benefit of the poor, January 8, 1767; ad hoc charitable relief societies, January 7, 1761, January 31, 1765, February 7, 1765; religious organizations for poor relief, November 9, 1755; religious organizations for relief of their own ministers and "their widows and children," June 5, 1760, November 27, 1760, March 19, 1761, July 22, 1762.

of working men in the years following the Seven Years War was hard to ignore. The increasing stratification of wealth during the decades before the Revolution benefited merchants and investors while causing economic dislocation and instability for laboring people.[62] Most Philadelphians could see the obvious ill effects of unemployment. One philanthropic group attempted to build a linen manufactory in 1764 to employ those who could not find work, recognizing that "many of them, especially in Winter, are reduced to great straits, and rendered burthensome to their Neighbors."[63]

Philadelphians increasingly emphasized the need to give the right kind of relief to poor men, particularly in the form of hospitalization, which would restore a man to working order, or institutionalization, which would prod him to industry. Women were largely left out of this equation, except insofar as officials, philanthropists, and others posited women's poverty as directly related to the unemployment of their spouses. Despite the fact that most women relieved by these organizations were not married, either because they were widowed or never married, and that the majority of the needy poor were women, officials increasingly focused on the rehabilitation of poor men as a solution to women's poverty. A resistance to appraising the sources and conditions of female poverty accompanied this insistence on male rehabilitation. This resistance was particularly striking in the case of the Pennsylvania Hospital for the Sick Poor, which would not admit poor women with children, "that the Hospital may not be burthened with the Maintenance of such Children, nor the Patients disturbed with their Noise."[64] In an essay appended to the hospital's annual report for 1764, the author opined that while "Of some Kinds of Charity the Consequences are dubious; some Evils which Beneficence has been busy to remedy, are not certainly known to be very

62. This subject has been treated at length in the literature. The best evidence of this stratification is in Smith, The "Lower Sort,", 224–229. See also Nash, "Urban Wealth and Poverty," and Salinger and Wetherall, "Wealth and Renting."
63. Fluctuations in the economy and wages, as well as a detailed comparison with typical household budgets for laboring people, can be found in Smith, The "Lower Sort," 92–125. See esp. pp. 109–112, for a discussion of the contributions of men and women to the household income of laboring families, and the vulnerability of those households to even minor changes in fortune because of illness or unemployment. On the linen factory see "Whereas the Number of Poor, . . . ", as quoted in Alexander, Render Them Submissive, 14.
64. "Rules . . . of the Pennsylvania Hospital," reprinted in the PG, March 24, 1752. Men comprised about two-thirds of the hospital patients. Nash, "Poverty and Poor Relief," 8. In the hospital reports of the numbers and illnesses of patients, pregnancy was rarely listed, suggesting that the hospital was designed largely to address the causes of male unemployment. See the hospital accounts reprinted in the PG for 1764–1775 and the report of July 19, 1765, which stated that the hospital was of importance to the community by virtue of its ability to return the recovered patients to gainful employment.

grievous to the sufferer, or detrimental to the Community," thus implic- itly questioning the benefits of direct poor relief to women. He continued that, instead, "no man can question . . . whether it not be worthy . . . to re- store those to Ease and usefulness, from whose Labours Infants and Women expect their bread."[65]

CONCLUSION

The institutional approach to poverty was a response to the increas- ingly obvious poverty of able-bodied men as well as the continuing co- nundrum of female poverty. An interest in enforcing gendered notions of female dependence and male independence also played an important role in the adoption of institutions as the sole provision for the poor. Bringing together the numerical predominance of women among poor- relief recipients and the significant role of gender in the discourse that shaped poor-relief policies and practices demonstrates how the rising rates of poverty in the late colonial period put enormous stress on the connections between gender and dependence that had previously in- formed poor-relief policies. Although there had never been a perfect fit between femininity and dependence, masculinity and independence (some women who refused to appear before the authorities as appropri- ately dependent had still received relief, for example), now the sheer numbers of the poor made attempts to ensure individual compliance al- most impossible. Rather than distinguish between the worthy and the unworthy, those suited for out-relief or the institution, or as the system's shorthand, simply between women and men, Philadelphia authorities focused more and more on the difference between the indolent and the industrious. These distinctions suited changing ideals of masculinity and of men's relationship to the economy and allowed authorities largely to ignore insistent, and consistent, female poverty, the roots of which were too deeply buried in Anglo-American culture to be uncovered.

The transition to institutionalization was hardest on unmarried women, dogged by economic uncertainty, the regular prey of poverty, and the primary recipients of regular poor relief. Insisting that poor women be committed to institutions was also one way of removing them from the public eye. In the next chapter, we will see how this at- tempted erasure of unmarried women echoed ways in which a reconsti- tution of political culture negated features of propertied women's com- munity positions.

65. "CHARITY, or Tenderness for the Poor . . . ," *PG*, July 19, 1764

[6]

Lydia Hyde's Petition:
Property and Political Culture

In November of 1765 Lydia Hyde joined with five other women shop-keepers, including her sister Elizabeth and her neighbor Magdalena Devine, to sign the resolution of "a general meeting of the merchants and traders" of Philadelphia protesting the Stamp Act and agreeing to forgo the importation and sale of British goods.[1] In endorsing the resolution, Hyde and other members of the mercantile community gave up a sub-stantial source of profits, just as their urban neighbors gave up goods they had come to rely upon, including finished cloth and tea. These nonimpor-tation agreements made and enforced throughout the American colonies proved very effective in combating British ministerial efforts to impose new taxes on the colonies. Confronted with this threat to their increasingly important American market, British merchants withdrew their support from such parliamentary policies.[2] Thus, Lydia Hyde participated in one of the most important political movements of her day. An unmarried business woman of property, Hyde acted as other women in colonial Philadelphia did, to protect her interests by political intervention.

Like the other women who signed the agreement, Hyde was a retailer; from her shop in Philadelphia's central Chestnut Ward, she sold dry goods and tea. A few of the other women, especially Elizabeth Paschall and Magdalena Devine, were quite wealthy and possessed substantial enterprises. Hyde's shopkeeping, on the other hand, was a modest affair, which kept her and her sister and partner, Elizabeth Hyde, in regular business over several decades but rarely, if ever, offered more than mea-ger profits. From the late 1750s, if not earlier, the Hydes had shared the

---

1. Non-importation Agreement, Philadelphia, November, 1765, Am 0337, HSP.
2. The boycotts that accompanied the Sugar and Stamp acts are discussed in Edmund S. Morgan and Helen M. Morgan, *The Stamp Act Crisis: Prologue to Revolution*, rev. ed. (New York, 1962), 50, 70, 118–119, 331–333, 369–370.

business with a third sister, Sarah, until her death in 1762. Then Lydia and Elizabeth continued on their own. Despite the humble nature of the Hydes' business, their participation in the boycotts of British goods signaled their involvement in the community in which they had long lived. To the organizers of the nonimportation movement, the Hydes' signature on the agreement provided evidence of the depth of Philadelphians' commitment to opposing British policies.[3]

During the pre-Revolutionary era, women's participation was critical to the success of boycotts as a measure of opposition to British taxation schemes. When male political leaders in seaports from Boston to Charleston called on women to demonstrate their resistance to British policies, they principally appealed to women as consumers. One Boston writer estimated in 1770 that "upwards of 300 mistresses of families, in which Number Ladies of the highest rank and influence," had responded to such appeals by signing a petition to "join with the very respectable body of Merchants and other inhabitants of this town . . . totally to abstain from the Use of Tea."[4] By refusing to consume such staples of urban life as tea and manufactured cloth, women were in a unique position to help defeat such measures as the Stamp Act and the Townshend Duties. Hannah Griffitts, the Quaker poet of Philadelphia, pointed out women's opportunities and liabilities as political actors in her 1768 exhortation "The female Patriots":

> Since the men from a Party, or fear of a Frown,
> Are kept by a Sugar-Plumb, quietly down.
> Supinely asleep, & depriv'd of their Sight
> Are strip'd of their Freedom, & rob'd of their Right.
> Let the Daughters of Liberty, nobly arise,
> And tho' we've no Voice, but a negative here.
> The use of the Taxables*, let us forbear,
> (Then Merchants import till yr. Stores are all full
> May the Buyers be few & yr. Traffick be dull.)
> Stand firmly resolved & bid Grenville to see
> That rather than Freedom, we'll part with our Tea

3. Information on the Hydes can be gleaned from the following sources: 1767–1774 Provincial Tax Lists for Chestnut Ward, HSP and VPL; 1775 Constable's Return, PCA; "A Directory of Friends in Philadelphia, 1757–1760," *PMHB* 16 (1892): 220–229; Phineas Bond Receipt Book, HSP; Frances Manges, "Women Shopkeepers, Tavernkeepers and Artisans in Colonial Philadelphia," (Ph.D. diss., University of Pennsylvania, 1958), 46, 50, 50n.

4. "Philagius," *Boston Evening Post*, February 5, 12, 1770, as quoted in Alfred F. Young, "The Women of Boston: 'Persons of Consequence' in the Making of the American Revolution, 1765–76," in Harriet B. Applewhite and Darline G. Levy, eds., *Women and Politics in the Age of the Democratic Revolution* (Ann Arbor, Mich., 1990), 196.

And well as we love the dear Draught when a dry,
As American Patriots,—our Taste we deny[5]

As Griffitts saw it, women had "no Voice," that is, women had no opportunity for direct political expression. But their "negative," as she pointed
out, could be a mighty weapon. Women could compensate for merchants' failure to heed the nonimportation agreements by simply avoid-
ing—and thus economically punishing—their shops. In this way, wom-
en's domestic role as consumers was transformed into a political one, and
their choice of consumer products became political statements of the
highest order.

Women's other primary role in the boycotts was as producers of alternative, domestically made goods. Through the public organized spinning bees as well as a developing discourse that lauded the wearing of
coarse "homespun" cloth, the significance of women's contributions was
made clear. In New England, where such public gatherings were most
common, sermons and singing accompanied spinning bees.[6] The purpose of home production was to subvert the growing dependence of
Americans on British finished cloth. The spinning bees made great political theater, and like the nonimportation agreements, they demonstrated
the political impact of economic activities.

Lydia Hyde, however, signed the nonimportation agreement not as a
consumer or a producer, but as a member of Philadelphia's mercantile
community. As an independent woman, that is, as an unmarried woman
of property, Hyde could claim a voice in Philadelphia's public realm. Like
the seventeenth-century English petitioners discussed in the Introduction, Hyde could take a political stance because of her marital status.
Those petitioners had asserted their right to be heard before the government "as we are not all wives." Similarly, Hyde's political access was
based on her marital status and on her position as a person of property.

Less than a year later, Isaac Zane of "the Society meeting weekly for
their Mutual Improvement in Useful Knowledge" queried the group
whether it was "advantageous to admit women into the Councils of
State." The group concluded that although women's natural abilities

5. Hannah Griffitts, "The female Patriots," in Catherine Blecki and Karin Wulf, eds.,
Milcah Martha Moore's Book: A Commonplace Book from Early America (University Park, Pa.,
1997), 172. This marginal note accompanied the poem, explaining which taxed items
Griffitts would address: "*Tea—Paper—Glass—& Paints.—"
6. On religious culture expressed through ostensibly patriotic spinning bees, see
Laurel Thatcher Ulrich, "'Daughters of Liberty: Religious Women in Revolutionary New
England," in Ronald Hoffman and Peter J. Albert, *Women in the Age of the American Revo-
lution* (Charlottesville, Va., 1989), 211–243.

and sensibilities would lend themselves to politics, their incursions into the public arena could have a subversive effect in the domestic realm. Should women exercise political power, they might "destroy the peace of Families."[7]

These two events, Lydia Hyde's participation in the nonimportation agreement, and the conclusion of the society men that women's political engagement would threaten the harmony of households, point to the complex position of women in Philadelphia's political culture and to the significance of marital status in shaping women's political experience. Although these two events happened only eleven months apart, they represent a larger, longer transition. Lydia Hyde's signature on the nonimportation agreement is evidence of the long-standing recognition that unmarried women who were property-owners possessed some civic standing, and therefore some, if limited, access to the political arena. In particular, it demonstrates the centrality of property to unmarried women's political access. That access became limited in the years of the pre-Revolutionary crisis and beyond, when public culture expanded to include more white men as it became defined in strictly racial and gendered terms. During the late colonial period, these two different ideas were complexly coexistent, and eventually the recognition accorded to women like Lydia Hyde as property owners would be eclipsed by other imperatives and by other measures of civic membership. Assuming women's married status, Isaac Zane and his circle had concluded that a woman's political actions should be evaluated in terms of its effect on her family. That assumption, and conclusion, would define women's political position well into the twentieth century.

Much of the historical literature on women's experiences and contributions to the American Revolution has focused on the expansion of women's political consciousness and opportunities during the conflict between Britain and the American colonies.[8] Scholars have also debated whether or not the Revolution actually benefited women as a group.[9] More recently, historians have begun to examine the ways in which the

7. As quoted in Carl Bridenbaugh and Jessica Bridenbaugh, *Rebels and Gentlemen: Philadelphia in the Age of Franklin* (New York, 1965), 24.

8. The considerable literature on women's political activity during this period includes Linda Kerber, *Women of the Republic: Intellect and Ideology in Revolutionary America* (Chapel Hill, 1980); Mary Beth Norton, *Liberty's Daughters: The Revolutionary Experiences of American Women, 1750–1800* (Boston, 1980); Hoffman and Albert, eds., *Women in the Age of the American Revolution;* Barbara Clark Smith, "Food Rioters and the American Revolution," *WMQ* 51 (January 1994): 3–38; Young, "The Women of Boston."

9. The classic statement on this subject is Joan Hoff Wilson, "The Illusion of Change: Women and the American Revolution," in Alfred A. Young, ed., *The American Revolution: Explorations in the History of Radicalism* (Dekalb, Ill., 1976), 383–445.

gendered language of the revolutionaries produced a new political environment that was exclusive rather than expansive and predicated on assumptions of white masculine privilege.[10] Lydia Hyde's participation as a signatory of the nonimportation agreement may be interpreted as evidence of any of these positions: women's new incursions into the realms of politics; the benefits that opposition to British policy would bring to some women (in this instance, merchants and retailers) or the failed promise of such opposition (because women's economic opportunities did not expand after the war); or the ways in which the composition of the community of merchants gathered to support boycotting evidenced the almost exclusively masculine nature of the group (given the few women retailers represented there).

Since the 1980s, historians of European and American women and gender have demonstrated the intensity with which revolutionaries on both sides of the Atlantic defined the republican citizen as white and male. In the course of defining this citizen-subject, these revolutionaries articulated elaborate discourses that explained both what was wrong with women's political place in the *ancien regimes* and what was right about their political position in the new republics. Joan Landes's argument concerning revolutionary France is the most fully developed, explaining how women who had possessed political authority before the revolution were marginalized and even demonized in the new political order. Gender was of paramount importance to the democratic movement in France. Women of the famous French salons wielded cultural and political authority, conveying in their choice of guests as well as in their own pronouncements their views on political matters before the royal court. In the republic, such women were stripped of their political authority, and the domesticated woman was celebrated as the republican ideal.

For historians of American women, charting the movement toward a more explicitly masculine political world has been more difficult, and the path of that movement itself has seemed less linear. Linda Kerber, Carroll Smith-Rosenberg, and others have elucidated the ways in which political discourse in the early Republic relegated women to a newly priva-

---

10. See in particular Linda K. Kerber, "The Paradox of Women's Citizenship in the Early Republic: The Case of Martin vs. Massachusetts, 1805," *American Historical Review* 97 (1992): 349–78; Joan Landes, *Women and the Public Sphere in the French Revolution* (Ithaca, N.Y., 1988); Carroll Smith-Rosenberg, "Dis-Covering the Subject of the 'Great Constitutional Discussion,'" *Journal of American History* 79 (December 1992): 841–873. See also Richard D. Brown, *The Strength of a People: The Idea of an Informed Citizenry in America, 1650–1870* (Chapel Hill, 1996); and David Waldstreicher, *In the Midst of Perpetual Fetes: The Making of American Nationalism, 1776–1820* (Chapel Hill, 1997).

tized domestic space, while men claimed for themselves a newly defined, highly gendered public space. They have shown how, through political discourse but also in law and political practice, American leaders restricted the citizenry of the new American nation by race and gender.

Yet the "before" picture in America—that is, the standing of women prior to the late eighteenth-century masculinization of the political realm—is more obscure and therefore somewhat less satisfying. In the French story that Landes relates, it is not difficult to see how women's political status declined. In the old order, elite women as well as men participated in the politics of influence before republican rhetoric and ideology moved women out of politics altogether. Across the ocean in America, however, the story line is not so evident.[11] A limited form of participatory governance already excluded women from voting and from jury service.

An obvious question is whether the masculinization of political culture simply authorized the political participation of a more inclusive group of men. Not necessarily. Political culture is the dominant set of ideas and values constitutive of authority, that is, a consensus about the requirements for the possession and exercise of authority. These ideas are often, but not always, played out in matters of formal governance. They are also made plain in the realms of commerce, religion, and other "public" arenas. In order to argue that the great democratic movements reshaped understandings about authority in ways that were much more attuned to gender than before, and that they reified the possession of independent masculinity in place of property as the prerequisite for political participation, then the ways in which gender shaped political culture before the American Revolution must be elucidated.

Examining the role of gender in colonial political culture, however, requires looking to specific regional contexts.[12] A close look at Pennsylvania and at the development of political culture within Philadelphia specifically shows that the political culture accommodated female political authority before mid-century.[13] The discourse and the forms of political participation were not so rigorously masculine as to exclude women. In particular, the claim to participation based on property was one key

11. See especially Cornelia Hughes Dayton, *Women Before the Bar: Gender, Law, and Society in Connecticut, 1639–1789* (Chapel Hill, 1995); Susan Juster, *Disorderly Women: Sexual Politics and Evangelicalism in Revolutionary New England* (Ithaca, N.Y., 1994).

12. Mary Beth Norton, *Founding Mothers and Fathers: Gendered Power and the Forming of American Society* (New York, 1996), esp. 3–24, 138–180.

13. Alan Tully argues that Pennsylvania was much more amenable to women's political activity than was New York. Tully, *Forming American Politics: Ideals, Interests, and Institutions in Colonial New York and Pennsylvania* (Baltimore, 1994), 350–351.

route to women's access, as was the religious authority vested in Quaker women. During and after the Stamp Act crisis, however, the process of masculinizing the political culture was already underway, eclipsing any space for feminine political authority. Quakers began to lose significant political power, and as imperial politics overshadowed local concerns and the imperatives of war celebrated masculinity in ways quite new to Philadelphia, the gender of political culture was transformed.

One weighty consequence of this transformation was the increasing conflation of "woman" and "wife." Women's dependence was much more vigorously asserted. A growing interest in distinguishing male independence from female dependence led Philadelphia officials to implement poor-relief policies that flew in the face of the obvious realities of urban poverty. Public officials acted as the rhetoric suggested they should and focused on the "problem" of male poverty and dependence rather than the more significant and persistent matter of female poverty.

This example of erasing unmarried women from public discourse was part and parcel of the transformation of political culture. In public representations of civic membership such as tax lists and in visual representations of the public such as militia parades, independent women figuratively and literally disappeared from view. Ironically, as her numbers increased, the unmarried woman—the woman who, whatever her economic circumstances, was independent at law and, in Philadelphia's early urban culture, was understood to be an independent person in the same sense as any male—lost her public position. This process had very real effects on women whose access to the public realm was a function of their position as unmarried women of property. As a consequence, women like Lydia Hyde became exceptional, rather than regular, participants in civic action.

This chapter looks first at the political authority conferred by property ownership, and the political expressions and actions of unmarried women in the early eighteenth century. It then turns to a consideration of the increasingly masculine character of Philadelphia's political culture, and finally to an analysis of the erasure of women's independence from public discourse.

PROPERTY AND POLITICAL AUTHORITY

Property formed the basis of Anglo-American political culture in two different ways. First, the ownership of property was a prerequisite for political participation. In England, of course, certain types of property guaranteed a political role, such as membership in the House of Lords, while in the colonies, the connection of property to political dominance was somewhat more flexible. Less property was required for voting or for office-holding in the colonies than in England, so that the proportion of colonists that was enfranchised was approximately three times the proportion of Englishmen. Furthermore, the practice of deferring to socioeconomic superiors in political matters was much less consistently practiced and much more contingent.[14] The second way property shaped political culture was through its bearing on local politics. The most important tasks in laying out new colonies, after all, were related to matters of property. From determining the order and process for the purchase of property to laying out roads, determining wharf space, and awarding contracts for local projects, colonists spent a great deal of time wrestling over matters of property.

Gender was a significant aspect of these connections between property and politics. Many men were politically enabled through property they acquired from women.[15] In Philadelphia, property was central to politics, and thus to propertied women's access to the political realm. Women petitioned in matters relating to property, women held positions as freemen of the city, and elite women participated in direct electioneering and political maneuvering. In all of these cases, women were treated as an unremarkable part of the political world. In only some cases, however, could they do so through the rights of property ownership rather than as a privilege of other connections.

As a result of the laws of coverture and inheritance practices that favored male beneficiaries, the vast majority of both real and personal property in the colonies was owned by men, and male property-owners tended to own far more than their female counterparts.[16] However, in different colonial contexts, due to different inheritance practices, the ratio of male-to-female ownership varied. In early New York, for example,

14. For a discussion of "deference" in colonial Pennsylvania and New York, see ibid., 365–381.

15. Terri Snyder and John Kolp, for example, have uncovered fascinating examples of Virginia women who transferred property to men for expressly political purposes. They cite the case of Anne Holden of Accomack County, who gave twenty-five acres to two men that they might "Vote at the Annual Elections for the most Wise and Discreet men." John G. Kolp and Terri L. Snyder, "Gender, Property, and Voting Rights in Eighteenth-Century Virginia," (paper presented at "The Many Legalities of Early America," Williamsburg, Va., November 22–24, 1996).

16. An important essay on women's ownership of property is Carole Shammas, "Early American Women and Control over Capital," in Hoffman and Albert, eds., *Women in the Age of the American Revolution*, 134–154. On inheritance practices, see Toby L. Ditz, *Property and Kinship: Inheritance in Early Connecticut, 1750–1820* (Princeton, N.J., 1986).

Dutch customs that stressed the community property inherent in marriage gave widows a much larger share of property than English law did. This practice changed in the eighteenth century, as inheritance patterns in New York became more anglicized, but even in the predominantly English colonies, there were important variations in women's ownership and control over property.[17] In the seventeenth-century Chesapeake, for example, where mortality rates and tenuous kinship ties made widows more likely to become beneficiaries and executors of estates, women probably controlled more property than they did in New England, where large families and an emphasis on male control over farm properties dominated from the outset.[18]

In eighteenth-century Pennsylvania, as elsewhere, men who wrote wills became more restrictive in regard to the property they left to their wives and daughters, increasingly favoring sons with real estate as well as other kinds of property. In the later eighteenth century, and especially after the Revolution, fewer women were named executors of their husbands' estates, and fewer widows were granted more than the mandatory "widows' third." Nonetheless, the proportion of women who owned property, and who could exercise important quasi-political leverage through this ownership, was significant. Particularly in urban areas, women tended to inherit more and to own more property. Philadelphia women's ownership of real property greatly exceeded that of their rural counterparts.[19] In addition, women themselves may have tried to ameliorate some of the effects of changing inheritance patterns by distributing more land, and more property overall, to daughters.[20] Thus, it is important to recognize that proportionately very few women were property owners, but it is also important to examine what those women's property ownership meant.

Women in Pennsylvania became owners of property through a variety of means, including inheritance but also outright purchase, and their share of property actually increased over time. One of William Penn's first tasks in planning the colony of Pennsylvania was organizing the sale and distribution of lands, some of which went to women. Among the "first purchasers" of property along the Dublin Creek, for example, were

17. On Dutch property law, New York inheritance practices, and anglicization, see David E. Narrett, "Men's Wills and Women's Property Rights in Colonial New York," in Hoffman and Albert, eds., *Women in the Age of the American Revolution*, 91–133.

18. For comparisons of various colonial regions with early modern England and with contemporary America, see Shammas, "Women and Control over Capital."

19. On the percentages of women taxables in each place, see Chapter 3.

20. Vivian Bruce Conger, "'If Widow, Both Housewife and Husband May Be'": Widows' Testamentary Freedom in Colonial Massachusetts and Maryland, in Larry D. Eldridge, ed., *Women and Freedom in Early America* (New York, 1997), 251–253.

Sarah Fuller, Eleanor Holme, Elizabeth Martin, Katherine Martin, Ann Salter, and Widow Shirter.[21] In this case the density of female property owners along a waterway would mean that any issues over water rights or access would require substantial negotiations with and interventions from women. When the lots for the city of Philadelphia were divided, similar situations occurred. Although women's original share of property in the colony was very small, it did increase over time, presumably largely because more women inherited. A brief look at the records of the General Loan Office demonstrates this trend. The Loan Office was established in the 1720s to generate mortgages on fee-simple owned property for the purpose of putting paper money into circulation. Mortgagers were primarily members of the economic elite, by virtue of their outright ownership of property, and thus it is not surprising that the overwhelming majority were men. Through the 1750s, the General Loan Office created roughly three hundred mortgages, of which only sixty-seven were made to women. Those women were among the most wealthy, politically connected, and astute in the colony, to be sure. But another fifty women were co-mortgagers with their husbands, and sixty-six more were the eventual satisfiers of the loan, meaning that they had now had some inherited rights in that property.[22] As a result, a substantial amount of city property was controlled by women by the late colonial period. In 1775, for example, fully 15 percent of householders in the city's High Street Ward paid their annual or quarterly house rents to women, and 22 percent of them paid ground rents to women. The largest resident landowner in High Street Ward may have been Mary Harrison, who collected ground rents from six of her immediate neighbors.[23] In neighboring Walnut Ward, 18 percent of householders paid house rents to women, and of the sixteen resident homeowners, one third was female.[24]

Although women's ownership of property increased over time, the meaning of that ownership changed as the colony developed. Early in the eighteenth century, property and political access had been explicitly linked through such mechanisms as the city corporation and implicitly linked by the workings of status, which accorded some elite women a po-

21. From the Thomas Holme map of original purchasers, reproduced in J. Thomas Scharf and Thompson Westcott, *History of Philadelphia, 1609–1884* (Philadelphia, L. H. Everts & Co., 1884), vol. 1, p. 108 (overleaf).
22. *Guides to the Mortgages of the General Loan Office of the Province of Pennsylvania, 1724–1756*, compiled by James M. Duffin. (Philadelphia, 1995). For more on the General Loan Office, see Mary M. Schweitzer, *Custom and Contract: Household, Government, and the Economy in Colonial Pennsylvania* (New York, 1987).
23. Other landlords had larger holdings, as indeed Harrison did. This refers to only one resident of High Street Ward collecting rents from other residents of that ward.
24. 1775 Constables' Returns, PCA.

litical voice. At the very beginning of the eighteenth century, the Philadelphia Common Council recognized women's economic position as the basis for political participation. Philadelphia was organized along the same lines as English borough corporations, with "freemen" annually choosing the mayor and his aldermen from among the members of the corporation. Both men and women who were resident in the city, who were over age twenty-one, and who possessed a freehold or estate over £50 could take out "freedoms" and qualify as members of the corporation. Notices of political events and pamphlets concerning political affairs were often addressed to the "freemen" of Philadelphia. Although no woman ever served as an elected official of the corporation, all freemen could vote for council members.[25] Propertied women could and did become "freemen" of Philadelphia.

Freemanship was also a commercial status, for the sale of "freedoms" facilitated market regulation. An early ordinance of the council, reflecting European ideas about legitimate commerce, restrained "those that are not admitted freemen of this city" from "keep[ing] open shops or be[ing] master workmen."[26] At the beginning of the eighteenth century, women, like men, claimed membership in the organization that governed the city and its commercial activity. In July 1705, nine women and eleven men were "admitted freemen and women." There is little evidence of the women's occupations, but after they became freemen, at least six of them married and one remained single.[27] Presumably, these women were admitted to freemanship for the same reason as their male counterparts: they wanted recognition of their right to trade and work.

A large group of Philadelphians was admitted as freemen in 1717. Among this group were another fourteen women, this time identified by occupation. A majority (nine) were shopkeepers, one was a baker, and one a "taylor." Three women were identified only as "widows," although they probably had occupations. Possibly the women not identified by marital status had never married. Mary Lock, for example, was identified as both a shopkeeper and a widow.[28] Another woman who was identified

25. Judith M. Diamondstone, "Philadelphia's Municipal Corporation, 1701–1776," *PMHB* 90 (April 1966): 183–201; *Ordinances of the Corporation of, and Acts of Assembly Relating to, the City of Philadelphia* (Philadelphia, 1851), 19–20.

26. *Ordinances of the Corporation*, 20.

27. Not much else is known of this group, except that at least five of the women were Quakers, one was Anglican, and one was Presbyterian.

28. It may have been important to identify who had been married, because women often had a connection to the city and council through their deceased husbands. In later years, for example, Sarah Paschall took over as tenant of the market's eastern stalls, and probably even briefly as clerk of the market after her husband, William, died. She had ongoing dealings with the council regarding market rents and repairs. Sarah Austin took

only as a widow in 1717 was a midwife. After 1717, few residents bothered to take out freedoms. As the city expanded, the provincial government eclipsed the corporation as the larger body moved to involve itself more directly in city matters. The decline in the corporation's influence attenuated what may have been independent women's most direct link to political power.

Despite women's lack of formal access to government through either the franchise or office-holding, they often played a role in politics. Examples survive of women making their views heard through petitioning, publicizing their letters to prominent male politicians, and outright electioneering. Petitions pertaining to land use were probably the most common way in which women attempted to affect the political process. In 1704, for example, a number of women joined their neighbors in petitioning the Philadelphia Quarter Sessions Court to alter the routes of proposed roads across their property. Mary Fletcher pointed out that a proposed road would "Divide said land into Such small Pieces that your Petitioner cannot clear any large field upon ye same."[29] Such participation is noteworthy for its commonplace nature.

Political gossip also gave women an important voice. In letters to her brother who was in Jamaica, Deborah Norris displayed a keen sense of the political implications of the news she conveyed. News of elections, the Maryland border dispute, Indian affairs, wars, and the complex intertwining of family alliances and political deals all sailed to Isaac in Deborah's letters. Deborah also warned Isaac that relatives and others were miffed by his failure to acknowledge their letters, and instructed him to communicate with "the Pro[prietor]" immediately. Thomas Penn "might . . . [have thought] it a slight to him." Deborah related that she "was at some Expence of spirits in making the usual apologies" for young Norris's neglect and had managed to convince several associates that it was necessary for them to open the correspondence.[30]

Deborah also wrote to Isaac of "weddings and Courtships . . . [and] In-

---

over a Delaware River ferry license when Samuel Austin died, but William Clark's widow decided not to maintain leases on city wharfs and ground near the Dock Street bridge. Both suggest that women were given the option of continuing whatever contractual arrangements their husbands had with the city. *MCC*, 609, 628, 631, 658, 687.

29. See the petitions of Mary Fletcher and others to the 1704 Philadelphia Court of Quarter Sessions at Philadelphia, in the Roads and Travel Collections, Box 1, file 3, HSP.

30. Alan Tully, *William Penn's Legacy: Politics and Social Structure in Provincial Pennsylvania, 1726–1755* (Baltimore, 1977), 3–22; Deborah Norris to Isaac Norris, Jr., Philadelphia, November 3, 1733, Norris Family Letters, vol. 1, p. 10, HSP. Hamilton seemed to collect feuds. See Katherine D. Carter, "Isaac Norris II's attack on Andrew Hamilton," 104 *PMHB* (1980), and Walker Lewis, "Andrew Hamilton and the He-Monster," *WMQ* 3rd Ser., 38 (April 1981): 268–296.

teligence of that sort."[31] Her information was neither trifling nor of only passing social interest. Reports of marital alliances were important because they often signaled the beginning or end of political and economic alliances. When James Hamilton was appointed Philadelphia County's prothonetary, a condition of the deal his father had cut with the proprietary party, James Logan began to consider him suitable son-in-law material. This news, Deborah reported, was "the talk of the whole Town."[32] Sarah Logan, young Hamilton's intended, was Isaac Norris's choice for a wife, and so the rumored match occasioned "a Shyness" between their fathers. Indeed Logan and Norris were to wrestle back and forth for a number of years. As two of the most senior, respected, and wealthy men in Pennsylvania, any spat between them reverberated through the Quaker community. Deborah was incensed at Logan's betrayal. "When I consider the friendship James has professed for father now thirty years or more," she wrote, "& in my oppinion how very different from a Common friend he has acted in severall things since thou Left us, I cant help thinking father will have no great Loss where they never to profess more than Common Civility one to the another." Deborah confessed to her brother that she was sure their father "would chide me" if he knew what she wrote about Logan; she nevertheless forthrightly stated that "it is an article of faith with me that no man can serve God and mammon."[33] Deborah's letters to her brother about the Hamilton-Logan-Norris situation combined marital ties and political infighting, and provided just one example of the way that such "news of the town" served multiple purposes for both sender and receiver.[34]

Despite the prevalent opinion that colonial women cared little for politics, the evidence from Philadelphia suggests that elite women had extensive political knowledge. One of the earliest of Deborah Norris's letters describes how she overcame a "resol[ution] not to meddle with politick" by her strong feelings about the issues at hand: "out of the abundance of ye heart the mouth speaketh."[35] Such disclaimers were not repeated. Six months later Deborah casually began a long discussion with

31. Deborah Norris to Isaac Norris, Jr., August 4, 1734, Norris Family Letters, vol. 1, p. 31, HSP.
32. Ibid., March 26, 1734, vol. 1, p. 23.
33. Ibid. Isaac Norris and Sarah Logan did marry, and after her death, James Logan continued to quarrel with his son-in-law over her dowry property, attempting to reclaim land already committed to granddaughters Mary and Sarah Norris.
34. For an analysis of the significance and operation of gossip and reputation in eighteenth-century Virginia, see Kathleen M. Brown, *Good Wives, Nasty Wenches, and Anxious Patriarchs: Gender, Race, and Power in Colonial Virginia* (Chapel Hill, 1996), 306–317.
35. Deborah Norris to Isaac Norris, Philadelphia, March 26, 1734, Norris Papers, vol. 1, p. 23 HSP.

the remark, "As for Polticks they are much the same as when I wrote Last."[36] Benjamin Rush was certainly being disingenuous when he wrote in the early nineteenth century that "[women] should not only be instructed in the usual branches of female education, but they should be taught the principles of liberty and government."[37] Rush knew very well that educated women of privileged backgrounds were well-versed in politics and political theory. One of the most politically active of Pennsylvania women, Susanna Wright, was in fact the subject of Rush's highest praise: when she died in 1785 he called her "the famous Suzey Wright . . . celebrated above half a century for her wit, good sense, and valuable improvements of mind."[38]

There are reported cases of women's direct involvement in elections, although it is unclear how often this occurred. The most remarkable case was probably Susanna Wright's participation in a hotly contested assembly election in the 1740s. Wright had long been involved in Lancaster County governmental affairs. As the sister of prominent politicians, the paramour of a key magistrate for the county, Samuel Blunston, and a significant landowner herself, she was well placed. In 1779, when she was over the age of eighty, one Lancaster County politician recommended to Joseph Reed, the president of Pennsylvania, that he seek out Wright, "who could give, I believe, a more satisfactory account . . . than I can" of a series of land disputes involving Indians.[39] In the earlier part of the century, Wright had served as acting prothonetary for the county during Blunston's illness, and her political views were often sought by Philadelphians.[40] In 1742, provincial secretary Richard Peters wrote to Pennsylvania proprietor Thomas Penn about Wright's collusion with Blunston in an election campaign. Wright and Blunston had composed a pamphlet designed to inflame partisan and ethnic passions, and she had distributed it during the actual election:

There is a she[et] in ye Box of Susa Wrights own handwriting & of her & Sam's composing wch was sent to every Presbytern Congregation in ye County & read at all publick meetings of ye Party: you'l see by it to what

36. Ibid., August 4th, 1734, vol. 1, p. 31.

37. Benjamin Rush, "Of the Mode of Education Proper in a Republic," in *Essays, Literary, Moral and Philosophical* (Philadelphia, 1806), as quoted in Rosemary Zagarri, "Morals, Manners, and the Republican Mother," *American Quarterly* 44 (June 1992): 206.

38. Lyman Butterfield, "Dr. Benjamin Rush's Journal of a Trip to Carlisle in 1784," *PMHB* 74 (1950): 443–56.

39. William Henry to Joseph Reed, Lancaster, November 27, 1779, reprinted in the *PMHB* 29 (1905): 122.

40. On Wright, Blunston, and the Norris family, see Wulf, "A Marginal Independence," Chap. 5.

Lengths a vindictive Spirit will carry people withot ye Restraints of Honr & concience: coud any one believe yt Susy cou'd act so unbecoming (& unfemale a part) as to be emply'd in copying such infamous stuff & to take her stand as she did at Lancas in an upper Room in a publick House & to have a Ladder erected to ye window & there distribute Lies & Tickets all ye day of ye Election?[41]

When Richard Peters decried Wright's actions, he invoked her gender (politics unsexed her), but mostly he complained about her tactics (writing a scurrilous political document and making sure it got wide play). Although women's direct participation in electoral politics may have been rare, there are other reported cases.[42]

Women's participation in politics, then, could extend from membership in the Philadelphia corporation to petitioning, to passing along vital gossip and electioneering. What distinguishes these various activities, however, is their contingent nature. Only petitioning and corporation membership were rights and not privileges. Susanna Wright could act in such a public way largely because she was an elite woman, and she was supported by male politicians (her friend Blunston and her relations). Deborah Norris's political news had consequences because she was connected to powerful men. Neither type of action was the kind women could claim as a result of their own status. As the eighteenth century progressed and the avenues for their direct participation as owners of property were closing, women had to rely more and more on such contingent access to politics.

FROM PROPERTY TO MASCULINITY

The transition in political culture from an emphasis on property, which allowed some women's attendance in the political arena, to privileging masculinity as the basis for political participation, did not occur uniformly. In Philadelphia, Quaker women, especially ministers, had also been allowed a public voice on political matters. The masculinization of political culture followed the removal of Quakers from political dominance and the intrusion of imperial politics into the daily political consciousness of colonists. Pennsylvania's political culture had allowed for

41. Richard Peters to Thomas Penn, November 17, 1742, Richard Peters Letter Books, vol. 29, p. 132, HSP. I thank Craig Horle for finally pointing me to the original of this letter, which I had long sought.
42. Alan Tully cites the case of Jane Hoskins's participation in a Chester County election. Tully, *Forming American Politics*, 351.

the inclusion of women based on either access to property or claims of spiritual authority. In the aftermath of the Seven Years War, both opportunities declined.

One of the most striking examples of Philadelphia's changing political culture can be found in the development of the militia during the mid-eighteenth century. All of the other colonies had organized militias from an early date, but Pennsylvania had refrained from forming such groups because of the pacifist principles of the Quakers, who dominated politics for so long.[43] During the military crises of the mid-eighteenth century, particularly the threats posed to frontier settlers by increasingly hostile Native Americans, backcountry residents and anti-Quaker politicians began to agitate more aggressively for a formal defense system. The result was a militia system that allowed for increasing public displays of masculinity and that generated a growing equation of public life with masculine, martial qualities. After Benjamin Franklin called for the formation of a voluntary militia in 1747, nearly one-third of adult white males joined a militia "association." Although they were never called upon to engage in any remotely dangerous activity, the new volunteer militia did provide a means for men of the lower sort to organize for the public good.[44]

The Seven Years War was a turning point for Pennsylvania. Quaker politicians could no longer resist entreaties for direct defense spending, and a host of Quakers resigned from the Pennsylvania legislature as a result of wartime politics. Although by no means all Quakers abandoned politics and the colony, especially Philadelphia, continued to feel Quaker influence, the war initiated a Quaker retreat from public life. Thereafter, major Quaker initiatives, such as the abolition of slavery, would be carried out through private means and organizations. While the militia had begun as an all-volunteer force, calls for mandatory service accompanied the outbreak of hostilities in the Pennsylvania backcountry that preceded (and followed) the Seven Years War. Franklin then oversaw the establishment of a legislatively authorized and publicly funded militia, and was elected colonel of the Philadelphia regiment.[45]

The creation of the new militia in the winter of 1755–and 1756 was the occasion for much celebration of masculine valor, especially in Philadel-

43. John K. Mahon, *A History of the Militia and the National Guard* (New York, 1983); Russell F. Weigley, *History of the United States Army* (New York, 1967).
44. Gary B. Nash, *The Urban Crucible: The Northern Seaports and the Origins of the American Revolution*, abridged ed. (Cambridge, Mass., 1986), 146; Tully, *Forming American Politics*, 108–109.
45. Tully, *Forming American Politics*, 151–152.

phia. The city had not shared in the celebration of masculinity held in other colonial locales; the annual processions of the city corporation paled by comparison with the regular militia musters held in other colonies. Those ritual events helped to cement the authority of whiteness, of masculinity, and of propertied privilege. By creating and then displaying organizations that required the participation of white men and explicitly excluded all others, colonial societies could create a cross-class alliance among participants. While in many places men could not vote or hold office without owning a certain amount of property, militia service required only the possession of a specific racial and gender identity and the ubiquitous gun.[46] In late December 1755, following the passage of a militia law and the election of officers by city ward, an announcement of the results appeared in the *Pennsylvania Gazette*. Accompanying the list of those who would serve their neighbors as militia captains, lieutenants, and ensigns was a declaration of the civic spirit that had motivated this action. "We can assure the Publick," the notice proclaimed, "that the excellent Spirit of Association, and . . . military Discipline, which so generally prevailed amongst us in the late War, and was, under the Blessing of Providence, our Security and Preservation at that Time, is now revived." Then followed an explicit assertion of the value of such undertakings: "If the same prudent and manly Steps are speedily taken in all the numerous Townships of this Province, we may reasonably hope soon to become the Terror of our enemies."[47] In other words, masculinity was equated not only with "prudence" and good judgment but with "terrorizing" one's enemies, something that by implication the feminized, imprudent Quakers had failed to do. In short order, a parade of the thousand men who had responded to this militia call was organized. Manliness could thus be asserted in print and demonstrated in the streets.[48]

This governmental sanction of the bonds uniting white men made explicit what had perhaps before been simply implicit in political life. Yet its very explicitness had profound effects. The example of the organization of Philadelphia's militia was quickly followed by the other counties in Pennsylvania and Delaware.[49] Subsequent militia acts of the legislatures, and amendments or addenda to those acts, stressed the importance of every white man's civic responsibility. When the new state of Pennsyl-

46. The significance of militia culture in colonial Virginia is treated in Rhys Isaac, *The Transformation of Virginia, 1740–1790* (Chapel Hill, 1982), 104–110; Brown, *Good Wives, Nasty Wenches, and Anxious Patriarchs*, 277–282. On the militia muster in Massachusetts, see Robert A. Gross, *The Minutemen and Their World* (New York, 1976), 70–74.

47. *PG*, December 25, 1755.

48. Nash, *Urban Crucible*, 169.

49. *PG*, March 25, 1756; December 29, 1757.

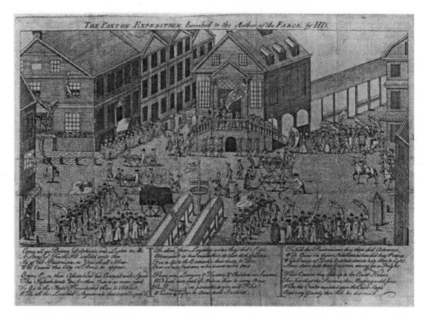

5. Philadelphians preparing to meet the Paxton Boys, 1764. Note the few women who appear in this depiction of events occurring directly in front of the city markets (under and behind the city hall, center). Henry Dawkins. Courtesy of The Library Company of Philadelphia.

vania passed a militia act in 1777, it was entitled "An Act obliging the white male inhabitants of this State to give assurances of allegiance."[50] Through the militia, the white men of Pennsylvania, whether German or English in national origin, Lutherans or Presbyterians, or merchants or laborers, all shared a common identity that was given new purpose and new expression.

An interesting representation of this masculinization of Philadelphia is the cartoon series surrounding the hotly contested 1764 elections when the question of armed action was again at the center. These were among the first depictions of the city's interior. A series of three shows men talking to other men, in dyads or small groups, with many of the men dressed in court attire. Another depicts Philadelphians ready to respond to the Paxton Boys, a group from the backcountry that threatened to march on Philadelphia to protest the insufficient defense provided by the government. Parading militia groups gathered in front of the city hall, with groups of male onlookers offering support. Women are entirely absent

50. Ibid., December 29, 1757; February 26, 1777; March 26, 1777; May 20, 1778.

from these depictions, except for two women among the many spectators for the militia muster. This absence is particularly marked because city hall, the backdrop for these illustrations, was located atop the city markets. At the center of commercial activity, the market and city hall was always thronged with crowds of women buying and selling. In these cartoons, though, men with weapons seem to dominate the urban landscape, while women's regular, prominent presence in the city was utterly erased.[51]

In the midst of this militarization and masculinization of public culture, Quakers made some last-ditch efforts to apply their distinctive style of politics to the crisis in the backcountry. These efforts illustrate how Quaker religious ideas and practices not only resisted an explicit emphasis on masculinity but also stretched Anglo-American concepts of political authority to include women. In 1755 Pennsylvania legislators, still predominantly Quaker, confronted the specter of war with the Indians. The British were already at war, and the Quakers' pacifism was being sorely tested. Allegiance to a theology of pacifism, loyalty to William Penn's vision of a relationship of mutuality with Native Americans, repudiation of Thomas Penn's policies of territorial aggression, and a desire to avoid conflicts with the crown created a tense and divisive atmosphere.[52] Held in the sway of a reform movement already concerned about Quakers' lapses from their faith, Quaker politicians were lobbied by emissaries of the Quaker men's and women's meetings to adhere to pacifism and avoid even the stain of wartime taxation.[53] Reform-minded ministers, including the English visitor Catherine Peyton and her travelling partner, Mary Peisley, played a key role in that year's meetings. Local women ministers also participated, but Peyton's activities in particular demonstrate the political opportunities available to women through religious authority. Peyton demanded and was granted access to the legislators and to their council on Indian affairs. When Quaker assemblymen met with a group of Indians in the hopes of arriving at an "accommodation," Peyton went along. She reported from this meeting that several Indian women also attended, explaining that "I was informed that they admit their most respected women into their counsels."[54] The

51. The cartoons for the 1764 election are reproduced in Martin P. Snyder, *City of Independence: Views of Philadelphia Before 1800* (New York, 1975), 76–80.

52. See, for example, the announcement in the *Pennsylvania Gazette* of Quakers' efforts to ameliorate concerns about their interests in backcountry settlers as opposed to Indians by collecting funds for the relief of the former who had suffered at the hands of the latter. *PG*, November 1755.

53. Jean Soderlund, "Women's Authority in Pennsylvania and New Jersey Quaker Meetings, 1680–1760," *WMQ* 44 (October 1987): 747–749; Tully, *Forming American Politics*.

54. *Memoirs of Catherine Phillips* (London, 1797), 142.

Quaker initiative failed, and their practice of accommodating women's public actions began to give way to the new imperatives of a masculinized political culture.

Quaker theology, with its explicitly egalitarian emphasis, was not perfectly translated into a social system predicated on gender equality. But if Quaker men did not grant women full equality and followed instead the Anglo-American legal tradition that kept women at distinct political and economic disadvantage, they did continue to recognize the religious authority that women could wield. More than any other religion that European Americans followed, Quakerism recognized women's capacity for religious leadership. Women in most Protestant denominations were recognized for their spiritual capacity, but in no other sect were women's speech and ministry so valued and so rewarded.[55] During the crisis over potential war in 1755, women exercised enhanced powers.

After 1755, Quakerism's influence in Pennsylvania declined. Although prominent Quakers continued to play a role in the colony's governance, many resigned rather than participate in the coming war. Others worked to accommodate both pacifist and militaristic goals, a highly problematic effort. Even outside the halls of governance, Quakerism's influence would continue to be important, but would be represented alongside the interests of the burgeoning backcountry of western Pennsylvania and an ever-stronger Anglican elite.[56] The withdrawal of Quakers from politics, and the parallel development of a political culture that emphasized masculinity, meant that women's access to public, political action was closing.

WOMEN, MARRIAGE, AND THE
TRANSFORMATION OF POLITICAL CULTURE

In 1980, Linda Kerber inaugurated an important debate about the gendered nature of political language during and after the American Revolution. In *Women of the Republic*, Kerber described the rise of the ideal of the "Republican Mother," a paragon of feminine civic virtue and domestic duty.[57] And yet the republican mother was an illusory model

---

55. Soderlund, "Women's Authority in Pennsylvania and New Jersey Quaker Meetings," also contains a good discussion of the invigorated reform-minded meetings of 1755 around the concerns over war, although not a specific discussion of Peyton's visit to the Indians.

56. Alan Tully argues that "civil Quakerism" continued to mark the colony's governance, but that was in stark contrast to the attempts at strict theological coherence demanded by the reformers of 1755. Tully, *Forming American Politics*, 147–155, 257–309.

57. Kerber, *Women of the Republic*; see also Ruth Bloch, "The Gendered Meanings of Virtue in Revolutionary America," *Signs* 13 (1987): 37–58; Carroll Smith-Rosenberg, "Domesticating Virtue: Coquettes and Revolutionaries in Young America," in Elaine Scarry,

for many women. If the republican mother's chief duty was to educate her sons for duty to the republic, then what of childless women? Jan Lewis subsequently noted that the model of the wife was similarly important. If a woman did not spend all her time shaping her children's morals, she should apply moral suasion to her husband.[58] Making sure that men were fit to rule became the province of the wife and mother. Historians have also noted how women then had to use the language of republican motherhood to gain access to the political arena. Unable to claim a direct role, women had to rely on their relationships to men and to their children to justify their public interests. Through charitable activities and even political rallies ostensibly directed at the morality of men, women could gain some political voice. Yet studies of the blossoming of charitable work in the early republic have repeatedly pointed to the overwhelming numbers of unmarried women within these groups, and the early republic inaugurated a sharp decline in marriage rates among white women.[59]

What could account for the significant impact of a political discourse that stressed women's relational and domestic nature at the same time that the numbers of unmarried women were actually increasing? What had transpired was a reformulation of notions of gender that more firmly tied women to dependence and thus to marriage.[60] In ways large and small, intimate and public, the discourse of gender in Philadelphia increasingly emphasized the importance of women's domestic lives and downplayed women's communal and public presence. Women's independence ran counter to efforts to connect masculinity more firmly with independence and femininity with dependence, and thus those women whose very existence challenged that construction were ignored and their traditional routes to the public realm were closed.

A very public confirmation of unmarried women's affront to the increasingly gendered nature of Philadelphia's political culture was the iteration of civic membership in the tax lists. Tax lists are symbolic docu-

ed., *Literature and the Body: Essays on Populations and Persons* (Baltimore, 1988), Zagarri, "Morals, Manners and the Republic Mother."

58. Jan Lewis, "The Republican Wife: Virtue and Seduction in the Early Republic," *WMQ* 44 (October 1987): 689–721.

59. Joan Jensen, *Loosening the Bonds: Mid-Atlantic Farm Women, 1750–1850* (New Haven, Conn., 1986); Margaret Morris Haviland, "Beyond Women's Sphere: Young Quaker Women and the Veil of Charity in Philadelphia, 1790–1810," *WMQ* 51 (July 1994): 419–446.

60. An interesting, almost reverse phenomenon occurred in England in the nineteenth century, when public attention and then public discourse coalesced suddenly around the "problem" of the unmarried woman. Martha Vicinus, *Independent Women: Work and Community for Single Women, 1850–1920* (Chicago, 1985).

ments that reflect far more than the simple enumeration of taxable property and the consequent tax obligations of the owners of such property. Rather, tax lists, like the laws they implement, reflect a culture's assumptions about what kinds of property should be taxed and what kinds should be excused from taxation, who should have to pay for owning such property, and who might be excused. In other words, the taxation process rewards certain kinds of property and thus certain kinds of economic and social behavior. One has only to look at the recurrent American debates about the home mortgage interest deduction or the so-called "marriage penalty" to understand that tax laws are as much about a society's cultural beliefs as they are about collecting revenues. In colonial Philadelphia, tax laws reflected not just assumptions about which kinds of economic behavior should be rewarded—improved land, for example, was taxed differently from unimproved land—but also the cultural values inherent in the taxation process itself. Petty officials, such as constables and tax assessors, applied communal standards of gender and civic responsibility to the taxation process, at times skirting and even outright evading the letter of the taxation laws.[61]

In the late colonial period, as Philadelphia's political culture became increasingly attuned to notions of gender and dependence, tax officials essentially wrote women out of the polity. Tax assessors regularly taxed women's property at much lower rates than men's, and they often excused women from taxation altogether, even women who owned significant taxable property. Philadelphia's provincial and city tax lists between 1756 and 1774 show a marked decline in the number and proportion of women among the taxable population. In 1756, for example, 189 women were taxed by the city of Philadelphia, comprising 8 percent of the taxable population. By 1774, only 154 women were on the provincial tax lists, comprising just 5 percent of the taxable population. In some areas of the city those figures were higher, but the overall trend toward smaller numbers and a smaller proportion was consistent.[62] Most important, even areas where very high proportions of households were headed by women showed quite small percentages of women taxed. In High Street Ward, for example, where in 1775 over 20 percent of households were headed by women, women accounted for only 5 percent of taxables. Some of this discrepancy can be explained by the high numbers of male boarders

61. A detailed analysis of the taxation process can be found in Karin Wulf, "Assessing Gender: Taxation and the Evaluation of Economic Viability in Late Colonial Philadelphia," *PMHB* 121 (July 1997): 201–235.
62. See Table 2.2 "Women as a Percentage of Philadelphia Taxables, By Ward, 1756–1774," in Karin Wulf, "A Marginal Independence: Unmarried Women in Colonial Philadelphia," (Ph.D. diss., Johns Hopkins University, 1993), 77.

who were taxed. But the fact remains that many women were simply excused from taxation, even if they headed households and owned taxable property.

Rachel Draper and Mary Sandwith, whose stories opened Chapters 3 and 4, respectively, are good examples of women who were never held accountable for paying taxes. By 1775 Draper had lived in High Street Ward for two decades, the last twelve years of which she headed her own household. She was a tavernkeeper, so she had both an occupation and an income, and she paid £14 a year in rent for her house, a not insignificant sum. Yet although the Constable's Returns listed Draper's household and its occupants, the tax assessor for High Street Ward never included her on his tax list.[63] Mary Sandwith lived within her sister and brother-in-law's home, acting as the family's "housekeeper" and as an additional parent to the couple's children. Sandwith had inherited money from her parents' estate. She was known to own ground rents in the city, and she had invested money with her brother-in-law, Henry Drinker. Yet Sandwith, despite this evidence of taxable property (rents) as well as income (taxable by law after 1764), was never assessed for a tax.[64] In addition, she never appeared on a Constable's Return as an inmate of the Drinkers' household. Without her sister's famous diary, we might never know where or how Mary Sandwith had lived. Her absence from the tax rolls raises the specter of much larger numbers of unmarried women, not just household heads, who may have lived in the city as residents in another's household but who never appeared on official census or tax documents.

Other women were taxed, but at very low levels. In fact, women generally were taxed at levels much below the actual value of their taxable property. For example, 50 percent of the women taxed in High Street Ward in 1767 were taxed at a level that represented less than half of the value of their taxable property. Meanwhile, only 17 percent of men were taxed at a level less than 90 percent of their property value.[65] The four surviving tax lists from 1767 through 1774 show this pattern throughout the city.[66] Assessors were reluctant to tax women on the full value of their property and just as reluctant to tax men much below the full value of their property.

The full import of this phenomenon needs to be explored. Colonial Philadelphians argued over the basis and the execution of tax laws. Pay-

63. Wulf, "Assessing Gender," 202–203.
64. On Sandwith's living arrangements and financial situation, see Chapter 3.
65. Wulf, "Assessing Gender," Table 4, 224.
66. Ibid., Table 5, 225.

ing taxes was understood to be a fundamental responsibility of every citizen. Tax revenues paid for public works, such as roads, lighting, and the city watch; taxation also supported more extensive undertakings, such as provincial defense. Paying taxes meant contributing to these basic services, as well as to the communal definition of the colony's health. Originally city and provincial taxes were applied only to specified kinds of property (including realty but also slaves and livestock). After 1764, however, occupational income was also assessed, thereby drawing in a new pool of taxables. Men who had never been taxed before, because they owned no taxable property, now found themselves paying taxes based on an assessor's evaluation of their income. Men who had not been invited or compelled to participate in the public rite of taxation now found themselves enumerated, assessed, and charged. This inclusion of more propertyless men into the ranks of the taxable population paralleled such men's entry into the political arena. At the same time that laboring men began to have a significant impact on political developments, they also had to take responsibility for paying their fair share of the polity's expenses.[67]

Women's civic status, on the other hand, was travelling an opposite route. As property became a much less significant qualification for political participation, and as the marker of independence was no longer property but masculinity, independent women were excluded from public recognition. Tax assessors who either greatly reduced women's tax burdens, or excused women from taxation altogether, as in the cases of both Rachel Draper and Mary Sandwith, were acting in accordance with this new cultural imperative. Draper was a widow of modest means, while Sandwith was a spinster from the Quaker elite, but their dissimilar socioeconomic conditions melted in the face of an ideal of gender that contraindicated women's independence. Because women increasingly could be understood or publicly represented only in a dependent posture, it followed that they could not be held accountable for the same kinds of civic responsibilities as could men. Thus, the independent status of Rachel Draper, a household head, was essentially denied, while the status of men in her neighborhood who boarded with other householders and who owned no taxable property at all was upheld. The process of taxation displayed in microcosm the broader changes in cultural connections among gender, dependency, and political status that were occurring in Philadelphia during the late colonial period.

Another document from the early years of the Revolutionary War pro-

---

67. The entry of the lower sort of men into Philadelphia politics is examined by Gary Nash in *Urban Crucible*, passim.

vides a fascinating look at the construction of femininity and marriage as inseparable. In the late winter of 1778, after Congress had decamped from Philadelphia to York, Pennsylvania, because of the British occupation, a manuscript circulated purporting to advertise books and plays "just published & to be sold by Matthew Minwell at York Town."[68] All of the authors were elite women, and the majority comprised a literary circle centered in the Delaware Valley.[69] Fourteen women's names were attached to thirty-two fictive publications. The titles of the farcical books and plays are as telling for modern analysts as they were surely meant to be instructive for a contemporary audience. A number of the books and plays centered on subjects common in the popular literature of the day, such as nature and friendship. A few addressed religious themes. But seventeen of the publications concerned matters of courtship and marriage, signified by such titles as "The Way to Win Him" and "The Lady's Magazine or a Treatise on *Visiting, Courtship, and Marriage.*" Two titles demonstrated the significance of the tight connections between femininity and marriage. One was "the female politician unbound," which was a title offered "by the compleat housewife, with some Thoughts on the education of Children." Here was a perfect demonstration of the value of the republican mother, whose chief responsibility was to raise virtuous children. The "female politician" could enter the realm of politics, or, put differently, the bounds of politics could be stretched to include her, only when the subjects at hand concerned housewifery and the instruction of children. One title alone suggested an alternative life course for women: "Serious Thoughts on Celibacy, or the life of a Nun." By associating celibacy with Catholicism, the satire was made plain. Surely no one would make such a choice. The discourse on poor relief, the creation of tax lists, and the circulation of even a satirical list of publications that included such works as "the female politician unbound" confirmed the importance of connecting women to marriage.

The erasure of unmarried women from the public marked the reorientation of Philadelphia's culture of gender and marriage. Property was no longer the marker of civic status and responsibility, but had been superseded by gender as the crucial determinant of membership in the polity. Property ownership not only failed to guarantee women a basic entree into political affairs, but its political irrelevance was made clear when petty officials excused female property owners from such basic as-

---

68. "Books just published & to be sold by Matthew Minwell at York Town Feby 1778," reprinted in the *PMHB* 15 (1892): 501–502.

69. For more on this particular literary circle, see Carla J. Mulford, *"Only for the Eye of a Friend": The Poems of Annis Boudinot Stockton* (Charlottesville, Va., 1995).

pects of participation in community life as paying taxes. The growing emphasis on masculinity as the testimony of independence and prerequisite for political access came at a cost. The expansion of the political realm to include more men of all sorts meant that propertied women could no longer be admitted to that circle. The political culture now treated all women, no matter their marital status and no matter their status as property -owners or heads of household, as fundamentally dependent creatures. They were not all wives, but the women of Philadelphia were now assumed to be possessed of those dependent, subordinated qualities that legally had been assigned only to wives and that previously had been much more flexibly applied and understood.

CONCLUSION

The famous exchange between Abigail and John Adams, wherein she asked him to "remember the ladies" and he effectively refused, has come to symbolize women's "new" political consciousness and ambitions during the Revolutionary era. But the Adams exchange, like Lydia Hyde's resolve to boycott British goods during the Stamp Act crisis, is actually emblematic of a very different phenomenon. Women like Adams and Hyde had always kept abreast of political happenings, and their tacit, if not active, approval of political developments was necessary for the smooth operation of local governance. The Adams exchange, therefore, does not mark a particularly new development.

The Adams's letters do, however, illustrate the cultural work that underlay the construction of a white, masculine republic. Creating that republic and its citizenry required writing all other contestants out of the public arena. Both Abigail and John Adams alluded to the implications of a new political world ruled by men, and their exchange echoed popular literary tradition by framing marital relationships as inappropriately hierarchical and subject to contestation. Abigail Adams not only asked her spouse to "remember" women's rights; she explicitly invoked the potentially disastrous imbalance of power in marriage: "Do not put such unlimited power into the hands of the Husbands. Remember all men would be tyrants if they could."[70] Here Abigail Adams identified the frightening potential of the Revolution to make some men all-powerful. While talk of liberty and equality abounded, this shift in white, proper-

70. Abigail Adams to John Adams, March 31, 1776, in Lyman Butterfield, ed., *Adams Family Correspondence* (Cambridge, Mass., 1963), vol. 1, pp. 369–371.

tied men's status would be bought at the expense of others' liberties. The Revolution would free some men from their dependence in relation to Great Britain, but she recognized that it would also entitle them to subordinate others.

Abigail Adams had only to wait for her husband's response to have this hunch confirmed. John Adams scoffed at his wife's claims that women would "not hold ourselves bound by any Laws in which we have no voice or Representation."[71] He immediately placed such demands alongside those of other groups whose political rights he could position as similarly ridiculous: children, Indians, and black slaves. "We have been told," he wrote, "that our Struggle has loosened the bands of Government every where. That children and Apprentices were disobedient— . . . that Indians slighted their Guardians and Negroes grew insolent to their Masters. But your letter was the first intimation that another Tribe more numerous and powerfull than all the rest were grown discontented."[72] After a week Abigail Adams replied, noting that she found it very ungenerous that "whilst you are proclaiming peace and good will to Men, emancipating all Nations, you insist upon retaining an absolute power over wives." She then predicted that this form of tyranny, too, would have to give way: "Arbitrary power is like most other things which are very hard, very liable to be broken."[73]

Abigail Adams was only partly right when she suggested that masculine, husbandly tyranny over women would be challenged and surmounted. It took another seventy-five years before New York was the first state to begin undoing the laws of coverture that had so hobbled married women. But by the time that legislation was passed, the real work on which John Adams and other Revolutionaries was engaged was completed. In the new Republic membership was strictly defined by race and by gender, and a model of domestic femininity, based on the experience of white, middle-class wives but rigorously applied to all women, had become hegemonic. Alternative models of femininity that had currency in colonial Philadelphia, the questioning of the hierarchical model of marriage, and the importance of the large numbers of unmarried women were pushed to the margins of cultural awareness.

To return to November 1765, when Magdalena Devine, Marcy Gray, Lydia and Elizabeth Hyde, Elizabeth Paschall, and Ann Pearson signed a resolution of "a general meeting of the merchants and traders" of Philadelphia protesting the Stamp Act and agreeing to forfeit the impor-

71. Ibid.
72. John Adams to Abigail Adams, April 17, 1776, in ibid., 381–83.
73. Abigail Adams to John Adams, May 7, 1776, in ibid., 401–403.

tation of British goods, how are we to understand these women's participation? In a moment of transformation in the political culture, their public, political action is revealing. Because there were so few women signers, some historians have explained their presence in terms of their relative importance among the mercantile community.[74] Others have read signing the nonimportation agreement as evidence of women's initiation into political partisanship.[75] However, the explanation that only exceptional or wealthy women participated in the non-importation agreement is complicated by the Hyde sisters' relatively modest property; their business was long lived, but precarious.[76] Neither of the other explanations is satisfactory either, because each assumes that women's access to public and political arenas expanded over the course of the eighteenth century, particularly in urban centers.

Instead, the opposite occurred.[77] While the growth of urban society made possible a myriad of connections, the nature of its development was driven by its distinctly gendered dimensions. What came to be identified as secular "public" life was masculine in orientation and membership. From political institutions and social organizations to Revolutionary groups like the committee movement, Philadelphians who acted collectively and publicly defined their groups as masculine.[78]

Rather than evidence of a newly political role for women, the inclusion of women shopkeepers and merchants in the non-importation movement represented a last gasp of the traditional colonial political culture of Philadelphia in the face of a new political culture that marginalized women's civic status. That such a small number of the many Philadelphia women involved in commercial activity signed the petition was indicative of a process by which only a few women could muster the civic

74. For this view see Frances Manges, "Women Shopkeepers, Tavernkeepers, and Artisans," (Ph.D. diss., University of Pennsylvania, 1958), 46.
75. Norton, *Liberty's Daughters*, 155–194. Alfred Young makes a similar argument in "The Women of Boston."
76. The constable in Chestnut Ward, where the Hydes lived and operated their shop, crossed them off the list of taxables. They were also never rated for a dwelling, for example. In 1767 each sister was taxed at £3, in 1769 at £5, and in 1772 and 1774 at £6. Those were very low assessments, and the Hydes were unique among taxpaying women for maintaining an independent existence on such meager holdings.
77. In an interesting parallel, some recent scholarship on women in early modern European cities suggests that, although women had considerable power and autonomy in the late medieval period, strictures on women's "public" activities tightened in the sixteenth and seventeenth centuries. For example, see Martha Howell, "Citizenship and Gender: Women's Political Status in Northern Medieval Cities," in Mary Erler and Maryanne Kawaleski, eds., *Women and Power in the Middle Ages* (Athens, Ga., 1988), 37–60.
78. Peter Thompson, "A Social History of Philadelphia's Taverns" (Ph.D. diss., University of Pennsylvania, 1989); David S. Shields, *Civil Tongues and Polite Letters in British America* (Chapel Hill, 1997).

resources necessary to counter the prevailing cultural trends and to participate in increasingly masculine urban institutions.[79] What each of the six female signers of the non-importation agreement had in common was their mutual participation in the dense economic, kinship, and religious networks that characterized Philadelphia's urban population. Although their economic statuses varied, for example, their residential status did not. Each was a long-time resident of a Philadelphia neighborhood. They also possessed connections to other families active in the non-importation movement. Elizabeth Paschall, for example, was a close friend and neighbor of one member of the retailers' committee assigned to organize the movement, and the sister-in-law of another.[80] Although politics was an increasingly masculine preserve, some women were so visible within their communities that they could not be ignored. As property owners and community members, they possessed the kind of civic status so important in the old order; as independent *women*, they were marginalized in the new order.

The women among this group were bound to their neighbors through a complex web of economic, religious, political, and kinship ties. Yet the networks among neighborhood residents that would come to dominate the attentions of the city and of historians were those created by the militia groups. With the onset of hostilities with Britain, radical committees and the Philadelphia Militia, composed partly of the "Lowest Sort," demanded a political voice for the propertyless, an early expression of hostility to what J. R. Pole has described as "the basic economic presupposition that the ownership of a specified amount of property was an essential guarantee of political competence."[81] Some contemporaries heralded a new spirit of politics, situated in "dramshops, tiff, and alehouses," that would turn everything "topside Turvey."[82] Within this contest for political legitimacy, masculinity was identified as the basis for political interest and participation. Gary Nash has written that the truly leveling spirit of 1776 gave the franchise to all taxpayers, rather than re-

79. On Philadelphia women shopkeepers, see Patricia Cleary, "'She Will Be in the Shop': Women's Sphere of Trade in Eighteenth-Century Philadelphia and New York," *PMHB* (July 1995): 181–202.
80. The members of the retailers' committee are listed in the appendices to Richard Ryerson, *The Revolution Is Now Begun: The Radical Committees of Philadelphia, 1765–1776* (Philadelphia, 1978).
81. Gary Nash, "Artisans and Politics in Eighteenth Century Philadelphia," in Gary Nash, *Race, Class, and Politics: Essays on American Colonial and Revolutionary Society* (Urbana, Ill., 1986), 252, 261; J. R. Pole, *Political Representation in England and the Origins of the American Republic* (New York, 1966), 273. See also, Nash, *The Urban Crucible;* and Rosswurm, *Arms, Country, and Class.*
82. Nash, "Artisans and Politics," 252.

stricting it to property owners, and John Adams worried at the time that this development would "prostrate all ranks to one common level." But Nash was wrong, and Adams need not have worried. The demand was only that any *man* be entitled to political rights.[83]

Women had long been among those groups, including children, slaves, laboring men, and other dependents, that were excluded from direct participation in political life through voting or office-holding.[84] But as potential household heads and as substantial property holders, women posed a special problem to those who would define public life in masculine terms. Women who owned property and were independent household heads had some traditional claim on membership, if not in the legislatures, then more loosely within the polity. Any emphasis on the inclusion of the propertyless in political life that was directly opposed to the privileges of property thereby undercut claims that women property owners and household heads could make to civic membership.

In the earliest stages of British settlement, women landowners and tradespeople were important in the local affairs that were essential to establishing colonies. Quaker women in the Quaker colony enjoyed unusual privilege and power. But as the eighteenth century progressed, women's activities were eclipsed and privatized. Quakers were surpassed in population and lost political power. More important, the locus of power and political significance changed, swinging away from local governmental functions that included women towards provincial and imperial politics that, in conjunction with other aspects of organized urban public life, excluded women.

Here we can see the outlines of a process whereby urban political culture increasingly denied women's civic status. Pre-Revolutionary political culture was not nearly so intensely gendered. The primary participants in political activity were men. By virtue of their larger claims to property and by their capacity to vote and serve on juries and in the assemblies, men constituted the government. But Philadelphia's political culture accorded some women civic status based on property, religious authority, and long-term residence. These qualities continued to have cultural currency, but were surpassed in political importance by the possession of masculinity and by activities defined or redefined as masculine.

83. Ibid., 261.
84. See the commentators noted in Carl Bridenbaugh, *Cities in the Wilderness, 1625–1742* (New York: Capricorn Books, 1964), 387–389.

Index

Index

Index

Netherlands, 8
New England, 9n, 19, 22n, 51, 66–67, 156, 183, 189; and patriarchy, 17n, 31n, 71; studies of, 9–10, 13, 17–18, 90n, 117n; and unmarried women, 14n, 15n, 30
New Jersey, 13, 19, 42, 87, 124n; Burlington, 33n, 44, 68, 85, 111
Newspapers, 96n, 98, 135n, 137, 139, 171, 177n; *American Weekly Mercury*, 36n; *Pennsylvania Gazette*, 34, 98n, 119, 141, 171, 197, 199n; as public literature, 22, 28, 50
New York, 19–20, 33n, 159, 186n, 188–189, 207
New York City, 125
Nonimportation agreements, 181, 183–185, 207–209
Norris, Charles Sr., 106–109, 116
Norris, Deborah, 53, 106–110, 192–193, 195
Norris, Elizabeth, 53–56, 62–63, 65–66, 68, 74, 106–108, 110
Norris family, 53, 62, 110, 116, 149n
Norris, Isaac Jr., 66, 106–108, 116, 192–193
Norris, Isaac Sr., 53, 106, 108
Norris, Mary, 108, 193n
Norris, Mary Lloyd, 53, 66n, 108
Norris, Sarah, 108, 193n
Norris, Sarah Logan, 66n, 107–108, 193
Northern Liberties, 92, 128n
North Ward, 93, 113, 124–126, 127n, 128–130
Norton, Mary Beth, 9–10
Novels, 40, 48

Occupations and professions: apothecaries, 139; artisans, 48, 125, 129, 135–136, 148; bakers, 129, 131, 134, 135n, 191; barbers, 161; blacksmiths, 129; bonnetmakers, 135n; booksellers, 134; botanists, 62, 128, 147n; braziers, 135n; butchers, 161; carters, 131; chandlers, 101, 120, 125, 135n, 149, 150n; cobblers, 131; cordwainers, 125–126, 149n; diplomats, 62; distillers, 134; dock workers, 131; doctors, 139–140, 165; domestic workers, 87, 121, 142n; dressmakers, 131; farmers, 10, 91, 93, 103; glovers, 115, 134; grocers, 35–36; hucksters, 96, 134, 144–145; innkeepers, 92, 135; laborers, 93, 41, 130–131, 198, 210; mantuamakers, 134; mariners, 97–98, 111; midwives, 129, 135, 139–140, 163, 176, 176n, 192; milliners, 104, 135n, 147; nurses, 139–140, 142, 158, 176n; pawnbrokers, 39; peddlers, 144; plasterers, 48; printers, 21, 41, 50, 62, 95n; scriveners, 4; sievemakers, 134, 135n; silver-

smiths, 127; skinners, 138; soapboilers, 134; spinners, 96, 134; tailors, 119, 125, 134, 161, 191; teachers, 16, 26, 45, 47, 49–50, 77, 111, 135; tinkers, 134; upholsterers, 96, 120, 129, 134; washerwomen, 135; whitewashers, 138, 141. *See also* Merchants; Ministers; Retailers; Shopkeepers; Tavernkeepers
Oestreicher, Richard, 130
Orphans, 43, 92n
Overseers of the Friends Public Schools, 48, 112
Overseers of the Poor, 154, 162n; and children, 97, 139–140; and poor relief, 156–157, 159–160, 162–164, 167n, 168–172, 174–175

Pamela, 48
Parliament, 1, 5, 188
Paschall, Elizabeth Coates, 129–130, 147n; Cedar Grove, 128; and medical advice, 122, 123n, 128; and nonimportantion agreements, 207, 209; as shopkeeper, 146–148, 181
Patriarchy, 19, 43–44, 57, 116–117, 173; and Anglo-American culture, 1–3, 28, 55, 88–90, 171; and law, 2n, 35; in New England, 17, 31n, 51
Paxton Boys, 198
Peisley, Mary, 111, 199
Pennsylvania Assembly, 62, 107
Pennsylvania Hospital for the Sick Poor, 139, 141, 160n, 168–169, 178
Penn, Thomas, 192, 194, 199
Penn, William, 12, 53, 189, 199
Philadelphia city wards. *See* entries for individual wards
Philadelphia County, 21, 91, 92n; Frankford, 85; Norriton, 108; Oxford Township, 92; Perkiomen Township, 91, 93; Skippack, 91
Philadelphia Quarter Sessions Court, 192
Phillips, Catherine Peyton, 60n, 69, 111, 199, 200n
Pietists, 20, 55–56, 75, 81
Plumstead, William, 4–5, 162n, 167n
Poetry, 30, 45–47, 54, 65n, 66n, 183n; "The Bachelor's Supplication," 42; "Choice of a Companion," 26–27, 29, 32, 42n; in commonplace books, 26–27, 32, 42; encouraging marriage, 38–39, 44; "Epitaph on a Man & his Wife," 89; "The Female Choice," 42n; "Few Happy Matches," 34; "The Maiden's Best Adorning," 42; "The Maiden's Choice," 27; "The Maid's Soliloquy," 42–43; "On Friendship," 64; "The

Index

Shammas, Carole, 12
Shopkeepers, 4, 99, 104, 181, 191, 209n; as female occupation, 96, 122–126, 131–132, 134, 135n, 144–146, 149; as female partnership, 114
Simler, Lucy, 93
Slavery, 17–19; and Quakers, 60, 108n, 196; slave trade, 103
Slaves, 13, 19n, 60, 78n, 99, 105, 149, 204; excluded from public life, 130, 207, 210; and household labor, 102, 108; manumission of, 78n, 103, 105, 108; as members of household, 13, 87–88, 91, 94–95, 136
Smaby, Beverly, 76
Smith, Billy, 141
Smith, Elizabeth, 44–45, 68, 73–74
Smith, Hannah, 77, 79
Smith-Rosenberg, Carroll, 185
Society for the Relief of Poor and Distressed Masters of Ship, 155, 167–168
Society of Friends. *See* Quakers
Sophronia, 39–40, 46
South Ward, 113
Southwark, Pennsylvania, 92
Spain, 8
Spinsterhood, 11, 14n, 31, 44n, 51, 62, 65; and radical religions, 75–81; and Quakers, 67n, 68–69
Spinsters, 6, 8, 15–17, 43, 54, 56, 150, 204; depictions of, 28, 30, 32, 38, 43, 106; and literature, 33, 45–48, 52; and work, 114, 125, 133
Stackhouse, Martha, 48–49, 112
Stackhouse, Mary, 49, 112
Stamp Act, 181–182, 187, 206–207
Steel, Mary, 143n, 146–147
Steel, Rebecca, 143n, 146–148
Stinson, Ann, 140–141n, 145
St. Paul's Church, 127
Strettel, Robert, 156, 167, 174
Susquehanna River, 62

Tavernkeepers, 125n, 138, 147; Draper, Rachel, 119–120, 124, 203; women, 92, 96, 114n, 119–120, 125, 132, 134, 135n, 147n

Taverns, 91–92, 96n, 102, 120, 125, 138, 147; Hen and Chickens Tavern, 132
Taxes, 99–100, 102n, 119, 124, 202–204, 206; British, 181–182, 185; poor tax, 156, 161–165, 163n, 175
Theology, 19, 51–52, 72–73, 75, 82, 117; Moravian, 80–81; Protestant, 28, 70, 89; Puritan, 17; Quaker, 54–56, 59, 61–65, 77, 199–200
Tomes, Nancy, 123
Tully, Allan, 12

Ulrich, Laurel Thatcher, 9–10
Upper Delaware Ward, 114, 115n

Venice, 15
Virginia, 9, 19, 188n, 193n, 197, 205
Virgins, 28, 30, 39, 43

Walnut Ward, 93, 129n, 190
War, 7, 12, 17, 187, 192, 196, 200n
Warner, Ann Coleman, 96, 101–102
Webb, Ruth, 145–146, 147n
Welsh immigrants, 78
Welsh Tract, 13
West Indies, 53
Whitebread, William, 125, 127
Widowers, 12, 14, 76, 106
Widowhood, 2–4; and economic strategies, 10n, 15, 18, 189; as metaphor, 107
Widows, 6, 8–9, 15n, 17, 44, 90, 92–93, 98n, 166; with children, 49, 96n, 97n, 151; and commercial activities, 119, 124, 128, 130–133, 135, 149–150, 204; as head of household, 15n, 88, 95–101, 116; and Moravians, 76–77; and poor relief, 153, 166, 177n, 178; in popular literature, 30, 41, 52; and remarriage, 12, 14
Wilson, Lisa, 100
Wishart, Ann, 101, 149
Wishart, Ann Battson, 101, 120, 149–150
Wishart, Thomas, 101, 149
Witchcraft, 30
Wright family, 62, 64n
Wright, Susanna, 45–47, 54–55, 62–67, 70, 194

CPSIA information can be obtained at www.ICGtesting.com
Printed in the USA
BVOW071954060113

309829BV00001B/147/A